Inventing American Religion

Inventing American Religion

Polls, Surveys, and the Tenuous Quest for a Nation's Faith

ROBERT WUTHNOW

OXFORD
UNIVERSITY PRESS

OXFORD
UNIVERSITY PRESS

Oxford University Press is a department of the University of Oxford.
It furthers the University's objective of excellence in research, scholarship,
and education by publishing worldwide.

Oxford   New York
Auckland   Cape Town   Dar es Salaam   Hong Kong   Karachi
Kuala Lumpur   Madrid   Melbourne   Mexico City   Nairobi
New Delhi   Shanghai   Taipei   Toronto

With offices in
Argentina   Austria   Brazil   Chile   Czech Republic   France   Greece
Guatemala   Hungary   Italy   Japan   Poland   Portugal   Singapore
South Korea   Switzerland   Thailand   Turkey   Ukraine   Vietnam

Oxford is a registered trade mark of Oxford University Press
in the UK and certain other countries.

Published in the United States of America by
Oxford University Press
198 Madison Avenue, New York, NY 10016

Library of Congress Cataloging-in-Publication Data
Wuthnow, Robert.
Inventing American religion: polls, surveys, and the tenuous quest for a nation's faith /
Robert Wuthnow.
p.   cm.
Includes bibliographical references and index.
ISBN 978–0–19–025890–0 (cloth : alk. paper)   1. United States—Religion. 2. Public
opinion polls—United States. I. Title.
BL2525.W866 2015
200.973—dc23
2014047894

1   3   5   7   9   8   6   4   2

Printed in the United States of America on acid-free paper

Contents

Inventing American Religion

I
Introduction

MIDWAY BETWEEN NEW York and Philadelphia, a large stone building known as Old Nassau stands as an icon of American history. Built in 1756 to house the College of New Jersey, it was seized by the British in 1776, fired on and retaken by Washington's troops, and then for four months in 1783 served as the seat of American government while the Congress of the Confederation convened in its second-floor library. The busloads of international tourists who now visit daily convene in front of the massive bronze tigers guarding both sides of the building's front entrance, pose for pictures, and hear the tour guide's practiced account of this small saga of Americana before resuming their journey toward Philadelphia, where they will visit Independence Hall and view the Liberty Bell.

An informed tourist would learn that Old Nassau played an important role in founding a distinctly American understanding of religion. It was here that John Witherspoon, the only signer of the Declaration of Independence who was a member of the clergy, presided for a quarter of a century over the fledgling college, teaching its required courses in moral philosophy. Gazing up at the towering ten-foot statue of Witherspoon that stands on the Princeton campus today, a visitor can imagine him to have been an austere lecturer who demanded nothing short of excellence from his students. Under his tutelage, many of the leaders who would shape the emerging nation—James Madison, Aaron Burr, William Bradford, and numerous others—learned the persuasive mixture of common sense, moral realism, and Christian theology on which the American experiment in democratic government was formed.

The version of American religion that grew from Witherspoon and Madison and from kindred spirits such as Jonathan Edwards and Roger Williams privileges the relationship between freedom and faith. It urges that a seamless connection be understood between natural law and divine grace, and, whether from firm belief or in unapologetic doubt, attests that an idea of inalienable, if not providential, regard for the rights of individual persons must be the basis for the nation's fragile undertaking of democracy. The understanding of religion that generations of Americans have learned at their parents' knees—the religion that so often becomes an object of litigation and of debate in the highest chambers of the land—is inscribed in the teachings of the nation's founders and in the nation's founding documents as an ideal. To respect the individual's freedom to practice religion, while at the same time prohibiting any particular religion from establishing itself as an element of government, is the ideal toward which the nation claims to aspire. Moreover, it is this ideal that periodically inspires the nation's leaders to seek God's blessings and to call for spiritual renewal, however partisan and contested those proclamations may be.

American religion in this historic manifestation embraces not only individual freedom but also individuals' responsibility to shape and interpret their faith commitments in personal ways. They do so in their families and congregations, experiencing the sacred in vastly diverse ways; making sense of their experiences through personal narratives; and finding support from family members, neighbors, and friends. To the extent that religion is distinctly "American," it exists as a framework for moral action and obligation, expressed in public and private acts of commitment. It necessarily centers on the aims and aspirations of individuals, expressed through their varied familial and community attachments, all of which are inherently local and therefore diversely experienced and diversely meaningful.

But there is another version of American religion that claims to be the latest, most factual, authoritative account of what Americans actually believe and do. It arises almost in the same breath as assertions about the nation's religious ideals because these revered standards beg for answers to the question of whether they are routinely upheld in practice. And if the ideals have necessitated continuing arguments about how exactly they should be framed, the realities of American religion have been no less difficult to establish with any degree of certainty. Indeed, the realities depend on assuming not only that they can and should be assessed but also on perplexing questions about whether anything as abstract as "American religion" exists at all apart from the local and diverse personal beliefs and practices of individuals.

Across the street from Nassau Hall, a Princeton landmark known as the Lower Pyne Building sits grandly at the intersection of Nassau and Witherspoon Streets. Named for benefactor Moses Taylor Pyne, the edifice dates from 1896, when it opened as one of a pair of Princeton dormitories. Modeled on Tudor-style English houses, its steeply pitched roof, cross gables, and massive chimneys in an earlier day embellished modest living space for students on the upper two floors and sheltered shops at street level—a charming mixed-use combination that F. Scott Fitzgerald once likened to "aristocratic Elizabethan ladies not quite content to live among shopkeepers."[1] Visitors today who wander across the street from Nassau Hall take photos of the pink and purple petunia-filled flower boxes that adorn the building's narrow upper-floor windows and venture for refreshments into the ground-level Starbucks. They undoubtedly have no idea that this building is as much an icon in American religious history as the one across the street, for it was here in rented third-floor space in 1935 that George Gallup designed the first national poll about American religion based on innovative scientific sampling methods.

Although polls and surveys had been conducted earlier, Gallup's methods, as well as his considerable ability to sell an interested public on the idea that what it thought and believed could be accurately measured, set in motion what would blossom into a billion-dollar-a-year industry in which a new understanding of American religion as numerically interpreted would emerge alongside a new understanding of the American public itself. The possibility of knowing about American religion as a reality and not only as an ideal played well in places as diverse as church conventions and news columns, appealing to notions about grassroots democracy and to a newer faith in science as the key to better living. In addition to those who considered it among the most exciting developments of their time, there were others who saw it as wasted effort, opening wide latitude for bias, misinterpretation, and downright abuse. And yet, within a few years, poll results purporting to describe American religion, not simply as the teachings of congregations but as a kind of generic category referring to the American public writ large, became commonplace, and a few decades after that, pollsters were among the most powerful interpreters of American religion.

As polling grew, it filled an apparent need for information about the public's mood as well as some of its more prosaic activities, such as what its purchasing habits might be and where it looked for news. Having considered itself a religious country in theory, the nation looked for answers in polls to questions about how often its citizens participated in religion and what they believed. Polling was never especially well suited to answering those questions. Its focus was on politics and public opinion, not on the deeply personal, complex, highly diverse beliefs and practices embodied in the many religious traditions of the nation. From the start, polling succeeded by selling brief, seemingly newsworthy results to newspapers. The results came from brief doorstep encounters in which strangers answered predesigned questions in predefined one- or two-word responses. Still, in the absence of other information and without much in the way of sustained criticism, polling gradually became a widely accepted way of thinking about religion.

By the twenty-first century, polls about American religion had become so common that it was nearly unthinkable to ask if its version of what American religion was made sense, for the answers were readily available in statistical results. An interested person could find the latest figures on religious membership, attendance at religious services, and belief in God by consulting a polling agency's website or catching a pollster's interview on cable television. To the casual consumer of this information, it simply made sense that this was a meaningful way to think about religion. It was easy to assume that the statistics were accurate and useful, especially when religious leaders themselves paid obeisance to them. Prominent television preachers considered it essential to have conducted a poll to ascertain the extent of the ministry's popularity, and an ordinary person of faith could well expect to hear from the pulpit that spiritual convictions and prayer should be emphasized more because the latest polls showed them to be in decline.

These are now a few of the ways in which polls about religion have become regular features of our world. They cast arguments about God and the Bible and about spirituality and participation in congregations very differently from the ones of preachers and prophets earlier in our nation's history. They invite readers and viewers to assume that because a poll was done, it was done accurately. They produce a veritable flood of information purporting to tell what the typical American thinks and what that hypothetical person believes and does. How did we get to this point? Why is it nearly impossible to think about American religion without polls? What have we gained? What have we lost?

Thinking about religion using numbers and percentages and notions of what is typical and what is atypical may be possible to take for granted, but it is important to recognize how recent this development is. If it is only in the past half-century that it became possible to think of something called American religion in these ways, being bombarded with new information from pollsters on a daily basis is more recent than that. In earlier times, faith would have been a matter of conviction grounded in the age-old teachings of particular traditions. It would have seemed strange to think of religion as public opinion.

Flooded with such information, the temptation may be to accept it without further thought—or to regard it with mild highbrow disdain. Certainly there is reason to wonder when one day's poll tells us one thing and the next day's tells us just the opposite. It may be interesting to see what pollsters say about the next election, but why it matters knowing that more people attended religious services this week than last week is harder to appreciate. Doubts of that nature were common when polling began, reflecting how peculiar polling seemed when newspapers started printing its results as if the numbers were truly meaningful and should be considered news.

But the polling industry's impact on American religion has been more significant than easy acceptance or quick dismissals would allow. As a nation, we know far more than previous generations did about what people believe, what they do to nurture those beliefs, and how those beliefs influence their opinions on important issues of the day. At the same time, polls are ill suited to capture the most meaningful aspects of our personal lives, let alone about the depth, superficiality, and complicated relationships we may have with religious traditions and practices. They rarely probe in depth the experiences underlying religious beliefs or the narratives through which those experiences become personally meaningful. The intent, rather, is to generalize and thus reinforce the otherwise tenuous idea that the religion of an entire nation can be aptly and succinctly described.

When polling began, it generated a vigorous discussion among social scientists about what it was and what it could and could not do. Social scientists were skeptical, not because they doubted the importance of research or the value of statistics, but because polling claimed so much and offered so little. Although the principal argument for the credibility of polling was that the results were scientific, the leading pollsters employed a sorely limited concept of science and were guided far less by social science, let alone the work of religion scholars, than by the need to produce terse headlines for newspapers and generate reasonably accurate predictions of presidential elections. As it became more familiar, the information polling produced came to be more readily accepted, partly because it received as much publicity as it did and partly because the era more broadly was a time when the nation cherished a robust and easily summarized characterization of what it was and what it believed. That was as true for information about religion as it was for information about political issues. Polls became the trusted oracles of the day.

The trust once evident, though, is now in serious free fall. When asked in polls what they think of polls, large and growing majorities of the public say they are skeptical. And yet, despite having more polling information than anyone possibly wants or needs, polling companies continue to reel out numbers and percentages, and news media long accustomed to thinking that numbers and percentages are news continue to publicize the results. This is happening despite increasingly serious difficulties in conducting polls and producing valid results. Not only are large majorities of the public skeptical of poll results, they are also unwilling to answer when pollsters call, leaving the reported results in danger of missed and unanticipated errors.

The time has come to ask what the place of all these polls is in our lives. The answer to that question may be straightforward with respect to politics and political campaigns, at least if it is assumed that policies and candidates should be guided by polling results. But can the same thing be said about religion? Does it make sense that authorities in the know would argue that the most influential person in American religion is a pollster? Are the numbers believable when 90 percent of the people who should have been included in a poll did not respond?

These are serious questions. Asking them does not suggest that polling about religion is purely a waste of time or that it should cease. Asking them should not be an occasion for polling firms yet again to argue that they do about as much as they can and generally figure they get it right. The questions run deeper than that. They require understanding and appreciating how polls are conducted, but also examining polling with a broader perspective on American culture and history.

What is truly sacred, Émile Durkheim observed in his famed work on the elementary forms of religion, is that which we take for granted. The taken for granted achieves the status of a mythic taboo because we never think to question it. We need to question whether polling about religion has come to be taken for granted in that way. Is it merely a tool that helps us collect information? Or has it influenced what we think religion is and what is important about it? When preachers cite polls as reasons why we should do this or that, shouldn't we wonder about this form of argument? When we hear American religion characterized in particular ways because of polls, we should ask what exactly "American religion" is, whose religion it refers to, and whether certain aspects of it are being emphasized while others are neglected.

Understanding the place of polls in American religion requires stepping back in time, looking at how this method of seeking information began, why it did, and what happened to bring us to where we are today. Taking a broader historical perspective reveals that polls have always been more than methods of measurement. They have been inspired by specific events and interpreted through the lens of those events, and they have in turn shaped how we think about the world in which we live.

An Unlikely Beginning

An 1895 church unity meeting in New York City is perhaps an unlikely place to seek the origin of polls and surveys about American religion. So is an 1895 meeting at a settlement house in Philadelphia. And so is a raucous 1904 meeting of the Chicago Federation of Labor. But they were.

The challenges confronting America's turn-of-the-century religious leaders were unprecedented. The frenetic church planting that brought Christianity to the expanding frontier was over. The frontier itself, Frederick Jackson Turner argued in his much-discussed 1893 lecture, was a thing of the past. As near as anyone could tell, religion's influence was declining.

Rural churches with decrepit buildings and poorly trained clergy were struggling. The situation in cities was no better. Estimates in several of the nation's cities suggested that fewer than 10 percent attended religious services. Congregations tried with little success to reach the growing masses of low-income, working-class families.

Immigrants came by the tens of thousands, creating priest shortages in the cities where they settled. Protestants' dominance seemed to be slipping away. Fundamentalists responded by arguing more vehemently than ever that the Bible was divinely inspired, word for word, free of error, and to be taken literally. Leaders who differed from fundamentalists looked to science, nonliteral interpretations of the Bible, and service to humankind as new sources of authority.

The challenge was theological as well as practical. Urban growth brought new ideas to education, science, and social philosophy. Scholars debated the meaning of true religion. They agreed that it could not be gauged by statistics alone. "Religion is fundamentally a disposition of the mind and the heart, largely irradiated with sentiment," a Jewish leader in Chicago observed. It was the source of reverence and awe, of joy and responsibility. It should be nurtured in the home. But was it still as central to the home as it had been?[2]

Conflict between labor and the captains of industry complicated congregations' work. News stories of strikes, lockouts, riots, closed shops, graft, corruption, and exploitation were daily fare. Congregations' financial support came from the expanding bourgeoisie. That made it harder for church leaders to speak on behalf of labor.

A few leaders took the bold step of identifying with organized labor. At the risk of being castigated as supporters of socialism, they argued that clergy and labor leaders should work hand in hand to secure better conditions for the laboring poor. It was an uphill battle. They faced resistance within the churches and skepticism from union members.

An alternative focused on the needs of working families. Instead of unions it emphasized the struggles of women and children, squalid housing conditions, inadequate public health, and the need for better education. It identified opportunities for volunteers and charitable donors. The social gospel meant caring for the poor, feeding the hungry, and assisting widows and orphans. It ranged from settlement houses and municipal reform to personal hygiene and temperance.

The question was how best to identify the prevailing needs. In small towns the needs were readily known. But in cities the needs were harder to assess. Not only was it important to know what the needs were; it was equally important to address them efficiently.

The view that efficient solutions could be found stemmed from two sources, one of which was business. If large companies could achieve efficiency, the argument went, a kind of social engineering could be applied to social problems as well. The other source was science, as it was understood at the time. Science opened possibilities for improved learning of how the world worked and making better use of those facts.

Science posed mixed blessings for religion. Fundamentalists saw it as a threat to biblical authority. Others embraced it as an alternative source of authority. If they were to solve the urgent social problems of the day, scientific information was an appealing option.

What was new? Not the idea simply of collecting statistics. The Census Bureau provided statistics on everything from population trends to employment and business patterns to schooling and health. Censuses since 1850 collected information about religious membership. The major denominations tallied statistics as well. They tracked membership, ordinations, church finances, baptisms, and enrollment in Sunday schools.

The new idea was collecting statistical information specifically for the purpose of church planning. That required information not only as it happened to be collected by the census or a denomination. It required deciding what information would be useful, collecting it, and making it available to local organizations that could do something with it.

The first efforts were community surveys. They anticipated and served as models for the public opinion polls that emerged several decades later but were quite different in purpose and design. Community surveys collected information by canvassing households and from informants, rather than from randomly selected respondents. Informants described the conditions in their neighborhoods and turned in figures about crime, poverty, and public health. The surveys included information about the various organizations that could assist in meeting the community's needs.

The surveys tallied data about churches because churches were among the organizations sponsoring the studies and hoping to use the information for community outreach. Researchers conducted surveys with funds from private donors and foundations. The most ambitious multicity survey was organized by church leaders and relied on thousands of volunteers from local churches to collect information. Besides information about social conditions, it included more detailed information about religious practices than any available from other sources.

Within a decade of those initial community surveys, church leaders were organizing surveys of churches in dozens of communities. This round of surveys focused specifically on church planning. They related community characteristics to the location, size, and memberships of local churches.

Although they lacked much in terms of later social scientific standards, the researchers who conducted the first community surveys justified their methods and results by arguing that these were the benefits of science. The studies' authority depended on facts and figures, rather than on speculation and theology. They attracted donors, were carefully planned and organized, and illustrated the value of church leaders working together across denominations.

Polling Comes into Its Own

The greatest strength of community surveys was that they were in fact done in communities and could, for that reason, provide information about specific needs, neighborhoods, and organizations. That was also their greatest limitation. News organizations wanted information about the nation, especially when national elections were in the news. Collecting and tabulating such information from tens of thousands of people living in scattered locations around the country was a monumental task that made it financially infeasible except on rare occasions. The breakthrough came in the 1930s when a young Iowan named George Gallup experimented successfully with a method of gauging public opinion by polling only a small representative sample of the nation's population.

Some of the first Gallup polls included a question about religious affiliation because of popular interest in whether Protestants and Catholics were likely to vote for different candidates. Within a few years, the polls added a standard question about attendance at religious services. The polls began asking questions about Bible reading and belief in God as well.

Interest in what the public believed about religion increased after World War II. In contrast with Western Europe and the Soviet Union, America became a nation of believers—not an assemblage of diverse traditions who taught distinctive beliefs and whose members varied in the intensity and content of their convictions, but a nation seemingly unified in a common, simple, easily measured faith. The evidence supporting this contention came from polls in which the vast majority of those polled claimed to believe in God. Whether Americans truly were united in common fealty to God or not, it was convenient to think that they were. This was hardly how old-fashioned revival preachers viewed America. It nevertheless fit the nation's Cold War image of itself.

Academic studies of religion took new directions in the 1950s as well. Earlier quantitative studies conducted in local communities or among college students and often with limited numbers of questions expanded as the social sciences expanded. Criticisms of studies conducted in other settings without proper regard to social scientific theories and methods came to the fore. Academicians claimed the term "survey" to describe what they did and disclaimed the "polls" that commercial polling agencies did. The distinction reflected academic social scientists' view that serious research should differ from what pollsters did, but, in reality, the distinction was imprecise. Without government data and with few sources for private funding, the first social scientific surveys of religion were financed mostly by religious organizations and were done for practical purposes. The publications emanating from these surveys nevertheless established the grounds on which a subsequent generation of scholars was trained and significantly enlarged the range of topics about religion to which survey methods were applied. Those social scientists would sometimes do studies similar to the ones conducted by polling agencies but, for the most part, would conduct different kinds of surveys and pay greater attention to qualitative approaches.

Few events had as significant an impact on polls about religion as Jimmy Carter's nomination for president on the Democratic ticket in 1976. Carter had stated that he was a born-again evangelical Christian. Thus, editors at national news outlets confronted the question: What exactly did it mean to call oneself a born-again evangelical Christian? Church leaders offered interpretations, but the question of whether there might be a large share of the electorate who shared Carter's views remained. National polls provided an answer. And with that answer they effectively defined what it meant to be an evangelical, as far as public discussion was concerned. That information and the large constituency it defined played a role in every subsequent presidential election.

A similar effect was evident among Catholics and to a smaller extent among Jews. Americans affiliated with each tradition could be distinguished not only in terms of affiliation but also on measures of belief and attitudes toward social issues. As polls proliferated, the nature of public commentary about religion shifted. New poll results counted as news as much as actual events did. Spokespersons were called on to interpret the polls. Pollsters increasingly became pundits.

Despite their growing popularity, an undercurrent of skepticism about polls remained. Clergy typically received stronger training in textual exegesis and the humanities than in social science and thus were often reluctant to view poll results as meaningful information. Religious studies departments thrived on qualitative research and teaching about the histories and practices of religious traditions. Social scientists themselves debated the merits of qualitative and quantitative approaches. Through the end of the twentieth century, funding from foundations and government agencies fueled a growing number of academic studies about religion. At the same time, commercial polling became less expensive and more common as a result of telephone sampling and computer-assisted interviewing. But its growing popularity also opened new questions about its value.

A *Shaping Influence*

Was it useful, critics wondered, to have new results about religious beliefs and practices week by week and month by month? Were the trends that polls purported to describe accurate? Were more sophisticated methods of statistical modeling providing better results or were they obscuring significant biases? Of particular concern, the public seemed to be tiring of pollsters' incessant phone calls. Response rates were notably lower than they had been in earlier studies. By the first years of the twenty-first century, poll watchers were generating computer simulations to assess the validity of polls. Some commentators predicted that the heyday of polling was over. Observers of religion increasingly expressed concerns about the nuances, diversity, and subtle changes that were being missed.

The story of polling about religion could certainly be told as a development that did nothing more than provide better answers to age-old questions. Religious leaders at the end of the nineteenth century had only their own impressions and a few statistics about church membership to guide their questions of whether religion was advancing or declining. They could only speculate about what people believed. A century later, religious leaders—and indeed anyone who might be interested—could know with hardly any trouble at all whether attendance at religious services was higher or lower this year than last. They could tell if the public mostly believed in God and thought that Jesus would return in their lifetime. And it was possible for political candidates to determine from polls if they needed to ramp up or downplay particular arguments to various religious constituencies.

All of that was good news for the occasional student or faculty person who might be interested in probing more deeply into the heart of American religion. A scholar who a half-century earlier would have had a single data set at her disposal and would have spent long nights waiting for results from an IBM mainframe computer could now download dozens of data sets onto her laptop in a few minutes. A person with the relevant computing and statistical skills could know everything a person wanted to know about religion. Or so it seemed.

That is a story worth telling, and it is part of the story I tell here. But the rest of the story must be told as well. Methods of measurement always depend on the purposes and audiences for which the measurements are made. Social scientists learn to guard against observer effects from whatever methods they use. In small ways, the worst of these effects can be minimized. But social scientists also caution that the "facts" we see are shaped by what we decide to study in the first place. As soon as the first community surveys were completed, a vigorous debate emerged about what was being studied and what was not. Critics suggested that the surveys were guided too much by programmatic agendas and too little by basic theoretical questions. As more studies were done, further questions were voiced about who and what was being left out.

My argument is that the polling industry has influenced—and at times distorted—how religion is understood and portrayed, particularly in the media but also to some extent by religious leaders, practitioners, and scholars. To have been influenced does not mean that religion has been fundamentally changed. But some perceptions of religion were reinforced while others were not. The evidence comes largely from scholars of religion carrying on a constructive dialogue that included criticisms of what they were doing. When polls suggested that Americans unanimously believed in God, closer investigation showed that doubt in varying degrees prevailed as well and that there were markedly different views of God. Tacit generalizations about "American" religion were shown to pertain mostly to white middle-class Protestants. The description of evangelicals that emerged from surveys in the 1970s came to be increasingly questioned by evangelicals themselves. African-American Christians, Jews, Buddhists, and Muslims, among others, found themselves missing from discussion in large national surveys. Additional concerns focus on what counts as religion, whether counting it is the appropriate metaphor, and if it is, whether adequate attention is given to the political and ideological forces that may be shaping the counting.

Such concerns notwithstanding, it seems unlikely at this juncture that polls about religion will cease being fashionable anytime soon. Besides the hundreds of commercial polling firms that include questions about religion in periodic press releases, a huge amount of private foundation money flows into the polling industry, yielding readily accessible results that busy journalists report without questioning if the findings are accurate and meaningful. The fine print about low response rates seems not to matter. Small upticks in percentages become evidence of major social trends, regardless of how much error may be involved.

The polling industry speaks through a large megaphone. It trumpets its characterizations of religion so loudly that criticisms can hardly be heard. Despite plummeting response rates and widespread public cynicism, polling companies and the news media keep on doing business as usual—asking the same questions, reporting confidence intervals that are no longer meaningful, and claiming that the latest numbers represent news. The working relationships that once connected pollsters and academic social scientists have become a chasm of distrust. Many of the polls about religion are of such poor quality that academic journals no longer publish articles based on them.

The road ahead will undoubtedly require an already cynical public to be even more critical of what it learns from polls. Religious leaders will need to be cautious about poll results, even when "Christian" pollsters produce them. Foundations that claim to be supporting respectable research will have to decide if spending hundreds of thousands of dollars on polls is worth the investment. And social scientists will find it necessary to teach students to be wary of polls—and to think about American religion in other ways.

2

The Survey Movement

ON APRIL 10, 1904, the featured speaker in Bricklayers' Hall at Monroe and Peoria Streets in Chicago was Charles Stelzle, a thirty-five-year-old Presbyterian preacher from St. Louis. Stelzle had been ordained four years earlier and earned a reputation for antisaloon activism, aggressive neighborhood evangelism, and an inner-city, working-class ministry that swelled to a church of fourteen hundred people, the largest Presbyterian congregation west of the Mississippi. His goal that afternoon was to convince the Chicago Federation of Labor to endorse fraternal relations with the city's clergy.

Had the meeting gone well, turn-of-the-century relations between religion and the growing needs of America's cities might have taken a different turn. As it happened, the meeting inadvertently contributed to the emergence of a new way of collecting information about religion and of using that information for strategic purposes.

The social survey movement, as it came to be called, emerged in the 1890s, grew significantly in the years just before the Great War, and extended into the 1920s. Although the information it produced fell short of later scientific standards, it served as a model for the polls that developed in the 1930s and 1940s. Religious leaders played a key role in formulating the methods and selecting the topics included in these early community surveys.

Seven years after the meeting in Chicago, Stelzle organized and directed the largest ever nationwide survey, collecting information about religion and social conditions in more than seventy cities. Part of the social gospel movement and what came to be known as muscular male-oriented Christianity, the survey set in motion efforts by churches across the country to survey their communities; they enlisted volunteers and attracted wealthy donors. As Stelzle turned to other challenges, his advocacy of scientific research continued and inspired others to take up the work.

But Stelzle was not the only person, or even the first, to experiment with community surveys oriented toward practical church outreach and ministry. In the 1890s, Reverend Walter Laidlaw in New York and W. E. B. Du Bois in Philadelphia were already engaged in projects to collect and tabulate information on urban neighborhoods. Both went on to other things, Laidlaw as a staff member for the Census Bureau, and Du Bois as the prominent African-American writer and civil rights pioneer, and yet it was in their efforts to conduct community surveys that new ideas about how to measure and, indeed, define American religion came into being. Of course they could not foresee those later developments. Their work was concerned with the immediate practical challenges of Protestant churches, which were long accustomed to ministering in small towns and rural areas but were now confronting rapidly growing cities with laboring families whose needs were obvious in general but only poorly understood in specific terms.

The New York Federation

Laidlaw was a Canadian, a graduate of the University of Toronto, who worked briefly at an uncle's law office, and then applied to Princeton Theological Seminary, entering in 1881. A letter of reference at the school described him as a "good young man possessed of much more than average ability, a successful student, and . . . endowed with just such gifts as are needful in order to guarantee success in the pulpit ministry."[1] Completing his seminary training in 1884, he studied sociology the following year at the University of Berlin, where Max Weber was also a student, and it is likely that they took classes together, perhaps from Georg Simmel, whose distinguished teaching career began there that year as well. Laidlaw returned to America after one year in Germany and pastored a church in West Troy, New York, before moving to New York City in 1893 as a minister at the Collegiate Reformed Church of America on Fifth Avenue. In 1896 he played a key role in founding the New York City Federation of Churches and Christian Workers, serving as executive secretary of the interdenominational hundred-church organization, and a year later finished his PhD at New York University. His work with the federation continued until 1922, and in 1919 he also became the general secretary for the New York City Census Commission, which he served until retiring in

1932. The training that shaped his work with the federation included the idea of cooperation among churches within a geographically defined area, resembling the parish system in Scotland, and the idea of using statistical information to understand the characteristics of those areas, which he learned from studying sociology in Berlin and put into practice as a pastor.[2]

The federation emerged at a time when Protestant church leaders were worried that denominational divisions were preventing them from ministering as effectively as they could to the nation's expanding urban population, especially where Roman Catholics' consolidated efforts seemed to be carrying the day. Laidlaw likened the federation to a "Grand Army" of denominational regiments marching under a single banner.[3] Its aim was to form a united force among the city's churches to better meet its growing population's needs, demonstrating God's love through the elevation and self-development of individuals, families, and the community. Private meetings to gauge interest among prominent New York clergy and business leaders convened during 1895, culminating in a public meeting in December, and then crystallized at a gathering hosted by John D. and Laura Spelman Rockefeller at their home on March 10, 1896, which secured a generous gift to cover the federation's expenses. The Rockefellers, their son John D. Rockefeller Jr., and the Rockefeller Foundation would play important roles in the shaping of American Protestantism, the social survey movement, and the social science of religion over the next three decades.[4]

Focusing on the Fifteenth Assembly District in Midtown West Side Manhattan where some forty thousand people lived, one of the federation's first tasks was to find out what the people's needs actually were. To that end, during the spring and summer of 1896, volunteers from eleven churches as well as the YMCA and YWCA, together with interviewers working for pay, conducted what they called a sociological canvass, or survey, of the densely populated twenty-three-square-block area. They collected information from each household to determine the occupants' nationality, employment status, days and hours of employment, and living conditions; how many people did or did not attend church and the denomination of the church (if any) to which they belonged; and the ages of children (if any) and whether they were in school. They combined that evidence with information about the location, finances, and activities of community organizations, including churches, libraries, schools, public baths, and health facilities. The survey reached 85 percent of the district's families. The total cost of the survey was less than $700.[5]

The idea of canvassing a neighborhood or town was not new. During the nineteenth century, canvassing for reasons other than church work went hand in hand with the growth of industrial production geared toward the consumption habits of middle-class families. By the 1870s, Americans with reasonably prosperous-appearing dwellings could expect periodic visits from paid canvassers selling everything from pencils and books to fire insurance policies, lightning rods, and magazine subscriptions. Suffragists and trade union organizers canvassed communities for support. Religious organizations were no exception. Women working for the London Sunday School Union canvassed neighborhoods as early as the 1830s, locating children lacking Sunday school training and classifying others by denomination.[6] In 1870, the American Bible Society reported having canvassed nearly two million families nationwide, finding that approximately 9 percent did not currently own a Bible.[7] Similarly, the National Temperance Society conducted statewide canvasses to solicit endorsements for prohibition bills and to raise funds.[8] In 1880, a pastor and two assistants surveyed the entire population of New Haven, Connecticut, to ascertain the names, addresses, and religious affiliations of the community's residents.[9] By 1895, individual churches and local church federations were conducting canvasses of other communities to determine families' denominational preferences and especially to identify persons having "no choice." A canvass of Jackson, Michigan, for example, divided the community into seventy districts, contacted nearly five thousand households, reported the names of those identifying a particular denomination to their respective clergy, and made special note of the 10 percent who indicated "no choice."[10] A canvass of Buffalo, New York, took the idea a step further, identifying a small portion of the community as "unbelievers" and an even smaller number as "infidels."[11]

The novelty of the New York Federation survey was that it not only included a larger number of households than church canvasses in smaller towns but that it also collected information about employment, health, living conditions, and other characteristics of families. Although much of the discussion when the results were tallied focused on evangelism, the federation's aim was to gather data that churches and other community organizations could use to remedy what Laidlaw and his collaborators saw as an alarming deterioration of social conditions in the city's slums. The federation's reports noted these conditions and observed with pride such ameliorative steps as the creation of a park, the founding of a new kinder-garten program, or the passage of a new tenement housing law.

Encouraged by the success of its first sociological canvass, and with funding from banking magnate Harvey E. Fisk, the federation conducted a second sociological canvass in 1897, focusing on the tenement section of the Nineteenth Assembly District in which a large number of Afri-can Americans lived, the results of which Laidlaw described in an article in the *American Journal of Sociology*. A third canvass was conducted in 1898, focusing on the fifteen thousand families living in the Twenty-First Assembly District. At a cost of less than $500, volunteers and paid workers achieved a response rate of 97 percent by making as many as fifteen attempts to contact each household. Following annual surveys of other legislative districts, the federation completed a survey in 1902 of all seventy-seven of the city's districts.[12]

One of the most innovative features of Laidlaw's surveys was the use of Hollerith punch cards. Devised by Columbia University graduate Herman Hollerith for the 1890 federal census, the punch card system in-volved a hole-punching machine, called a pantagraph, that office workers used to translate questionnaire responses into holes in the cards—which resembled later IBM cards in size and shape except with fewer columns—through which electrical current was passed by a piano-sized machine to produce a statistical count.[13] Hearing that the system saved the Census Bureau more than half a million dollars, census departments in Austria, Canada, and Russia adopted it as well. Laidlaw saw it in use during a visit in 1897 to the New York Board of Health, where it produced daily tabula-tions of the city's deaths. Realizing its potential for the federation's work, he contacted Hollerith, now serving as president in Washington, DC of the Tabulating Machine Company, and Hollerith provided the federation with one of the machines free of charge. Laidlaw proudly described it as a money saver that "works with lightning's swiftness and a recording angel's accuracy."[14] It enabled the federation's data not only to be summa-rized efficiently but also to be cross-tabulated—for example, to show that residents living greater distances from churches were less likely to attend, and to produce graphs of population densities, age distributions, and na-tionalities by block locations—or, as an enthusiastic writer observed at the time, "tabulated as to wring from them their fullest meaning."[15]

The federation's 1898 report of its third sociological canvass made full use of the Hollerith system of cross-tabulation, providing more than a hun-dred pages of detailed tables, summaries, and interpretations. It included nearly every conceivable cross-tabulation of the district's family units and individual residents according to the block where they lived, their age and gender, thirty different ethnic and nationality groups, level of schooling, employment status, insurance coverage, weekly wage rate, length of residence in their current dwelling and in the city, how many rooms they occupied and the kind of bathing and toilet facilities they had, the amount of rent they paid, whether anyone in the family used a public library, their membership in labor unions, and whether any of the children might be working illegally. All that provided measures with which to cross-tabulate information about religious practices, which included information about the denominational preferences of Protestants or identification as Roman Catholic, Jewish, Greek Orthodox, or Confucian; and membership in a congregation, attendance at worship services, whether that attendance occurred within or outside the district, whether individuals were baptized, and whether families owned a Bible. The report included breakdowns of this information by nationality, length of residence, location, and family size. Among other things, it showed, for example, that 32 percent of the families in the district were Catholic; 52 percent were Protestant (the largest number of whom were Episcopalian, Presbyterian, or Lutheran); 7 percent were Jewish; and 7 percent did not have a religious preference, were nonreligious or agnostics, or identified themselves in some way other than through religious belief (for example, by nationality, a response of no religion was highest among Germans and Hungarians).

By its tenth anniversary, the federation's "sociological inquiry bureau" was collecting and tabulating detailed block-by-block statistics of this kind and combining them with census and tax exemption data for use not only by the churches and by congregations affiliated with other religious traditions but also by the city's major charities, trade unions, and tenement organizations. Its publication department published an estimated 2.6 million pages of material in these years, and federation affiliates were giving lantern-slide public lectures and sponsoring vacation Bible schools. Through its program of "civic evangelism" and "cooperative ministry," it claimed to have significantly reduced the number of New York residents who were religiously unaffiliated and contributed to better tenement housing laws and public health. When he retired, Laidlaw was known for his work not only on behalf of the federation but also as a census official, credited with having originated the idea of census tracts, which he first proposed in 1906, and which the US Census Bureau implemented in New York City and seven other large cities in 1910.[16]

Du Bois in Philadelphia

The idea for a survey in Philadelphia originated in 1895 at the home of Quaker philanthropist Susan Wharton. She lived in the predominantly African-American Seventh Ward and was a member of the executive committee of the Philadelphia College Settlement Association, which served the neighborhood in ways similar to Jane Addams's Hull House in Chicago by providing classes and vocational training. Wharton contacted University of Pennsylvania Provost Charles C. Harrison on May 30, 1895, asking if the university might be interested in cooperating on a sociological study of the community. Harrison in turn wrote a fundraising letter, in which he quoted Columbia University President Seth Low, who was interested in similar practical scientific work in New York because "those who despise the poor . . . and declare that nothing can be done for their uplifting have failed to learn a great lesson that Christ would teach us." Low was one of the organizers of the New York Federation of Churches and Christian Workers and an honorary vice president for Laidlaw's survey.[17]

On June 8, 1896, Du Bois received a telegram from University of Pennsylvania President Norvin Green, notifying him that an appointment for the project was approved with a salary of $900 for the year. Du Bois held a PhD from Harvard, which he had completed the previous year, and was teaching at Wilberforce University in Ohio. With his wife of three months, Du Bois moved to Philadelphia and set to work. The stated aim of the project was to obtain accurate statistics about the "social problem" represented by the city's Seventh Ward, including especially information about residents' occupations, the occupations from which they were excluded, and how many of their children were going to school.[18] A draft questionnaire was drawn up in the fall and circulated for suggestions, which included the idea of incorporating questions from 1890 and 1895 censuses in order to compare results with other locations. The "family schedule" used for the study consisted of thirty-four questions asking the age, sex, and place of birth of each member of the family; their length of residence in Philadelphia; whether they could read and write; if they had been ill during the past year; and whether the children had attended school. Those employed were asked about their place of employment, occupation, and earnings. Additional questions included whether the family had participated in varied activities, including athletics, music, house parties, picnics, and "church entertainments." In interviews averaging fifteen to twenty-five minutes, usually with women, the survey achieved almost 100 percent coverage of the Seventh Ward households. Unlike Laidlaw's study in New York, Du Bois conducted the interviews himself, personally talking with some five thousand persons. As would become standard practice in subsequent surveys, residents who answered the questions were informed that their responses were confidential and that the information would be used only for "scientific purposes."[19]

Data from the survey, supplemented with extensive observations, field research, and qualitative interviews with community leaders, formed the basis for *The Philadelphia Negro: A Social Study*, which Du Bois published in 1899. The book went well beyond reporting results of the Seventh Ward survey, tracing the history of African-American migration to Philadelphia, describing the rise of its neighborhoods and social institutions, discussing the history of discrimination and violence, charting changes in its population in comparison with other cities, and presenting census statistics on age and gender to put the Seventh Ward in perspective. Du Bois provided additional context for the survey by describing the neighborhood's housing, streets, and general appearance and, despite the survey's high response rate, cautioning about the possibility of a "large margin of error." Dozens of tables presented detailed information from the survey on marital status, family size, migration, schooling, health, incomes, and occupations, frequently including tabulations by gender and age categories.[20] The result was "not merely a census-like volume of many tables and diagrams," one of several impressed reviewers observed, but a book in which the author interpreted statistics "in the light of social movements and of characteristics of the times."[21]

Although the survey touched on religion only in passing, Du Bois highlighted several of the twenty-two clergy it included; quoted from his interviews about their ministries; discussed clergy salaries in large and small churches; considered how clergy were trained and why they became pastors; and provided information from other sources about the history of Philadelphia churches, church publications, the value of church property, congregations' activities, worship styles, and even the possible health hazards associated with church crowds attending services in poorly ventilated auditoriums. The frequency with which people in the survey mentioned church activities persuaded him that churches not only were places to express religious devotion but also functioned as the center of community social interaction, providing the occasions for holiday celebrations and family gatherings, enlisting adults in committee work, giving better-educated young people opportunities to socialize, and passing important moral teachings from generation to generation.

At a meeting of the American Academy of Political and Social Sciences in Philadelphia, Du Bois reflected on what the study might suggest for future investigations. "The best available methods of sociological research are at present so liable to inaccuracies that the careful student discloses the results of individual research with diffidence," he said. "He knows that they are liable to error from the seemingly ineradicable faults of the statistical method; to even greater error from the methods of general observation; and, above all, he must ever tremble lest some personal bias, some moral conviction or some unconscious trend of thought due to previous training, has to a degree distorted the picture in his view." Nevertheless, he contended, the problems facing society demanded investigation. "We must study, we must investigate, we must attempt to solve," he urged, "and the utmost that the world can demand is not lack of human interest and moral conviction, but rather the heart-quality of fairness and an earnest desire for the truth despite its possible unpleasantness."[22]

Well in advance of national polls becoming the hallmark of statistical investigations, Du Bois cautioned against the kind of generalizations they would offer. "General statistical investigations," he advised, were "apt to be dangerously misleading" when dealing with complicated topics, which in his view suggested a preference for "intensive studies carried on in definitely limited localities."[23]

Du Bois moved on to other things, playing an important role as one of the nation's leading African-American public intellectuals, but *The Philadelphia Negro* established both his reputation and that of systematic sociological research involving house-to-house surveys. "Few people ever read that fat volume," he wrote in his autobiography years later, "but they treat it with respect, and that consoles me."[24] It was true, as the scant interest the study initially received suggested, that Du Bois was underappreciated as a founder of American sociology until later. And yet, for the generations of social scientists who did read it, it set the standard for excellence in scientific investigations of social conditions. Its enviable response rate and the care with which Du Bois interpreted the results while also cautioning against their limitations were hallmarks of high-quality research. It demonstrated, too, that tabulations and numbers, perhaps especially about religion, were better employed in discussions that included information about neighborhoods and their histories and leaders and families, rather than being presented as stand-alone statistics. Because of the

exceptional talent that Du Bois brought to the project, and perhaps because the academic context in which he worked insulated him from the
more practical uses to which his donors hoped the information would be
put, the book became a classic that social scientists would look to as one
of their most important pioneering community studies.[25]

Men and Religion Forward

Stelzle's inner-city work in St. Louis and Chicago resembled Du Bois's in
Philadelphia and Laidlaw's in New York, but his path to becoming a Presbyterian minister was unique. Unlike Laidlaw, whose well-educated, middle-
class family made it only natural for him to enter a profession such as the
ministry, and unlike the many Protestant preachers raised on farms and
in small towns, Stelzle's father ran a saloon, and, after his father died,
Stelzle's mother moved the family into substandard tenement quarters
on New York City's Lower East Side, where she earned a few dollars a
week sewing cotton wrappers. Stelzle began working at a sweatshop at age
eight, working at various jobs until he was fifteen, and then working at the
warehouse of a large company that manufactured printing presses, which
gave him the opportunity to complete a machinist certificate in 1890 and
join the International Machinists' Union. While working ten-hour days,
six days a week, he managed to teach Sunday school, hold office in the
YMCA, and become a Presbyterian lay leader. As his interest in church
work increased, he negotiated with his employer to spend two afternoons
a week holding services at a small mission in Brooklyn. Quitting his machinist job in 1893, he spent a year studying in Chicago at the Moody
Bible Institute, which attracted young people from low-income families
by enabling them to work for their room and board. Stelzle's goal was to
minister to workingmen like the ones he knew in New York. After three
years at an inner-city mission in Minneapolis, he returned to the Lower
East Side, spending two years ministering to a mission church there in
his boyhood neighborhood, and then relocated to St. Louis, becoming ordained in 1900. He was "as strong of purpose as of physique," had "peculiar, albeit pretty eyes," and was "forceful without becoming roused to
excessive animation," a reporter for the *St. Louis Dispatch* observed.[26]

Over the next three years, Stelzle and his wife (trained in music at the
Moody Bible Institute) turned the Menard Street Mission (also known as
the Markham Mission Church) into a flourishing congregation with what
was said to be the largest number of Sunday school children anywhere.

In cooperation with twenty local pastors and lay leaders, he served as a founding trustee of the St. Louis Anti-Saloon League and with fellow Presbyterian clergy organized citywide evangelistic meetings attended by tens of thousands. His goal, as he saw it, was not to engage in traditional slum ministry, working with drunkards, thieves, and murderers ("those who are either past redemption or are so low in sin and shame that the most optimistic worker has little hope of lifting them from their moral filth"), but to evangelize, educate, and assist working families "in communities whose inhabitants earn mere pittances, where some lives are passed in honest poverty, but where the Word of God is respected, is wanted and is listened to with the simplest reverence the world knows." The idea was not only to preach but also to follow the "institutional plan" embraced by the settlement house movement of organizing boys' and girls' clubs, singing societies, drum corps, public baths, reading rooms, dispensaries, and other programs of community self-government.[27]

Creating and facilitating the activities of organizations in low-income, working-class neighborhoods necessarily meant thinking about the role of labor unions. Stelzle believed his membership in the Machinists' Union would open the door to cooperative relationships between churches and union leaders. However, his first effort to explore that possibility—his first foray into survey research—produced sobering results. To the questionnaire he mailed to two hundred labor leaders, the replies registered widespread skepticism toward organized religion. They viewed the churches as servants of wealthy capitalists, staffed by clergy who were lazy at best and hypocritical defenders of the status quo at worst. They considered the churches more as enemies than as allies.[28]

Although Stelzle's work in St. Louis would have been enough to occupy his full attention, he aspired to greater accomplishments involving more than a single city. By the end of the nineteenth century, the old-line denominations that had populated American Protestantism from the beginning were evolving into centralized bureaucratic organizations with specialized offices responsible for activities ranging from fundraising and publishing, to foreign and domestic missions, to bookkeeping and communication.[29] New endeavors still required debate and approval at meetings of clergy and elected lay representatives, but the way to put those activities into practice was by starting a specialized agency with one or more dedicated persons in charge. Stelzle's dream was to initiate and operate an agency within the Presbyterian denomination to work especially on activities of interest to laboring men and women. In 1903, against the backdrop of labor unrest and evidence from surveys, like the ones Laidlaw was conducting in New York City, of worsening slum conditions and large numbers of families without church affiliations, Stelzle proposed and won approval from the Presbyterian General Assembly for a plan to establish a Department of Church and Labor.[30]

Nowhere were the challenges facing the nation's rapidly expanding industrial labor force more evident than in Chicago. Between 1880 and 1900, the city's population tripled from just over half a million to 1.7 million. Its rate of increase in the 1890s was the fastest of any city in the nation. Of roughly one million adults, 60 percent were foreign born. And in 1894, the city was rocked by the Pullman strike, which included riots brutally quelled by the police, militia, and US troops. Following years in which smaller separate labor unions formed, the Chicago Federation of Labor (CFL), originated in 1896, was composed of more than 250 local unions. By 1903, its membership totaled more than 245,000, constituting one-sixth of the nation's total American Federation of Labor membership and making Chicago rivaled only by London as the trade union capital of the world.[31]

That year, through the cooperative efforts of the CFL, Federated Women's Clubs of Illinois, and Women's Catholic League, the Illinois legislature passed a child labor law that prohibited children under fourteen from working for anyone other than a parent and limited children under sixteen from working longer than eight-hour days. The measure illustrated what could be accomplished if church groups and civic clubs worked together with unions. But the CFL was also fraught with corruption, including dubious election practices, resisted reforms, and was known for fractious floor arguments about which unions' delegates should be seated and which should not. This was the context in which Stelzle appeared in 1904 in hopes of persuading the assembled union leaders to accept a plan under which clergy could participate as fraternal partners.

Stelzle had been having modest success thus far in promoting the idea of cooperative relations between churches and unions, mostly by traveling around the country and speaking at Presbyterian churches in large cities. In his talks and through accompanying newspaper stories, he presented himself as a member of the Machinists' Union and a supporter of organized bargaining between unions and employers. He was there as a pastor who had worked with laboring people through his churches in Minneapolis, St. Louis, and New York; was part of a pioneering effort by the Presbyterian denomination to reach working people; and had the blessing of several prominent labor leaders. Besides his appearances at churches, he spoke at Rotary dinners, at Chautauqua meetings, and occasionally at synagogues. Those were appreciative audiences who agreed in principle at least that churches should do what they could to help deserving working people in poor neighborhoods. Speaking to labor assemblies was a different matter.

The meeting at Bricklayers' Hall on Sunday afternoon, April 10, 1904, did not go well. Stelzle, in conjunction with an alliance of Chicago clergy, had been trying without success that spring to persuade the CFL to establish formal relations between its member unions and clergy. A letter from Stelzle in late March drew comments from union leaders questioning the pastors' motives and fearing that union sessions would become embroiled in creedal disputes. The mass meeting on April 10 was Stelzle's chance to pitch the idea directly to union members. The proposal, he explained, was for clergy to send elected delegates to CFL meetings, serving as nonvoting members to build bridges by learning about union activities and in turn communicating ideas about church activities. Stelzle pledged his personal belief in unions' efforts to protect workers from unscrupulous employers, acknowledged that he held some reservations about union activities, and expressed hope that his plan would garner greater understanding of the churches. "The chasm between the workers and the church is due to mutual misunderstandings," he contended. "Each needs the other. The success of the labor movement is due to the fact that the church has blazed the way. The church was started by workingmen. I should not be surprised if its early leaders belonged to the trade guilds of the day."[32]

It was a hard sell, even if Stelzle had not insulted the assembled unionists by crediting the church with originating union work. Although it was true that churches were fighting for child labor regulations and Sunday closing laws, the city's churches were making headlines that spring mostly for the Law and Order League's efforts to shut down saloons and, in the case of Presbyterians like Stelzle, the Chicago Presbytery's mass revival meetings to covert sinners to Jesus. Better laws were not the answer to the "chattel slavery" in which industrial workers lived, Leo Tolstoy advised the CFL in a letter that spring, but fundamental reforms empowering working people to change legislation. The audience at Bricklayers' Hall "challenged practically every statement he made," a journalist who listened to Stelzle's speech reported. "In what way has the church ever aided the workingman and proved its friendship for him?" a listener asked. "From my youth I was taught in the church to be docile and humble and to do the bidding of those above me," another said. "I want to know what you would advise in case of a strike. Would you counsel the workers to be careful not to harm the capitalist?"[33]

In his autobiography, Stelzle recalled the CFL effort as one of the most difficult he ever encountered. "I never yet saw a preacher who did any work," he remembered one of the labor leaders saying. "I have yet to see the preacher who hoed potatoes or sowed a patch of cabbages," said another. "I have yet to see the garment woven by a preacher. We have had to do all of that for them. We have had to carry the preachers on our backs, just as we have the other parasites of society. I never saw a preacher yet who did not pose as the workingman's friend; but if they are his friends, let them prove it by getting off the backs of the workingmen."[34] Newspapers across the country carried the story.

Stelzle comforted himself, believing that the meeting's most vocal critics were socialists who simply held the churches in contempt, trying instead to give their own movement a religious flavor, and noting that he did, after all, have good relations with American Federation of Labor President Samuel Gompers. But the meeting redirected Stelzle's thinking about how the churches could span the chasm separating them from labor. Although unions in other cities proved more amenable to accepting clergy as nonvoting fraternal delegates, efforts to organize other activities, such as noon-time shop meetings at plants in Chicago, achieved less success than Stelzle hoped, as much because of clergy disinterest as from union leaders' resistance. Tackling the gap by working with churches, rather than with unions, increasingly became Stelzle's focus. Church audiences warmly received Stelzle's argument that church involvement in unions' affairs could curb vice and crime and graft, but Stelzle also wanted them to consider the conditions in which industrial workers lived. To that end, he realized that churches needed to understand better the needs of working-class neighborhoods, which meant, as Laidlaw and Du Bois had recognized, better information collected through scientific means.

An event that may have sparked Stelzle's interest in research occurred in 1905. Stelzle, now working in New York City as secretary of the Presbyterians' Church and Labor Department, attended the tenth-anniversary dinner of the New York Federation, where he heard Laidlaw describe the surveys he had been doing in the city and the practical purposes to which the results were being put to use. According to the federation's newsletter, Stelzle "declared that no better evangelizing work could be done in the City of New York than to present to the laboring men of the city, who

conceive that the Church is devoting itself simply to post-mortem purposes, an account of the activities of the Federation in the betterment of
living conditions."[35]

The mandate for Stelzle to conduct research came two years later when
the Presbyterians' General Assembly created a Department of Immigration and asked Stelzle to direct it in addition to his work with the Department of Church and Labor. Among other things, the Department of
Church and Labor was charged with serving as a bureau of information to
engage in sociological research about the social conditions and religious
lives of immigrants. Meanwhile, interest in community surveys continued on other fronts, most significantly in 1908 when the Russell Sage
Foundation for the Improvement of Social and Living Conditions, organized by devout Presbyterian Olivia Slocum Sage following her husband's
death in 1906, funded a comprehensive survey in Pittsburgh of the city's
sanitary, industrial, and moral conditions, the results of which were published in six volumes from 1909 to 1914.[36]

Stelzle's large-scale survey, which began in late 1911 and continued
into 1912, collecting information in more than seventy of the nation's
largest cities, was conducted in conjunction with what he called the
Men and Religion Forward Movement. The movement was inspired
by Stelzle's efforts especially to reach workingmen affiliated with labor
unions and by a parallel attempt to enlist men in middle-class churches
to assist in these efforts. The focus on men was motivated by church
leaders' impressions that men's involvement in churches fell considerably below that of women—an impression verified by information about
religious bodies collected by the US Census Bureau. The centerpiece
of the movement was to be a series of social service institutes or conferences to educate churchgoing men about the history of industrial
work and organized labor, the threat of socialism, and what churches
could do to combat that threat. Other topics dealt with community problems ranging from sanitation and crime to municipal administration
and immigration with information from the latest sociological studies. After discussing methods of church advertising, the institutes concluded with practical instruction in conducting field surveys, including
how to write questionnaires, where to look for available statistics, the
importance of being accurate and securing facts rather than opinions,
and how to produce charts and publicize the results. Enlisting the assistance of clergy and lay volunteers, Stelzle printed thousands of blank
questionnaires and asked congregations to collect information about

social service work, Bible study, union activities, evangelism, and missions. He did this in person as well as by mail. With James "Railroad Jim" Smith of the YMCA and Fred B. Smith of Men and Religion Forward, Stelzle stumped the country, lecturing in churches, holding special afternoon meetings, talking to journalists, and posting newspaper essays. The idea behind the survey, he explained, was to make the churches run as scientifically as modern railroads and construction companies. "A new principle has been born for the science of religious revival," he told his audiences.[37]

The survey was ambitious in scope, but differed from the ones Laidlaw and Du Bois conducted in that most of the data it obtained was from informants and pertained to blocks rather than individuals. The house-to-house canvass that volunteers conducted asked for the family's name and address, nationality and race, church preference, ages and gender of children, and whether each member of the family held membership in a Sunday school or church. Each home visitation card remained in the hands of the local church for later use, while the information submitted to Stelzle's bureau in New York was aggregated into block-level summaries. The block-level summaries were then supplemented with information about the location of churches, settlement houses, hospitals, libraries, schools, dance halls, police stations, motion picture theaters, private kindergartens, saloons, charitable organizations, pool halls, and parks. Block maps color-coded by dominant nationality included symbols showing the location of each community organization. For each town, additional information was tallied, including the proportion of each nationality represented, changes in population, detailed questions about community government, the assessed value of real estate, school enrollment and educational attainment, whether free public lectures were given, the number of volumes in libraries, employment patterns, crime, public health, the condition of streets, family incomes, and how families spent their earnings.

While much of the information could be obtained from censuses and municipal statistics, the survey was exceptional in including questions about informants' assessments of conditions in their communities. It asked their opinion of how much influence churches had on the community's social, political, and economic affairs; what contributed to or inhibited residents from feelings of common cause with other residents; whether people gathered to express popular will mostly in public halls, schools, churches, or out of doors; their impressions of employees' working conditions; where young men and young women gathered; and what informants perceived governing officials' attitudes to be toward housing regulations and saloons.

Additional information was obtained from clergy about the composition and activities of their congregations. The congregation survey included questions about methods of church advertising, uses of the church building for recitals and social gatherings, how many evangelistic meetings were held, how many people of each age group and gender attended the meetings, the number of Bible classes held, what study guides and equipment were used, who attended worship services, whether mixed-gender or separate-gender classes worked better, how the church raised money, whether discussions had been held about topics such as child labor and immigration, and what social service activities the church provided for the community.[38]

What the survey lacked in precision, given the number of questions informants were expected to answer, it made up for in scope, providing unprecedented compilations of facts and figures for dozens of communities and hundreds of churches. Without the knowledge required for complex statistical analysis, the information was summarized in charts and on maps. Believing that churches would benefit mostly from replicating the survey in their own communities, Stelzle produced and circulated an eighteen-page pamphlet composed of forty-six charts, summarizing the overall results with little narrative interpretation, but including instructions for churches interested in conducting their own surveys. Because its primary audience was expected to be the institutes sponsored by the Men and Religion Forward Movement, the featured charts included topics such as the numbers of men's and boys' Sunday school classes, the percentage of boys who were in Sunday school classes, the kinds of offenses for which boys were accused in juvenile courts, the nationality of their parents, truancy among boys, employment among boys, labor union membership, and arrests among adults by gender.

Stelzle also published a lengthy volume, titled *American Social and Religious Conditions*, with chapters on women and children, immigrants, African Americans, Spanish-speaking Americans, Indians, social agencies, and churches. Framed with observations from Malthus and Aristotle and including a brief history of the decline of farming and the rise of cities, the book presented statistics from the 1900 and 1910 US censuses, discussed the recent conclusions of Theodore Roosevelt's Country Life Commission, summarized statistics about liquor consumption, examined the history of suffragist efforts in relation to shifts in women's employment,

showed maps of immigrant origins and destinations, provided information about comparative infant death rates by race and ethnicity, considered
literacy and schooling among Native Americans and Spanish Americans,
and described the various social movements and charitable organizations currently responding to changing social conditions. The purpose of
understanding this statistical information, he argued, was to render the
church more scientific, and thus more efficient, in conducting its business, just as businesses were doing: "If God thinks it worth while to adopt
a system in His economy does it seem unreasonable to insist that He
expects men to be scientific in carrying on His work?" He believed the
churches should adopt "scientific management" and, for that purpose,
should organize a "national bureau" to "make comprehensive surveys."[39]
Almost as an afterthought, more illustrative of what could be done than
of what had been done, the book included appendices summarizing the
results of the multicity survey, giving only a brief overview of the results
and offering little in the way of detail about how many people actually participated and whom they represented. The survey nevertheless anticipated
the kinds of surveys that would occur later in which information would
be collected about congregations and related to data about congregations'
community contexts.[40]

Making surveys, he wrote a few years later, "was an utterly thank-
less job" because usually "the facts produced were not especially compli-
mentary."[41] And yet, besides conducting his own surveys, Stelzle became
an enthusiastic user and promoter of other surveys and statistical data.
Drawing overly precise estimates of the total number of Protestants, Catholics, and unchurched adults and children by inferring numbers from
the 1910 census, he produced charts suggesting that churches were falling behind and needed to work harder. With no training in sociology, he
nevertheless called himself a sociologist (even though the term was un-
popular in church circles and was sometimes confused with "socialist"),
believing that the discipline's scientific methods were the way forward.[42]
In 1912, as superintendent of the Presbyterian Church's Bureau of Social
Services, he arranged for paid investigators to conduct interviews with
nearly a thousand workingmen at meetings in New York City, the results
of which served as the basis for George E. Bevans's 1913 Columbia University dissertation *How Workingmen Spend Their Time*. Stelzle produced
his own summary of the results and drew up a plan to present them at
churches and at evangelistic meetings for workingmen throughout the
city. He found especially interesting the extent to which saloons, theaters,

and pool halls competed with churches for workingmen's time, observed that church attendance was highest among men age forty-six and older and among married men, argued that workingmen would benefit from shorter hours and more leisure time, concluded that shorter hours would not necessarily increase church attendance, and noted the potential for churches to promote improved understandings of citizenship and democracy.[43]

On a smaller scale, surveys similar to Stelzle's were taken in other cities. In Syracuse, New York, for example, Shelby M. Harrison, who had worked on the Pittsburgh survey and who would continue to work with the Russell Sage Foundation as director of its Department of Surveys and Exhibits, conducted what he hoped would be considered a social survey of a "typical American city" by enlisting the support of the Ministerial Association (representing more than a hundred churches), the Chamber of Commerce, and the Central Trades Assembly. From community leaders and census information, the survey compiled statistics on demographics, immigration and ethnicity, housing, employment, education, juvenile delinquency, child labor, and "betterment agencies" (including churches, hospitals, Christian associations, and settlements). Forty of the town's clergy preached sermons about the results, and evening meetings were held at churches and schools to discuss practical implications. In 1914 a similar survey was conducted in Springfield, Illinois, followed, according to Harrison, by some hundred and fifty other community surveys over the next decade and a half. "All over the country little groups of people who a few years ago met together to cultivate a taste for literature and art are now studying their local communities and devising plans to reform them," sociologist Robert E. Park wrote in 1917. "This is the survey movement."[44]

Stelzle's work for the Presbyterian Church ended in 1913, stemming from criticism of his support for workers during the bloody McKees Rocks Strike in Pittsburgh in 1909, including accusations that he was an agent of the American Federation of Labor, and prompted by what he perceived as rising capitalist-funded fundamentalism within the denomination. Billing himself as an independent "consulting sociologist," he conducted a survey of social conditions in Wilkes-Barre in 1913, complementing a simultaneous Russell Sage Foundation study of Scranton, and one in Jersey City the following year, declaring, "A survey is not mere gratification of curiosity, it is made entirely with the view to outlining a definite practical program of sufficient scope to serve as a guide to the efforts of a community for a number of years." He assembled statistics about social conditions for the YMCA in 1915; worked for the American Red Cross during World War I, publicizing the organization's needs among religious bodies; and, after a year with the Methodist Church's Centenary Celebration, worked with the Interchurch World Movement (IWM)'s short-lived billion-dollar fundraising effort—a project he found to be top-heavy and doomed by human frailties.[45]

The Religious Life of America

In 1926, as president of the Church Advertising Department of the International Advertising Association headquartered on Madison Avenue in New York City, Stelzle organized what he hoped would be a path-breaking study of American religion. The idea was to move beyond the canvasses of organizations and the information about communities that the social survey movement had been collecting. The plan was to poll individuals directly to find out what they believed religiously and how they put those beliefs into practice.

With input from a multidenominational panel of clergy, Stelzle drew up a questionnaire that asked about church membership and attendance, attitudes toward religion, and beliefs about God, immortality, and prayer. Through the Advertising Association, he then persuaded two hundred daily newspapers around the country to print the questionnaire, asking readers to send in their answers. The results were to be published in the newspapers and discussed in pulpits and at meetings of church leaders.

Stelzle expected the research to have a profound impact. "I believe that the information procured," he told a reporter for the *New York Times*, "will become classical in the religious life of the world for years to come. It will be used in public addresses and in the [printed media] as an authentic presentation of the religious life of America."[46]

The response was enormous. Approximately 125,000 people filled out the questionnaire. They overwhelmingly affirmed that religion was important: 91 percent said they believed in God; 88 percent, in immortality; 88 percent, in "prayer as a means of personal relationship with God"; 85 percent, that "Jesus was divine as no other man was divine"; and 85 percent, in the Bible "as inspired in a sense that no other literature could be said to be inspired." The responses also showed that 77 percent were active church members, 76 percent regularly attended religious services, and 87 percent thought "religion in some form is a necessary element of life for the individual and for the community."[47]

Religion in America, Stelzle concluded, was now thriving, contrary to earlier pessimistic appraisals. The nation was not composed of Philistines, he observed. Despite the popularity of short skirts, jazz, and motion pictures, the populace had not become irreligious. Nor was it composed of backsliders, as fundamentalists argued, who no longer believed in God or the Bible. Religion in America was on the whole conservative, even old-fashioned, and, at the same time, he cautioned, the churches needed to work harder to activate the public's interest. That was especially true, he noted in New York City, where only 50 percent attended religious services regularly.

But Stelzle's hope that the poll would be received as "authentic" and "become classical" was not realized. The newspapers that printed the questionnaire immediately cast doubt on the results. It was surely biased for the questionnaire to have invited replies by noting, "every man has some kind of religion." There were certainly more atheists than the survey suggested. Fundamentalists seemed to be replying more often than modernists. Having said a table grace as a child with words that could no longer be remembered was being counted as having been raised in a religious home. Religious belief was too personal and too diverse to be measured with simple yes-or-no questions.

"The returns from the questionnaire on religion, recently printed by newspapers in nearly 200 cities, are being used, as statistics always are, to prove almost anything that anybody wants to demonstrate," a columnist for the *Nation* wrote when the final results were tallied. The best statistics from the Church Advertising Department itself, the author noted, estimated that 43 percent of the population were church members, not 77 percent, as the survey suggested.[48]

In 1927, the Church Advertising Department under Stelzle's direction conducted a follow-up to the 1926 poll, this time with questionnaires distributed to thirty thousand students at a hundred colleges and universities. With the intent of selling religion, the poll suggested that religion was indeed a promising market, even among college students who commentators believed disinterested if not downright skeptical toward religion. The poll registered belief in God among 98 percent of the students responding. In nine additional questions, the proportion of students giving "orthodox" responses ranged from 52 percent at Dartmouth to 96 percent at Oklahoma Baptist and Kentucky Wesleyan to a high of 99 percent at Providence College in Rhode Island and Pacific Union College in California. Like the other survey, this one evoked criticism from newspaper editors who questioned who the responses represented and whether the survey's response categories were adequate. "The only thing demonstrated is the misuse of which the questionnaire is susceptible," one editor remarked. Ironically, the best summary of the criticisms appeared in the *Literary Digest*, which a few years later would be embarrassed by a poll of its own erroneously predicting the results of the 1936 presidential election.[49]

It would be nearly a decade before serious attempts were again made to assess the nation's religious beliefs and practices with polling. In the meantime, several studies using similar questionnaires in newspapers and magazines were conducted, but they received little interest or comment. Stelzle's work also shifted. He continued to conduct and promote research, but his research returned to the earlier style of the social survey movement. His surveys were inventories of community statistics drawn from state, federal, and municipal censuses. The closest he came to another attitude survey was a questionnaire distributed to Presbyterian pastors asking for detailed information about the activities of their congregations, including beliefs about the kinds of topics considered appropriate to address from the pulpit. In the 1930s, his fundraising on behalf of the World Alliance for International Friendship through the Churches still emphasized research, but by that time he had in mind collecting factual materials and statistics from other studies, not conducting original polls.[50]

Stelzle's research never produced the detailed systematic evidence that Laidlaw's did and fell far short of the excellence Du Bois achieved in writing about Philadelphia. He differed from both in preferring church work to scientific inquiries, and his interests in advertising and public opinion put him closer to anticipating what polling would later try to accomplish than either of the other two. However, he agreed with Laidlaw and Du Bois in appreciating the value of studying local conditions rather than seeking broad national generalizations. "When local men and women engage in such studies," he wrote, "they will constantly make 'original' discoveries."[51] And, acting on that belief in 1930, with funds from the Chicago Federation of Churches, Stelzle conducted almost the same kind of citywide survey there that Laidlaw and Du Bois had pioneered in the 1890s, tabulating door-to-door information about social conditions and churches and making extensive comparisons by race and ethnicity and between inner-city neighborhoods and suburbs.[52]

Continuing the Work

In March 1917, Stelzle met with forty-one-year-old John D. Rockefeller Jr., who a few years earlier had been excoriated in the press for the Ludlow massacre at his Colorado Fuel and Iron Company, which left twenty men, women, and children dead. Despite Stelzle's history with labor, he took a different view of Rockefeller. In an account of their hour-long conversation in New York City, Stelzle wrote, "I have come away with the feeling that here is a man, who, although he probably will some day be the richest individual in the world, nevertheless thinks more deeply and sincerely about big moral and ethical problems than he does about financial questions." If Stelzle discussed Rockefeller's Baptist upbringing, he did not mention it in the essay, instead quoting Rockefeller to the effect that "every man must work out his own salvation" and that the teachings of Jesus could not be specified as dogmatic ethical laws. Stelzle commended Rockefeller mostly for his "social spirit," including his support of a recent survey about social hygiene and prostitution.[53]

Stelzle was canny enough to know that describing Rockefeller this way might encourage Rockefeller's philanthropy, even to support Stelzle's own projects. It was in fact Rockefeller who footed the bill for much of the IWM's work over the next several years, in which Stelzle played a small part. But it was not through Stelzle's work that surveys about religion continued. Like it had for Laidlaw and Stelzle, the Presbyterian Church played an instrumental role in organizing the IWM, but the key agency was now the Foreign Mission Board, rather than the Home Mission Board, and the impetus came from church leaders' desire to assist Europe at the close of World War I. The IWM formed on December 17, 1918, a few days after the armistice, as a gathering of 135 church leaders interested in the feasibility of a joint fundraising campaign. The armistice, though, also sharpened conflict between steelworkers and employers, resulting in the "great steel strike," which closed plants around the country in September 1919, and prompted the IWM to form an Interchurch Department of Industrial Relations to investigate the struggle. The IWM only lasted through the end of 1920, despite Rockefeller's generosity and participating personally in a two-week cross-country fundraising tour. But in the interim, it conducted an investigation of the steel strike, including the role of churches, and produced what it called a "world survey," which for the United States summarized in dozens of charts statistics about rural and urban populations, divorce, fertility, migration, race relations, and trends in church membership; and for the rest of the world summarized statistics about population, economic conditions, health, and education, insofar as such information was known. In appearance more like an almanac than a research study, nearly all the US information was drawn from the 1910 census and the 1916 census of religious bodies, as well as information from surveys conducted by hospitals and charities. Like Stelzle's work, the report encouraged local churches to conduct their own surveys and proposed topics that would be of particular value to study. However, compiling the information brought together a team of researchers with the skills and funding needed to carry forward the survey work that had begun during the previous quarter-century.[54]

When the IWM disbanded, enough interest in research had been generated that a Committee on Social and Religious Surveys formed in New York City made up of some of the church leaders and researchers who had participated in the IWM. The committee then formed the Institute for Social and Religious Research. The key member of the new institute's board was Raymond B. Fosdick, a 1905 Princeton graduate who earned a law degree in New York City three years later, observed the appalling conditions of the Lower East Side, and in 1913 became the head of Rockefeller Jr.'s Bureau of Social Hygiene. When the institute formed, Fosdick was a board member of the Laura Spelman Rockefeller Memorial, which provided its financial support.[55] One of the researchers was H. Paul Douglass, a Congregational pastor who had spent his early career as superintendent of education for the American Missionary Association, worked on race relations in the South, wrote several books, traveled to France with the YMCA to assist with the demobilization of African-American soldiers, and most recently managed the Agricultural Labor Branch of the IWM. Douglass joined the institute in 1921 and in 1922 directed a citywide survey of Springfield, Massachusetts, enumerating, with the help of a thousand volunteers on a single Sunday, sixteen thousand households.[56] Douglass continued at the institute for the next thirteen years, directing forty-eight research projects and authoring or coauthoring numerous books. While most of the studies focused on congregations, Douglass also conducted surveys among seminary faculty, clergy, and laity. One of the principal themes of the studies was that church leaders needed to make use of modern scientific studies because impressions and even membership figures were faulty indicators of religious trends. Another conclusion was that Protestant churches in particular were suffering from apathy and failing to keep pace with population growth.[57]

The Institute for Social and Religious Research disbanded in 1934, but Douglass continued collecting data and writing, becoming secretary to the Federal Council of Churches' Commission to Study Church Unity in 1937 and chair of the council's research department in 1943. Douglass was revered as the leading church researcher of the 1920s and 1930s because of his prodigious output and the prominence of the Institute for Social and Religious Research. Two of his collaborators—C. Luther Fry and Edmund deS. Brunner—carried on the tradition of research he started, well into the 1950s. Although Douglass came late in his career to religious research, he continued longer and produced more than any of his predecessors. He was, however, not the only researcher who gained prominence through the Institute for Social and Religious Research.

Ironically, the study that did "become classic," as Stelzle hoped his would, did not have national scope but was the intensive investigation conducted in the single community of Muncie, Indiana, that became known as *Middletown*. Although it employed a different method, it too began as church research. With support from Rockefeller, the Institute for Social and Religious Research decided in late 1922 that it would be valuable to conduct another survey of a small city similar to the one Douglass had directed earlier in the year in Springfield, only this time in the Midwest, and in 1923 Robert Lynd was selected as the investigator for the study. Lynd was a Princeton graduate and had taken courses at Columbia University and Union Theological Seminary before pastoring a church in Wyoming while deciding whether to continue as a minister. Lynd and his wife, Helen, moved to Muncie in 1924 to pursue the institute's objective of learning about churches, but soon broadened the research to produce the exhaustive account of the community's social, cultural, and political life published as *Middletown* in 1929.[58]

Middletown was unlike any of the church surveys that Douglass and others had done; it was more similar to Du Bois's study of Philadelphia, but different from it as well. Although *Middletown* included some statistical evidence the Lynds collected by conducting a survey, the Lynds considered it more an example of ethnographic research of the kind anthropologists did, including field observations and qualitative interviews, and that was how the book was received. As a predecessor of later polls and surveys about religion, its influence was thus different but no less important.

In her detailed discussion of the book's reception, historian Sarah E. Igo argues that *Middletown* captured—and indeed contributed to—an emerging national consciousness as no other social scientific study did at the time. Written in an engaging style with ample narratives and quotes, it was widely reviewed in nearly every major newspaper and magazine, became required reading in courses at dozens of colleges, and went through six printings in its first year alone. Unlike the surveys church leaders and social reformers had been doing in low-income urban neighborhoods, *Middletown* described people with whom the average middle-class reader could identify, whether that person lived in a small town, suburb, or city. The research, in fact, basically ignored African Americans, immigrants, and ethnic diversity, instead presenting an image that could be characterized by newspaper editors and columnists as typically American, at least for their predominantly white readership.[59]

If *Middletown* contributed to an emerging sense of national identity, it did so in ways that posed several important implications for the national polls that followed a few years later. In suggesting that there was such a thing as a typical American or a typical American town, it opened itself to criticisms, of which there were many (especially from social scientists), stating that information from one town in the Midwest could not, in fact, be considered representative of the national population. That criticism set the stage for national polls that could claim to be representative. In addition, *Middletown* provided a framework for thinking that generalizations about white middle-class families could be regarded as representative of the population. That assumption also carried forward in interpretations of polls. A third implication was more complicated and is most evident in how *Middletown* was received compared with Stelzle's 1926 survey. Both offered interpretations of what Americans believed, but readers regarded *Middletown*'s observations as more credible than Stelzle's. The reason was that *Middletown* offered a more nuanced view because of the field observations and verbatim quotes included, whereas readers considered questions in polls simplistic.

For understandings of religion, *Middletown* encouraged scholars to use ethnographic methods rather than quantitative surveys. The Lynds' 1937 follow-up study sparked additional interest that in turn prompted ethnographic community studies in the 1940s and 1950s, such as W. Lloyd Warner's *Yankee City* and Arthur J. Vidich and Joseph Bensman's *Small Town in Mass Society*. *Middletown* contributed to understandings of religion in one other way that was subtler and that was shared by the pollsters and survey researchers that followed.[60] The assumption was that religion was best understood by viewing it from a distance, no matter how close and personal the methods were, because doing so provided objectivity that in turn reduced bias. *Middletown*'s observations about religion were critical and presented from a distance—like an anthropologist studying an alien culture. The social scientific studies that followed, whether quantitative or qualitative, were often similarly critical of religion, suggesting, as the Lynds did, that ordinary people's beliefs and attitudes were fraught with self-deception. That was a point with which pollsters would disagree, viewing public opinion as both credible and thoughtful.

Toward Polling

The social survey movement of the 1890s through the 1920s anticipated many of the characteristics that were to become hallmarks of public opinion polling a few years later. The impetus for conducting surveys was to move beyond anecdotes and impressions by collecting scientific statistical information. Door-to-door canvassing was the preferred method for obtaining information about individuals and families. The framing and phrasing of questions was important, as was the necessity of representing the entire population of a community and interpreting the results as objectively as possible. Trained researchers were better than amateur volunteers for conducting surveys, and cross-tabulations were essential for understanding the relationships of religious activities to age, gender, nationality, and race. Under Laidlaw, even the idea of using electronic tabulating machines was present.

And yet, the social survey movement was rarely concerned with public opinion. Its aim was to collect information about behavior, whether in the form of churchgoing and participating in Sunday school classes, or about employment, wages, illnesses, schooling, or leisure activities. The emphasis on behavior reflected the researchers' interest in understanding social conditions. It also underscored a particular view of how research could benefit religious organizations. The purpose was not to find out what ordinary people thought, but to document the hard facts of what religious organizations were or were not doing in relation to facts about social conditions.

It was not that public opinion was unimportant. Public opinion grew in importance during the late eighteenth century and by the 1830s was one of the distinguishing characteristics that Alexis de Tocqueville described in his famous treatise on American democracy. From time to time, later discussions of public opinion included remarks about Americans' faith in God and interest in religion. It was not common, though, to speak generally about American religion let alone to regard religion as a matter of public opinion. Those understandings were secondary to conceptions of religion featuring churches and other religious organizations.

The clearest exception involving surveys was Stelzle's effort to determine what percentage of Americans and American students believed in God. The criticism the attempt received was more telling than the results. The charge was that something as subtle and complex as religious beliefs could not be captured with simple survey questions. The survey evoked skepticism not only because the questions were crude, but also because it was hard to know what it meant to describe something as general as "Americans" that way. It was perhaps instructive, too, that the survey was conducted in newspapers, rather than by religious organizations, and for the purpose of advertising—to persuade religious leaders and newspaper publishers that advertising about religion and to religious people was good business. *Middletown*'s more favorable reception rested partly on the fact that it did not appear to be selling anything.

It made more sense at the time to conduct scientific studies about religion within local communities, even if those communities were as large as New York City and Chicago. For the practical ends to which religious leaders might put them, local surveys produced information about specific needs and the specific community organizations that could address these needs. For academic purposes, as Du Bois most clearly argued, local research provided firsthand knowledge not only of aggregated statistics but also of the specific contexts in which those statistics occurred. For Laidlaw and Stelzle, and especially for Du Bois and the Lynds, religion was best understood by linking survey results with information from interviews and observations about communities' histories and particularities. Those understandings would continue to inflect studies of religion but would soon be accompanied by a new way of conducting surveys that would bring with it different understandings of religion.

The era of social surveys demonstrated, too, that the institutional contexts in which research was conducted profoundly influenced the topics that were studied and thus the perceptions of religion that resulted. Although the surveys conducted in these early years aspired to be scientific, and despite the fact that researchers called themselves sociologists and either held advanced degrees in sociology or consulted with those who did, surveys about religion occurred largely outside of colleges and universities. The investigators worked as church leaders, received funds from churches or in a few cases from foundations and private donors, did not teach, and did not train students. Academic social scientists who occasionally read and reviewed church researchers' publications were rightly critical of the methods involved and the lack of statistical rigor. Located outside of academia, and yet seeking the imprimatur of social science, put church researchers in an awkward position going forward. The open question was whether religious organizations would continue to serve as the principal sponsors through which information about religion was obtained, whether academic-based social scientists would play an increasing role, or whether commercial polling would enter and redefine the field.

3

Measuring Belief

THE FIFTY-THIRD ANNUAL Triangle Club Show on the Princeton University campus took place in late November 1941. Each year, the show satirized noteworthy recent and current events. Except for the annual gridiron rivalry with Yale, it was the festive highlight of the year. A few days later, the attack on Pearl Harbor would plunge the nation into war. But on November 21, a thousand people filled the McCarter Theater auditorium for the Triangle Club Show's opening night. The theme that year was "Ask Me Another." Its inspiration was the Gallup Poll. The skits included students pretending to be Gallup interviewers asking compliant members of the public ridiculous questions. The opening number, performed by the cross-dressed, all-male chorus line, was called the "Gallup Poll Gallop." The *New York Times* gave the event a rave review. *Variety* wrote that "the Princeton lads really have something this year," asserting that the opening number was a "socko" bid for curtain-call applause. Mr. Gallup was reported to have lauded the event as a "perfect job."[1]

George Gallup was arguably one of Princeton's most famous citizens—better known than the university itself. A former journalism professor at Northwestern University, Gallup visited Princeton in 1934 as a guest lecturer, came again in 1935, and purchased a farm eight miles north of town that reminded him of the one he had grown up on in Iowa. He founded the American Institute of Public Opinion that year in rented third-story office space across the street from the university. Funding to conduct national polls came from an arrangement for weekly columns in thirty-five newspapers. After successfully predicting the 1936 presidential election, which the much larger survey conducted by the *Literary Digest* failed to predict, Gallup's method of scientific sampling attracted national attention. By 1938, the number of newspapers carrying his columns grew to sixty, and Gallup's six hundred field researchers were conducting weekly interviews in selected locations around the country. It was through his columns that tens of thousands of readers every week saw the byline, George Gallup, Princeton, New Jersey. Early in 1939, the *Saturday Evening Post* published an eight-page article with photos of Gallup, his wife and sons, and several of the staff, and described in detail who Gallup was, his ancestry, his start in polling, and how the polls were done.[2]

From the beginning, Gallup polls included questions about religion. For the first time, interpreters of American religion could base their assessments on something other than membership figures and conjecture. Churchgoers could know if they were in the majority or minority in their part of the country, and church leaders could compare the success of their efforts against national trends. By the time a new generation came of age in the 1960s, all of this would be taken for granted. But when polling began, it was unclear if questions about religion could be asked, and if they were, whether anyone would care. How polling and religion came together was a process that unfolded slowly and in unexpected ways.

Scientific Polling

If 1936 was the year Gallup polls gained national attention, 1938 was the year that saw them become fully integrated into the regular news cycle. From week to week, the polls monitored Roosevelt's popularity and how the public felt about him seeking a third term in office. The polls included questions about the Supreme Court and the federal budget. They queried the public about the business climate, whether they thought the railroads should be publicly owned, and what people thought about state and local dry laws. They documented regional differences in attitudes toward a federal antilynching law. When the New York State legislature proposed a bill requiring expectant mothers to be tested for syphilis, a poll documented widespread support for the idea. By year's end, Gallup's press releases in each of the newspapers carrying them appeared seventy times.

Besides national polls, Gallup conducted statewide polls asking voters their preferences in congressional primary elections. Polls monitored trends in closely contested elections in Colorado, Georgia, Kentucky, North Carolina, and Pennsylvania. A Gallup counterpart to the American Institute of Public Opinion conducted regular polls of the British population as well. Readers in the United States could see periodically how people there felt about preparations for war on the continent and prospects for American involvement.

Gallup's arrangement with the newspapers gave him complete freedom to ask questions about any topic he wished, the only constraint being that he needed to produce newsworthy material to fill the weekly columns. Most of the polls, for that reason, dealt with politics and pending legislation. Events that happened to be in the news occasionally sparked deviations from that pattern. A poll in which 39 percent of the public registered approval of restoring the whipping post as a means of punishing certain types of criminals, for example, was prompted by a cat-o'-nine-tails flogging of a Baltimore printer convicted of beating his wife.

The polls' publicity put Gallup in high demand as a speaker at community events. Municipal advertising clubs invited him to talk about polling. They wanted to know how the polls were conducted and what potential they held for marketing products. Oil company executives were interested too, as were local and national leaders of both political parties. They were eager to hear in person from this expert who for the first time seemed to be using science to investigate public opinion. Here was a technique, they realized, that could be used to influence opinion as well as measure it. One listener suggested a poll be conducted to show that immigration should be stopped. Another published the results of a hypothetical Gallup poll suggesting that women would probably want to purchase a new line of fur jackets.

Audiences wanted to know if the methods were sound. They especially wanted reassurance that the polling was nonpartisan, that candidates and special interest groups were not slipping Gallup money behind the scenes to skew the results, and that all the results were being reported openly and honestly. There were rumors that Roosevelt's minions had secretly worked with Gallup to swing the 1936 election. Questions surfaced in 1938 about the timing of press releases and whether some results were being suppressed.

Writing from Emporia, Kansas, where he had paid close attention to the contest between Roosevelt and Kansas native son Alf Landon, Pulitzer Prize–winning editor William Allen White saw polling as the wave of the future but worried about its implications. It grew from radio and marketing research, he observed, in which "trick questions conceived by intelligent psychologists" were used to tap into underlying sentiments. He predicted that the public's penchant for numbers would draw them to poll results claiming to be accurate within a tenth of a percentage. Polling, he averred, was democracy's "latest accessory gadget"—"cuter and handier than a windshield wiper." But he also thought people would try to give agreeable answers that would put them on the winning side.[3]

One of the prevailing questions was how polling as few as a thousand people could yield credible results. Sampling seemed to be a difficult topic for newspaper readers to grasp. They still wondered if perhaps the *Literary Digest*'s larger numbers might not be preferable. To make his case, Gallup reported the results of a poll he conducted in 1936 in which 30,000 people were asked if the National Recovery Act should be revived. Among the 30,000, 55.5 percent said no. An almost identical result (54.9 percent), he said, was obtained from only the first five hundred polled.[4]

Not everyone was convinced. The most frequently publicized criticisms focused less on sampling and more on whether the idea of polling at all made sense. They ventured that polls captured a certain kind of public opinion, and might even be redefining the meaning of public opinion, but were hardly a substitute for the reasoned debates that used to be understood as the basis of informed public opinion. Were the results interesting? Were they meaningful? "Dr. George Gallup goes galloping ahead, buttonholing the man in the street and reducing him to snappy percentages on everything under the sun," syndicated columnist Jay Franklin observed. He doubted that the percentages captured much of how the public felt.[5]

Letters to editors and letters sent privately to Gallup echoed similar mixed reactions. People wrote to express approval of poll results they liked and disapproval of the ones they did not. The ones they disagreed with prompted remarks about how the polls were probably biased, would likely be proven wrong in the next election, and might fall into disrepute like the 1936 *Literary Digest* poll.[6]

Gallup understood that something as new and as potentially powerful as polling depended on earning the public's trust. The successful prediction in 1936 was key. The predictions in 1938 proved to be accurate as well. In addition, Gallup cultivated his academic credentials as much as he could. Although he sometimes did and sometimes did not include "Dr." in the byline of his newspaper columns, he was widely known by that title. He acknowledged that one of the advantages of writing from Princeton, New Jersey, was its reputation as a college town. In 1937, the new *Public Opinion Quarterly*, published across the street at the university, provided a forum to which Gallup became a frequent contributor. "The science of measuring public opinion is only in its infancy," he wrote in 1938. "Many things have still to be learned." This was the context in which polling about religion began.[7]

Polling Religion

Had polling about other topics attracted less interest than it did, the technique might have taken longer to include questions about religion. But nearly everything Gallup asked about drew interest. The more serious topics, such as attitudes about going to war and conscription and opinions about Social Security and labor unions, attracted attention. Other topics did too. What did the public think about women wearing shorts in public or men wearing topless bathing suits at the beach? Gallup had the answers. Which automobile did the public consider best designed or most beautiful? What should children learn in school? If Gallup had not already asked about certain topics, then readers suggested that he should.

Like politics, religion was a topic that etiquette books said should not be discussed in polite company. But newspapers and now polling established that politics certainly could be discussed. Religion was available for discussion as well. With some fifty million Americans on the membership rolls of various denominations, it made sense that religion was a frequent topic in news stories and editorials.

Gallup and his wife were members of Trinity Episcopal Church in Princeton, and while George was traveling and giving lectures to publicize the Gallup Poll, Ophelia served on church committees and hosted church gatherings at the farm. George's lectures emphasized science and the value of polling and seldom if ever mentioned religion—except on one occasion when he speculated that statistics could probably prove the existence of God. Whether from personal interest or if he knew that religion was generally important, or both, Gallup began asking about religion almost as soon as he started national polls.

A 1935 poll asked interviewees, "What is the most vital issue before the American people today?" Employment, unsurprisingly, was mentioned most often, but religion and morality were among the top twenty. The polling in conjunction with the 1936 election compared voter preferences among Catholics, Jews, and members of several Protestant denominations, concluding that religion was not the significant factor it had been in the 1928 faceoff between Herbert Hoover and Al Smith.

Neither result suggested that religion was particularly important in shaping public opinion, but in 1937 Gallup asked interviewees if they were members of a church. Seventy-five percent said they were. Another poll asked how people felt about all Protestant churches in the United States combining into one church, finding that 44 percent thought it was a good idea and 56 percent did not. Yet another poll showed the Bible to be the book Americans most often mentioned when asked about interesting books they had read. The Bible result was newsworthy, Gallup thought, not because the Bible came in ahead of *Gone with the Wind* and *Anthony Adverse*, but because older people named it more often than younger people. Maybe religion was declining after all, he speculated.[8]

A controversy about church lotteries prompted another early poll question about religion. When an Episcopal bishop in New York denounced the Catholic Church for raising money by promoting gambling, Gallup decided to see how Protestants and Catholics felt about the issue. Results released on June 3, 1938, showed a deep divide. By a margin of 58 percent to 42 percent, Catholics approved of churches "raising money by lotteries and games of chance." But among Protestants, only 21 percent approved, while 79 percent disapproved. If it seemed strange to poll the public about this topic, Gallup explained that churches were suffering because of the Depression and were being forced to consider new ways of raising money.[9]

The first Gallup Poll to probe religious participation in detail was conducted in late February 1939. The poll asked about possibility of war between Russia and Japan, job opportunities in the United States, and labor relations before turning to questions about church membership and attendance and related topics. Thirty-seven percent of those interviewed said they "happened to go to church last Sunday," and 52 percent said they attended less often than their parents did. Eight percent said they would like church better if no sermons were included. Thirty-one percent said they had listened to a church service on radio the previous Sunday. Views were mixed about the influence of religion in interviewees' communities: 29 percent thought it was increasing and 34 percent thought it was decreasing.[10]

At the suggestion of a staff person in New York from the American Bible Society, which for decades had been sponsoring an annual "Bible Week" climaxed by "Universal Bible Sunday," Gallup included several questions about Bible reading in the 1939 poll as well. Thirty-two percent said yes when asked, "Have you, yourself, read the Bible or any part of it within the last month?" Five percent said they read the Bible every day, 26 percent said yes when asked if they had ever read the Bible all the way through, and 46 percent said they liked the New Testament better, while only 19 percent preferred the Old Testament.

Having speculated before about religion's decline, Gallup picked up the theme again in emphasizing conclusions from the 1939 poll. He considered it worrisome that so many people were attending church less often than their parents did. While city dwellers thought religion's influence on their communities was increasing, people in small towns were more likely to say it was decreasing. In contrast to his columns about elections and public policy, Gallup included a list of suggestions for churches wanting to improve their influence. These, he noted, were not his but ones offered by the persons interviewed. Hiring more intelligent clergy topped the list.[11]

Speculation about religion's decline took a different turn when Gallup asked questions about Bible reading in 1942. Although the small proportion who read the Bible every day (6 percent) was about the same as in 1939, 8 percent said they had changed their reading habits because of the war, and 59 percent reported having read the Bible at home sometime within the past year. In 1943, the number rose to 64 percent, following heightened efforts by the American Bible Society and an endorsement of Universal Bible Sunday by President Roosevelt.

Then in 1944, Gallup asked a new question about religion: "Do you believe in a God?" An overwhelming majority (96 percent) of those polled said they did. Nearly everyone gave the same response, whether they were young or old, resided in cities or small towns, or lived in different parts of the country. The nation might be divided on how it viewed the president or what it thought about church gambling, but on this topic, believing in God, it was united.

In the history of polling about religion, this was a landmark event, less because of the results than because it represented an effort to capture something as personal, complex, and subjective as religious belief. It went beyond asking about something people had or had not done and could easily remember, such as going to church in the past week or reading the Bible. This was the kind of belief that had formerly been reserved for catechetical instruction and creedal assertion. If interesting and credible results could be obtained, perhaps polling could open a new era in how the public understood its position on basic church doctrines and teachings.

Americans may have considered themselves a God-fearing people. They had heard often enough during the war that God was on their side. They hoped that righteousness would prevail in the battle against tyranny.

Many of them attended religious services where they heard sermons about the importance of believing in God. They had no way of knowing if their fellow citizens actually did, unless they remembered Stelzle's poll and were among the few who believed its results. The same sermons warned against heresy and disbelief. Many of their neighbors did not participate in religion at all. It was impossible to know if America was a nation united in faith or if it was composed of diverse religious organizations waging an uphill battle against a rising tide of secularity. Only now, when someone said America was a nation of believers, there was proof. Nearly everyone did, in fact, believe in God.

By any indication, the Gallup evidence of Americans' nearly universal belief in God was profoundly important. Hardly anything, other than the nation's commitment to winning the war, evoked that much agreement. Opinion was usually divided. It certainly was about Roosevelt's domestic policies. But here in the question about belief in God was evidence that Americans were truly united. They shared a common conviction.

There was every reason to think that Gallup's report about belief in God would be received as important news. Gallup's headlines that fall about the presidential election were widely discussed. Besides the news-papers in which his syndicated columns appeared, other newspapers carried stories of the poll's latest predictions. The news about belief in God came a few weeks after the election. It circulated shortly after the nation had paused to attend Thanksgiving services at their various places of worship and as they began preparing for Christmas. The American Bible Society's Bible Week and Universal Bible Sunday were being spon-sored in some 120,000 churches representing fifty-five denominations. All Americans, Roosevelt urged, should be reminded of the eternal truths for which the nation's loved ones on the front lines were fighting.

If polling were to directly shape how the public thought about reli-gion, this was the moment when that effect should have been evident. The long history of fire-and-brimstone preaching in which the nation was called to repent for its wicked ways should have at least been modified. There should have been calls for the nation to put its faith into action since it did so universally believe. When leaders argued that God was on America's side, they could have noted that Americans were also on God's side. It would not have been surprising for pundits to debate whether it was really true that America was a nation of believers, and if it were, what that meant. Gallup did his best to heighten interest in the story. The cities were not godless after all, and young people were not as iconoclastic and skeptical as they probably appeared, he observed, and it was reassuring to see such widespread faith amid the grim reality and mass slaughter of the war.[12]

In fact, the poll received relatively little attention. Beyond the newspapers in which the syndicated column appeared, few mentioned it. Letters to the editor did not comment on it. The countless sermons that newspapers routinely printed ignored it. The report included details that commentators might have found interesting. It showed that belief in God was slightly less universal among younger people than among older people and perhaps a bit less common in large cities than on farms and in small towns. There was evidence, too, that belief in life after death was not quite as universal as belief in God. Seventy-six percent said they believed there is life after death, 13 percent said they did not, and 11 percent were undecided.[13]

Why the poll attracted so little attention is impossible to know. It may have been that nobody was truly surprised. They had, after all, heard time and again that America was a nation founded on biblical principles by people who believed in God. Perhaps there was no need for polling as proof. Or perhaps there was already sufficient evidence. Perhaps people remembered Stelzle's poll or, more likely, were persuaded that people believed in God because the ones they knew best routinely said they did when reciting the Apostles' Creed.

The coverage the poll did receive, though, suggested another reaction. Religious leaders were skeptical of the results and the methods by which they had been attained. *Christian Century*, which served as the leading magazine among mainstream Protestants, was critical both of this and of other Gallup polls. Writers described polling as an inexact science, questioned whether polls were useful, and discussed why they were inaccurate. If the methods themselves were not at fault, doubts remained about how informed the public was and whether the opinions people expressed in polls should be taken seriously. *Christian Herald* Editor Daniel A. Poling, who also served as president of an evangelistic organization called World Christian Endeavor, reported the Gallup results but was unconvinced. He felt the public was massively indifferent toward religion and had little understanding of how the troops were experiencing God on the front lines.[14]

The criticisms were notable because church leaders were by no means allergic to polling in other contexts. The surveys that Stelzle and H. Paul Douglass had done in the 1920s and early 1930s evolved into polls on specific topics. In 1936, a committee under the supervision of a Lutheran bishop conducted a multidenominational poll in which some ten thousand clergy expressed their views about going to war. A 1937 poll of Disciples of Christ members showed reluctance about bearing arms unless an actual attack occurred. The same poll registered widespread support for freedom of religion and freedom of the press. Congregationalist leaders a few months later enlarged the idea, polling their members on topics ranging from unemployment and relief to tariffs and capitalism in hopes of seeing if church teachings about the kingdom of God were shaping attitudes about these issues. In 1939 the New York YMCA polled the city's youth to learn if they had received religious training at home, were going to church, and looked to religion for guidance. Other polls were conducted on college campuses to see how students viewed the Ten Commandments, thought about morality, and were influenced by religious training. One of the largest polled more than 54,000 students at 182 Catholic colleges and universities, asking questions about conscientious objection to military service and attitudes toward the eventuality of war.[15]

Few of the polls religious leaders conducted in these years were based on systematic representative samples. Most followed the earlier procedures of canvassing based on church membership and clergy lists or among enrolled students. The response rates were as low as 10 percent. What the polls indicated, nevertheless, was that religious leaders were interested in knowing what their constituents thought. The key word was *constituents*. Religion was organized. It mattered what people affiliated with those organizations thought. Their opinions either reflected church teachings or were relevant to being instructed by church teachings. In contrast, the results from a Gallup poll of the nation might be interesting, but not in the same way. There was less of an obvious connection to what particular religious organizations needed to know and hoped to do.

Another reason the poll may have received little attention is that polling, as Gallup said, was still in its infancy. Gallup's success depended as much on his sales ability as on his numbers. He had to explain to audiences not only how the polls were done but also why they were important and what they contributed to the democratic process. Most of all, he had to generate public interest. Despite the attention polls received in conjunction with presidential elections, many people remained unaware of them. A few weeks before the 1944 presidential election, a Roper poll asked, "Have you ever heard of a public opinion poll?" Only 57 percent of those who were polled said yes. And of those, one in three were unsure if polling reports were honest and accurate, and only one person in five said they followed the results of any public opinion poll regularly in any newspaper or magazine. Unlike a few decades later, when preachers could mention a recent poll knowing that their congregation would understand the reference, a preacher doing that in 1944 would have had some explaining to do.[16]

The fact that poll evidence of widespread belief in God did not attract immediate interest is telling. It suggests that if polling shaped how Americans thought about religion, this effect did not occur immediately and it was not attributable simply to how a question was asked or how those interviewed responded. It was rather that polling initiated and corresponded with a broader shift in how public opinion was understood. That shift occurred gradually. It reflected the social circumstances of the time. Its relationship to public understandings of religion took until the late 1950s to become fully evident. The process involved an affirmation of long-standing emphasis on the wisdom of ordinary people, public pronouncements associated with the Cold War, and a selective redefinition of what was truly important about religious belief.

Intelligence of the Masses

Like the social survey movement a generation earlier, polling in the 1930s positioned itself as an advance based on science. Although Gallup became a cultural icon for seeming to have invented polling almost from thin air, there was in fact precedent for the methods Gallup used. By the early 1920s, academic social scientists were extending the work of the social survey movement by conducting surveys based on sampling rather than canvassing entire communities. Writing in 1924, University of Minnesota sociologist F. Stuart Chapin argued that the survey method had become so familiar in economics, political science, and sociology that examples could be found at nearly any major university. The Russell Sage Foundation, the Carnegie Corporation, and the Commonwealth Fund were providing financial support. The American Sociological Society had a standing committee that focused on survey research. The National Social Science Research Council had been organized in 1923 to plan and coordinate research across the disciplines.[17]

The ability to conduct sample surveys and arguments for conducting more of them went hand in hand with social scientists' faith in science and their desire to be scientific. To scholars like Chapin, it was distressing that public policy was so often based on impressions and opinions instead of scientific facts. It was even more distressing that social science journals were filled with articles based on impressions and opinions. The kind of progress that the nation hoped for in the 1920s could only be furthered, the argument went, by conducting studies in which the rigorous standards of sampling and experimental design were employed.

Several of the studies that employed scientific sampling in the 1920s included measures of religion. A study published in 1927 of a New England town, for example, contributed to the growing literature on community life by selecting a random sample of households and then asking questions about the various activities in which each member participated during the week.[18]

It did not take long for the idea of scientific sample surveys to shift from studies of time use and poverty and marriage and agricultural practices to research about public opinion, at least in local contexts, well before Gallup polls. Prompted by questions about how much the 1924 presidential election may have been influenced by newspaper coverage, a major study was conducted in Seattle in which a random sample of nearly a thousand residents were interviewed to see how their opinions varied in relation to which of the city's major newspapers they read.[19] Another study selected a random sample of farmers in Minnesota and asked about their attitudes about cooperative buying and selling arrangements and how those related to the farmers' marketing decisions and participation in rural cooperatives.[20]

The Seattle study concluded that the newspapers did not significantly influence public opinion in that city. Residents apparently were able to think independently about candidates. The Minnesota study drew more critical conclusions. It argued that farmers' reasoning was generally deficient. They reasoned from simple analogies, confused correlation with causation, too often followed generally accepted but unproven opinions, and were more easily swayed by personal appeals than by solid policy arguments.

The Minnesota study illustrated a larger long-standing quandary about public opinion. Were average Americans reasonably intelligent and thus capable of forming valid opinions about important social and political issues? Or were they on the whole deficient in this respect, either as the voting population in general or among selected segments of that population? If the latter, which segments were most deficient: farmers, recent immigrants, African Americans? And was the purpose of studying public opinion to identify these deficiencies, correct them, show that they did not exist, or what?

As polling on a wider scale evolved, these questions remained. Pollsters' faith in science posed a potential difficulty for thinking about the very information their polls were collecting. The common person was not trained in science and did not think scientifically. If scientific information was preferred, why bother with the opinions of ordinary people at all? This was the question that critics of public opinion had raised all along. It should at least be enlightened if it was to count for anything, they argued. Polling's emphasis on science reopened the question but did not answer it. An argument did, however, emerge as polling prompted further consideration of what public opinion was and why it was important. It evolved with three emphases.

The first emphasis reasserted familiar arguments about democracy essentially being the voice of the people in contrast to the rule of elites, even the elites who might have been elected to represent the people. In an informal talk to the Princeton Alumni Association in January 1939, Gallup expressed his views on this topic more candidly than he generally did in other settings. He was far more interested in assessing public opinion, he said, than in predicting elections. The latter was simply a necessary evil, the price to be paid for securing the funding and attention needed to conduct polls of public opinion. "These forecasts do not prove anything nor are they of any special value except to indicate the accuracy of our polls in general," he said. Although the poll's 1938 predictions had largely been accurate, Gallup wanted his listeners to know that error was likely. Predictions could never be closer than 3 percent, he cautioned, and elections could vary more than that because of weather or corruption. Assessing opinion on other topics was more interesting, he thought, and, although it went without saying, was less risky as well. Election forecasts could be wrong. Opinions could not be independently verified.[21]

But if that was so, why was it useful to know what the public thought? The answer was that ordinary people's views mattered. "I am confident that the masses can be as right on public questions as any smaller and select body such as for example Congress itself," Gallup asserted. His audience probably agreed. This was the populist view of democracy that regarded the common person as a citizen whose opinions should be taken seriously and that was inherently skeptical of public officials and others in power.

The second part of the argument held that ordinary people were actually smarter than commonly assumed. Gallup stressed repeatedly that the masses among which his polls were conducted were capable of analyzing and thinking intelligently about public issues. That did not imply that they had scientific evidence at their disposal. It was more a response to criticism that polls elicited only knee-jerk responses. If that were true, there would be little justification for asking what the public thought. Gallup's argument, though, was that the polls elicited thoughtful responses.

The notion that ordinary people were intelligent enough to offer reasonable responses when pollsters asked played well in the popular press. It played especially well in the South and Midwest, where grassroots populism had fueled resentment against Washington bureaucrats and New York plutocrats for a long time. Following a speech by Gallup to the Georgia Press Institute in 1939, a local newspaper editor remarked, "The collective intelligence of the American people is amazingly accurate." He was not referring to the polls' accuracy in predicting election results but to the credibility of the opinions expressed. "There is a prevalent belief among certain 'smart' cliques in this country that the so-called masses in America, generally speaking, are notoriously dumb," he noted. But that view was wrong. The polls in fact revealed "remarkable knowledge" among the general public, and if lawmakers followed the opinions expressed, democracy would be better for it.[22]

The third argument related most clearly to polling. It held that intelligent public opinion had to be measured scientifically in order to avoid biases and misrepresentations in how it was interpreted. Skepticism toward public officials mirrored doubts about other opinion leaders as well. Polling a representative sample of the public was a way to circumvent the potentially misleading arguments expressed by pundits in the press and perhaps in the professions and pulpits.

The unresolved question was how much the decisions of those in authority should be guided by public opinion. This was a question that had to be addressed carefully. If persons in authority were to be guided by principles instead of opinion, then it mattered to poll public opinion only to know how much persuasion leaders might have to exert. But if public opinion was to have a significant effect on decisions, it was important that polls only measure and in no way influence it.

Critics argued that polls did influence public opinion rather than merely measure it. A few days after the belief-in-God results, members of a congressional committee visited the Gallup offices in Princeton to see the operation firsthand. They wanted to know how polling was done and how it might be used in postwar planning. They were particularly interested in how the results that fall might have influenced the election. Two weeks later, Gallup took the train to Washington to respond in greater detail.[23]

Gallup explained that the polls were scientific, paid for by the newspapers in which the results appeared, and never subsidized by any political party or candidate. All the ballots collected in the polls were archived at Princeton University, he said. He insisted that the polls only collected and reported the facts about public opinion. The idea that poll results influence the readers of those results, he contended, was a "widely held delusion" that ran contrary to a mountain of scientific evidence.

But the hearing illuminated another way in which polling's influence might occur. Gallup contended that the principal reason for conducting polls was not to predict elections but to use those predictions for developing and testing the accuracy of polls on other topics. Presumably, doing so would advance democracy because public officials could then determine quickly and efficiently what the public wanted and then act accordingly.

Peacetime conscription was a case in point. When asked in 1944 about continuing the draft or requiring universal military training after the war, two-thirds to three-quarters of the public favored the idea. Noting those results at the hearing, one of the representatives observed that church leaders were nevertheless urging Congress to go slowly in considering the matter. Gallup's response was that church leaders' views did not represent the views of rank-and-file members, which was objectively true, but that was not all. Polling provided a check on church leaders' claims. That was how it furthered democracy.

The argument connected well with the idea that democracy should privilege public opinion. It did not mean that church leaders' views should be ignored, but if the leaders were incapable of persuading their own members, then public opinion polls could be used against them. Where there had been one voice in the past, now there were two. Leaders' opinions could be challenged. Polls provided the evidence to do so.

It was a compelling argument as long as the evidence could be trusted, as Gallup claimed it could be. Implicitly, though, the hearing revealed two reasons for caution. Poll predictions in recent elections at the state level were off by as much as 12 percent, which meant that they could be in error on other topics as well, especially if the topic pertained to Methodists or Baptists rather than to the public at large, and if there were no election results to check their accuracy. The other was that pollsters decided whether to poll the public on some topics and not others and determined when the results would be publicized.

Postwar Polling

The question of accuracy and inaccuracy in polling results surfaced most prominently in 1948 when Gallup erroneously predicted a victory in the presidential contest for Thomas E. Dewey over Harry S. Truman. It mattered less if the polls about religion were or were not on target because there were no external standards of comparison. To those paying close attention, though, it was evident that polling still had a long way to go to establish itself as an accurate indicator of public opinion and behavior.

From 1935 through the mid-1940s, Gallup polls deliberately underrepresented women, Southerners, and African Americans because they voted at low rates, and the polls' aim was to represent the voting public rather than the public at large. As few as 10 to 15 percent of those polled were from the South, for example, despite a third of the public living there, and the proportion polled who were women ranged from only 30 to 35 percent.[24] That made it necessary when interpreting Gallup polls about church attendance and religious beliefs, which varied by gender and region, to consider the figures separately for various categories, rather than taking the result for the nation at face value. When later polls were conducted using different methods, though, the trends reported rarely took these differences into account. In addition, the early polls did not require interviewers to go house to house based on a specified sampling design. Instead, interviewers frequently found interviewees in the most easily available locations. "Personally, I find the public parks are the best in summer and large railroad stations best in winter," one interviewer explained. Said another, "I personally do the greater part of my work in the parks and along the streets, the shoppers' lounges, small shops and stores, suburban railroad stations, and busy corners."[25]

By 1945, more systematic sampling methods were in use, but religion questions produced results that did little to inspire confidence. Polls conducted by the various agencies that had begun competing with Gallup estimated that as few as 65 percent and as many as 80 percent of the public were church members, all within a few months. Following yet another poll result about Bible reading, the editor of *Theology Today* voiced caution, arguing that other methods of investigating the cultural impact of the Bible should be considered. Noting with confidence the extensive research being conducted at the University of California at Berkeley on the roots of anti-Semitism in authoritarian personalities, sociologist Arnold Rose contended that commercial polling in general was being taken over by marketing firms that had little respect for rigorous standards.[26]

And yet, the idea that polls could accurately characterize important aspects of religion was gradually catching on. Poll results about church attendance, God, and the Bible were increasingly in the background of public commentary about religion. When a poll in 1945 suggested that church attendance was declining, Archbishop Richard J. Cushing of Boston took the occasion to warn that patriotism would likely diminish as well. A 1948 Gallup poll showing that 94 percent believed in God, down 2 points from the 1944 result, prompted a banker in Alabama to worry that materialism was on the rise. Later that year, *Ladies' Home Journal* conducted what it called a Gallup-style poll in which 95 percent attested to believing in God, 62 percent considered themselves to be following the Golden Rule, and 25 percent claimed even to love the nation's enemies. *Time*'s report of the results cautioned, though, that what people said in polls should not be taken at face value. "A profound gulf lies between America's avowed ethical standards and the observable realities of national life," it stated. "What may be more alarming is the gap between what Americans think they do and what they do do."[27]

The most extensive religion poll to date occurred in 1952 when the *Catholic Digest* commissioned the Ben Gaffin and Associates polling firm to conduct a large study asking detailed questions about beliefs and practices. Although the earlier Gallup polls suggested that Americans were mostly united when it came to basic religious beliefs, the new information further demonstrated the extent to which that was true. Ninety-nine percent of those polled said they believed or at least were pretty sure they believed in God, and when asked if they were absolutely certain, few differences were evident among members of the major denominations: 93 percent among Baptists, 92 percent among Catholics, 90 percent among Presbyterians, 86 percent among Methodists, and 80 percent among Lutherans.[28]

To some interpreters, it was almost as exciting that science was able to determine what people believed as it was to know what they believed. "Modern science has been striving to discover as much as possible about what makes people behave the way they do," a lengthy 1952 *Los Angeles Times* article observed. "Leading psychologists and sociologists have realized that to do this they must discover what people believe. And to this end, scientists have pooled their efforts to determine the religious attitudes and beliefs of men and women of every age and walk of life."

Nine out of ten Americans definitely believed in the existence of God, while only one in a hundred could be classified as an atheist. Belief in God, moreover, was higher in the United States than anywhere in Western Europe. The God Americans believed in and prayed to, moreover, was a personal God. And, while many Americans did not attend religious services regularly, those who did tended to be better educated and had the highest earning capacity. Here at least was a "concrete picture of what America believes."[29]

Cold War Proclamations

Arguably, polling about religion was gaining acceptance as polling more generally became more common. The extent to which Americans came to think of themselves as a nation of believers in God, though, cannot be understood in terms of polling alone. It was rather the conjuncture of polling with the cultural suppositions of the times that mattered most. Those suppositions held that it was important for Americans to believe in God, to affirm their belief and find unity in it, and to have evidence that they did in fact believe. Those were the suppositions about religion that prevailed in tandem with rising concerns about the Cold War.

The fact that more than 90 percent of Americans in polls said they believed in God did not have to be cited specifically in claims that belief in God was the common thread in Americans' faith. The statistic was there in the background in case anyone doubted the veracity of these claims. "All the great religions represented in this organization," President Truman told the National Conference of Christians and Jews at a meeting in 1949, "acknowledge this belief in God as the Father and Creator of mankind. For us, therefore, brotherhood is not only a generous impulse, but also a divine command. Others may be moved into brotherhood only by sentiment. We acknowledge brotherhood as a religious duty."[30]

A year later in a broadcast from the White House, Truman again emphasized the nation's shared belief in God. He called on the nation to participate in the Crusade of Prayer currently under way, enlisting it as a common cause of spiritual renewal. This was the source of courage and wisdom, he said, that would strengthen the nation in the fight against the tyranny of communism. "Communism is godless. Democracy is the harvest of faith—faith in one's self, faith in one's neighbors, faith in God. Democracy's most powerful weapon is not a gun, tank, or bomb. It is faith—faith in the brotherhood and dignity of man under God."[31]

With encouragement like that from the White House, it was probably not surprising that the *Catholic Digest* poll showed nearly universal belief in God. Yet in framing the questions, there was little effort to disguise the most socially acceptable answers. "How do you think of God—as a loving Father who looks after us, as some kind of supernatural power but don't know what, or how?" Put that way, 79 percent of those asked took the God-as-loving-father response. "Do you believe the Bible is really the revealed word of God, or do you think it is only a great piece of literature?" Eighty-three percent said the Bible was the word of God. Unlike later polls that teased out differences in how people interpreted the Bible, the point here was simply that nearly everyone believed the Bible was the word of God.

The apparent national unity in the polls was as much fiction as fact. If it seemed reassuring in the face of godless communism to believe that Americans were united in their faith in God, the reality was that many Americans doubted the loyalties of their fellow believers. Asked in 1950 if Jewish people were more likely than other people to be communists, 11 percent of those polled said yes, and among that number nearly half thought many or most Jews were communists.[32] Among Catholics in the *Catholic Digest* poll, 21 percent thought there was ill feeling toward Jews among fellow Catholics. In the same poll, a quarter of Protestants thought there was ill feeling among Protestants toward Catholics.

True to form, *Christian Century* still expressed reservations about polling, acknowledging in 1952 that Dr. Gallup's "omniscient tribe" had improved their methods but describing them as "less than an infallible guide to the mind of the public" because of questions asking for snap judgments with little substance behind them.[33] The public, however, appeared to be taking a more favorable view. In a survey conducted by the National Opinion Research Center at the University of Chicago in November 1952, 60 percent of those polled thought "public opinion polls are a good thing for the country" while only 3 percent thought they were a bad thing, and 56 percent thought polls were right most of the time in predicting elections, while only 25 percent thought the record was not good.[34]

Whether there was solid poll evidence that interest in religion was increasing or decreasing, the impression that it *was* increasing fed discussions of its importance in the 1952 presidential election. Eighty-eight percent in one poll said they belonged to or attended a church. A quarter said they usually agreed with their church leaders' views about candidates for public office, and one-sixth said they personally talked about politics at church. Another poll suggested that church leaders were leaning toward

Republican candidates over Democrats by nearly two to one.[35] Correspondents covering the 1952 presidential campaign noticed that Eisenhower increasingly talked about his family's religious roots and emphasized the need for spiritual strength. Putting Adlai Stevenson's name in nomination as the Democratic candidate, Truman also encouraged the nation to call on its faith and work for the betterment of all God's children.

The Eisenhower administration carried forward the nation's Cold War emphasis on unity under God. As leaders considered adding the words "under God" to the Pledge of Allegiance, Gallup weighed in with supporting evidence. Asked in early 1953 if they believed in God, 99 percent of those polled said they did. Gallup followed the question with an opportunity for believers to say why they believed, in which comments about creation, life, Adam and Eve, and the Bible dominated. Then, when asked if they favored or opposed adding "under God" to the Pledge of Allegiance, 69 percent said they were in favor, and only 21 percent said they were opposed.[36]

It was not a good time to be an atheist; only one in a hundred Americans, the polls found. As fears of communists operating in the United States spread, denying the existence of God was as good as admitting that one was a communist. One of the high-profile targets of Senate investigations in 1953 was Roger Lyons, the director of Voice of America's religion programs, whom former coworkers accused of having once claimed not to believe in God. Lyons rushed to Washington to plead that he did in fact believe in God. In remarks broadcast on the nation's four television networks in 1954, Eisenhower declared that atheism "leads inevitably to domination and dictatorship."[37]

The time *was* good for polling, especially polls that showed not only what the public thought but also what leaders should do and why they should do it. In 1952, when the National Council of Churches entertained plans to locate its headquarters in New York City (which it eventually did), *Christian Century* put aside its usual skepticism of polls and conducted its own (unscientific) poll of clergy to argue that somewhere in the Midwest, presumably Chicago, would be the preferred choice. That year the National Council of Churches itself conducted a poll of delegates to one of its conventions, concluding that public officials who ignored the moral indignation of church people concerning economic injustice did so at their peril. Another survey concluded that clergy should preach more often about prayer.[38] Other polls examined attitudes toward segregation, church unity, and interfaith cooperation.

Few of the polls were as rigorous or claimed to be as scientific as the ones conducted by Gallup. Even the Gallup polls rarely got the numbers exactly right. They called the 1948 election for Dewey, misestimating the actual vote by 5 percent, and erred again in 1952 by more than 4 percent. Nevertheless, polling had become a flourishing business. When the *Saturday Evening Post* profiled Gallup again in 1956, Gallup's income was more than a million dollars a year, and the polling industry's combined efforts were estimated at nearly $200 million.[39]

The most noted result from polling about religion, though, was support for the idea that America was a nation that believed in God and in various ways expressed its religious faith. Eisenhower followed Truman's example by repeatedly declaring that America was founded on religious faith and by calling on the nation to strengthen its faith commitments. In the speech in which he condemned atheism, he declared, "It is faith that has made our nation—has made it, and kept it free." He kept a red leather Bible by his bedside, he told *Time* reporter Stanley High, and from reading it, he believed that nothing was more sorely needed than a rededication of the nation to its religious values and conduct.[40] At an interfaith gathering in Washington in 1954, billed as the National Conference on the Spiritual Foundations of American Democracy, Eisenhower expressed confidence that democracy would prevail against communist tyranny as long as Americans understood their value as individuals before God.[41]

But was that what Americans actually believed, or was it only the president's hope about what they should believe? One of the speakers at the Washington conference was Reverend Theodore M. Hesburgh, president of the University of Notre Dame. Hesburgh was confident that Protestants, Catholics, and Jews were God-loving and God-fearing Americans who would stand united against those who denied God. Another speaker was Rabbi Will Herberg, who saw what he termed biblical realism as a unifying element in the American public.

In 1955, Herberg published *Protestant, Catholic, Jew: An Essay in American Religious Sociology*, which gained immediate attention in the popular media and became known as one of the most influential treatments of religion in the United States of its time.[42] Herberg made extensive use of Gallup polls to show that Americans *were* united in a common faith. They overwhelmingly believed in God, according to the polls, and, as far as he could tell, it had become a mark of being American to locate oneself as a Protestant, Catholic, or Jew. Granted, these convictions were not always as deep in theological understanding as religious leaders might wish, but he was certain that American faith was strong.

The polls suggested that Herberg was right. Notwithstanding the various polling results, it became fashionable to observe that nearly everyone believed in God and felt it important to obey the biblical law of love toward one's neighbors. Eighty percent of the public arguably belonged to a religious congregation. Moreover, the president's urging seemed to be bearing fruit. Gallup polls over the next few years showed that 90 percent of Americans believed in the divinity of Jesus and more than 50 percent attended services at their houses of worship in any given week, up from only 41 percent in 1939. In one poll, 81 percent thought religion could answer "most of today's problems." Another poll revealed that 46 percent of the public thought religious leaders were doing the most good for the country of any group, up from 17 percent in 1942. And whether religion's influence was increasing or not, two Americans in three thought it was.[43]

Imagining American Religion

Herberg's argument was that religion in America had become Americanized, submerging its ethnic and denominational differences into a common culture that included basic agreement about religious faith. Religion as a common denominator rested on the assumption that nearly all Americans believed in God and had somewhat the same views about who that God was and what eternal rewards came with that belief. It was a kind of civil religion, Robert N. Bellah would argue a few years later, similar to the one Rousseau had suggested would be especially conducive to mutual happiness and tolerance in a democratic republic. More simply, it was American religion.[44]

At the time, discussions of American religion were surprisingly rare. Their rarity was surprising in view of the extent to which churches and seminaries and theological arguments were, in fact, woven into the very fabric of the nation. It was not that America had become thoroughly secular. It was rather that the term "American religion" did not quite capture the reality that people experienced. The reality was that there were Methodists, Baptists, Catholics, Jews, and so on; believers in Jesus; devotees of the Blessed Mother; members of a particular congregation to which they went regularly, sporadically, or not all; and those who did not affiliate with any of the aforementioned. American religion was not a notion that spoke to those local, personal, and familial identities.

When American religion was discussed, as it was from time to time, its meanings illustrated why it was not the first language in which Americans customarily described their faith and the faiths of their neighbors. One usage was in academic publications, lectures, and discussions. Examples included *Religion in Our Times*, published in 1932 by Gaius Glenn Atkins, the author of several books about religious history, cults, and religious movements; *Varieties of American Religion*, published in 1936 by sociologist Harry Elmer Barnes; and theologian H. Richard Niebuhr's *Kingdom of God in America*, published in 1938. These and similar publications saw that American religion could be characterized by its history and distinctive features but also understood that terms such as "religion in America" or the "culture and institutions of American churches and denominations" provided a more accurate description.[45] A second usage was in discussions of religion's relationship to politics or the federal government and its contributions to democracy. Religion in these discussions was as likely to refer to the ideals of religious freedom and separation of church and state as to the realities of various religious organizations. A third usage occurred in occasional references to or from the perspective of outliers, such as American Buddhists, socialists, dissidents, and other marginal groups, which presented the possibility of drawing contrasts with something central, mainstream, and dominant.

The common aspect of these usages was the interpreter's distance from the topic under discussion. The stance was external, unlike that of an insider who directly experienced particular beliefs, practices, and traditions, and was acquainted with the customs of others in his or her community. That external view permitted religion to be objectified and regarded as if it was one thing. The whole could be seen instead of only the constituent parts. It was as if a person was looking at America from another country and imagining it as a nation with a national religion, rather than seeing just the trees and rivers and steeples and towns. The stance was similar to Tocqueville's, only now it was the perspective taken by the occasional commentator from within who created enough distance from the issue to discuss it in those terms.

Polling provided a new way in which to view something that could be called American religion. Polling necessitated taking the stance of an external observer. This was what it meant to be scientific, to regard public opinion as an object to be measured and to be reported about objectively. Whatever the pollster's own religious opinions might be, those were to be bracketed so that the opinions of a representative sample of the public could be described. And it was in that notion of representing the public that "American" could be attached to religion. The opinions might in the first instance be those of particular individuals, but, by aggregating them, a new reality came into being, a description of religion, not of individuals, but of a collective entity—the nation. Religion, in a general sense, was ascribed to the collective and not just individuals, thus creating a national identity founded on shared, albeit overly simplified, religious beliefs.

Polling about religion pushed the idea a step further. Besides asking the people being interviewed if they believed in God and attended religious services, the polls regularly asked people their opinion of religion as well. They were asked if religion as a whole was increasing or losing its influence on American life. The question assumed they would somehow know and that the results would somehow be meaningful. It very likely was shaped by what they read in newspapers and saw on television as much as by their personal experiences. But it did not ask about personal experiences. It characterized the topic the same way that polling results did, as an aspect of the nation, as American religion.

Polls alone did not invent American religion. They contributed to the public prominence of that invention and to how it was understood. Before polling, it was possible to conceptualize something as American religion by viewing it externally as if it were an object. With poll results, it was possible to concretize that object by associating it with numbers obtained through a scientific process of data collection and measurement. The numbers both described and instantiated themselves as part of the public reality that was known as American religion. Having contributed to the public visibility of that reality, pollsters would, in coming years, be called on as the authoritative interpreters of it. They would be accompanied by academic social scientists whose approach was similar but at the same time would serve as a critical voice.

4

Scientific Studies

ON JUNE 21, 1951, a small group of researchers met in New York City to discuss how to carry on the work that H. Paul Douglass had done in the 1930s to apply scientific methods to the study of religion. They agreed that a new organization was called for and to that end founded the Religious Research Association. Two years earlier, a separate group had organized a committee also to promote social scientific studies of religion. That committee evolved into the Society for the Scientific Study of Religion in 1956. By that time, the American Catholic Sociological Society, founded in 1937, was focusing more of its attention on research as well.

None of these organizations expressed a particular preference for polls and surveys over other modes of investigation. But their founding members did believe that science was a valuable tool for advancing understandings of religion. They regarded themselves not merely as scholars but as social scientists, and they embraced rigorous empirical inquiry. And that soon put them on the path of conducting surveys, which in turn competed with the methods and perspectives on religion being advanced by nonacademic polling agencies.

The studies these academic researchers initiated differed significantly from the polls that Gallup and a few other commercial pollsters were doing. The differences stemmed less from intellectual disagreements, although there were indeed disagreements, than from institutional locations. Academic surveys and commercial polls reflected the same general assumptions about the importance of rigorous methods, the value of sampling, and the possibility of measuring public opinion. Researchers agreed that studies could and, indeed, should be of practical value for religious leaders. But academic researchers had limited means at their disposal for conducting large-scale studies and yet entertained convictions about the importance of such studies for descriptive purposes and for testing theories about the sources and effects of religion. Unlike the Gallup Organization with its hundreds of field researchers in selected locations across the country, academic researchers seldom had resources beyond their own colleges and universities. Some worked on projects funded by religious organizations or piggybacked onto studies concerned with other topics.

But academics enjoyed an enviable degree of intellectual freedom that only colleges and universities provided. They were not constrained by the need to craft studies capable each week of tantalizing the nation's newspaper editors. They could take their time and direct their attention to different questions. As such, they not only became occasional collaborators with pollsters and sounding boards for polls about religion but served as critics as well. They did this not only by producing statistical studies of their own but also by interacting directly and regularly with scholars using other—mostly historical and ethnographic—methods of research.

Over the next quarter-century, academically based scientific studies of religion would grow both in numbers and quality and in the topics addressed. The organizations founded specifically to promote these studies initiated professional journals, held annual meetings, and attracted growing numbers of members. Leading scholars in their respective fields produced landmark surveys that resulted in major books and scholarly articles. The academic researchers existed both in harmony and in tension with commercial pollsters. Sometimes researchers used the best polls for further analysis because no comparable information was available, at other times they criticized polls for being superficial at best and deeply biased at worst, or academics simply ignored some polls, deeming them unworthy of serious consideration.

The growth of survey research about religion from the 1950s through the 1970s established a pattern that continued through the end of the century. It was a curious trajectory shaped as much by what else was happening in the social sciences, polling, and academic studies of religion as by the surveys themselves. Few subfields of social scientific interest reflected as complicated a set of influences as survey research about religion, or if they did, those influences have rarely received careful attention. On the one hand, survey research about religion borrowed the theories and statistical methods in use among the most respected social scientists who studied other topics. And religion researchers benefited from the legacy established by Douglass and the Lynds and from the continuing interest and support church bureaus provided. On the other hand, church-based interest and support, driven as it was by practical and, indeed, confessional aims, put researchers specializing in the study of religion at an awkward distance from social scientists who eschewed such applied purposes and wanted research to be, above all, theory focused.

Except for the role that polling about elections played in relation to political scientists, academic researchers studying religion faced the unique challenge of having polling as their leading competitor—by defining the topics that should be studied and publicizing poll results to such an extent that academic research hardly mattered beyond the dusty shelves of college libraries. Criticizing, embracing, ignoring, or politely mentioning polls was always part of the backstory against which academic research about religion developed. With commercial polling as the most influential alternative, academic researchers competed for the support of church bureaus and on occasion went to considerable pains to demonstrate that polling firms' understanding of science and statistical methods was flawed.

This occurred while suspicion about the usefulness of numbers for studying religion existed in two important camps. The larger public continued to doubt the validity of polling and believed, at least half-heartedly, that statistics and lies went hand in hand. Second, the most respected academic scholars of religion—whose interests were shaped by theology, history, and philosophy—were doubtful that much of anything under the banner of positivist science could be helpful for understanding religion. Thus, the doubts that emanated from existentialism and phenomenology and that inspired comparative and historical investigations of religion created, at least for a while, a sharp intellectual divide regarding polling about religion, and yet that divide left polling's capacity to define the public character of American religion free of what otherwise would likely have been an important source of criticism.

Making a Start

Although the specialty organizations that formed in the early 1950s were the clearest step toward sustained social scientific studies of religion, the story of how those studies were shaped by the concurrent intellectual tides requires looking more closely at academic social scientists' responses to public opinion polling in the 1940s. Gallup's recurring refrain that his polling was scientific and the frequency with which the media referred to him as "Dr. Gallup" and mentioned his PhD in psychology aided in erecting an intellectual bridge to the ivied halls of academia. His location near a university, his articles in *Public Opinion Quarterly*, and his frequent conversations and occasional collaboration with his neighbor and friend Hadley Cantril, the distinguished Princeton psychologist, furthered the bridge-building effort as well. On a broader scale, annual meetings of the American Association of Public Opinion Research, founded in 1947, occasioned opportunities for discussions of polling methods between academically based researchers and the best-known polling researchers such as Gallup, Elmo Roper, and Archibald Crossley, as well as representatives from organizations such as NBC, the Opinion Research Corporation, and the Texas Poll.

From academic quarters, surveys based on scientifically drawn samples were in vogue, as previously mentioned, during the first decades of the century, and by the 1930s researchers' efforts were focusing increasingly on surveys of public opinion. In 1937, the Rockefeller Foundation funded a research project to ascertain the effects of radio on public opinion, locating the project at Princeton's School of Public and International Affairs (founded in 1930), with sociologist Paul Lazarsfeld as its director and Cantril, along with Frank Stanton of CBS, as members of its research team. The 1938 Orson Welles broadcast about a Martian invasion, supposedly happening less than five miles away at Grover's Mill, New Jersey, provided an exceptional opportunity to examine these effects. Cantril, in collaboration with Gallup, conducted a nationwide survey to find out how many people had been frightened by the broadcast and why some had been more susceptible to mass hysteria than others.[1]

Lazarsfeld moved on to Columbia University, where he founded the Bureau of Applied Social Research, which continued the work on radio and communication and served as the training ground for the coming generation of survey researchers. An Austrian immigrant of Jewish parents, Lazarsfeld had come to America in 1933 through a two-year fellowship from the Rockefeller Foundation, under which he also met and was influenced by researchers Luther Fry and Robert Lynd, both with interests in religion.[2] Like Gallup, Lazarsfeld sought, but without much success, to attract businesses as commercial clients, and he retained an interest in studying patterns of consumption; however, his publications contributed increasingly to the development of academic concepts, theories, and statistical methods as the foundations for survey research.

Besides the bureau at Columbia, centers focusing on basic and applied survey research emerged in the 1940s at several other locations. Following six years of employment with Gallup, during which he directed polls in England and France, Harry H. Field formed the People's Research Corporation in 1939, which morphed into the National Opinion Research Center, located at the University of Denver in 1941, and then moved to the University of Chicago in 1947. At the University of Michigan, the Board of Regents established a Survey Research Center in 1946 with the stipulation that it should be self-supporting, and by 1949 the center's success resulted in the formation of the more ambitious Institute for Social Research. And with Rockefeller support, Alfred Kinsey founded the Institute for Sex Research at Indiana University in 1947.[3]

While, on the surface, these centers did similar research to that conducted by Gallup, Roper, Crossley, and other polling firms, their agendas and understandings of social science were quite different. Gallup's emphasis on science undoubtedly reflected the appreciation for science he acquired during his graduate training in psychology at the University of Iowa, but in practice it meant little more than utilizing ideas about representative sampling for conducting his polls. Although he attested at a 1944 congressional hearing to his organization's carefulness when wording questions and reporting results, he also complained that the newspapers carrying his columns prevented him from asking more detailed questions or reporting results with additional evidence about the procedures involved. The legislators convening the hearing felt it necessary to receive more authoritative counsel about the procedures from University of Chicago demographer Philip Hauser, serving concurrently as assistant chief statistician for population at the Census Bureau.

The pressure from Gallup's sponsoring newspapers not only limited the length of his weekly columns but also led commercial polling in a direction notably different from its academic counterpart. Although Gallup expressed interest in identifying the sources of variation and change in public opinion, Gallup polls rarely, if ever, included any serious attempts to assess those sources statistically, instead drawing inferences only from temporal variations that seemed without further investigation to be related to public events, such as a campaign speech or the outbreak of war. To avoid the unwelcome prospect that door-to-door interviewers would face an increasingly resistant public, the polls seldom lasted more than fifteen to twenty minutes and sometimes included as few as a dozen questions. That made it difficult, if not impossible, to examine consistency among responses to similar questions or to explore the relationships among opinions on varied topics. And while the polls did a reasonably good job of phrasing questions in understandable language, the extent to which focus groups or qualitative interviews were used to develop and interpret those questions was minimal. Given these limitations, commercial pollsters' best argument that what they were doing was meaningful rested on the claim that poll results truly represented "the voice of the people" and that upticks and downturns in public opinion should be regarded as valid barometers of important cultural trends.

It was true, of course, that commercial and academic researchers alike considered it important to properly draw probability samples and develop appropriately unambiguous questions. Areas of common concern included cost, efficiency, interviewer training, and relationships with clients. At meetings of the American Association of Public Opinion Research, discussions nevertheless diverged, with academic researchers paying greater attention to the design of panel surveys, drawing causal explanations from cross-sectional data, problems associated with the construction of variables, nuances of sampling (such as in rural areas), advanced statistical techniques, and interdisciplinary perspectives, as well as the abiding question of what public opinion was, after all, and how best to study it. The range of interests was well illustrated by David Riesman, whose 1950 book *The Lonely Crowd* became the best-selling book of all time by a sociologist. Riesman was intensely interested in public opinion and its relationship to what he perceived as large shifts in American character. For those reasons he participated in discussions of public opinion and published essays about how to conduct and interpret interviews; he believed wholeheartedly in the value of qualitative interviews over quantification.[4]

In later years, when funding agencies and church boards determined that it was just as good, or better, to have polling firms conduct research about religion, rather than academic social scientists, the decision rarely took full account of these differences. To their credit, polls were cheaper, quicker, and better positioned to garner attention from news media, but polling firms had different traditions and operated with different assumptions than social scientists in academic settings. Covering whatever topics happened to be in the news, pollsters rarely brought in-depth knowledge of religion to the questions they asked about religion, nor did the standards governing the publication of poll results go beyond basic criteria about the reporting of percentages and sampling errors to include peer review of how the results were interpreted.

The contrast with academic surveys was most evident in the fact that polls usually took only a few days to conduct, with another poll going into the field a week or two later, whereas social scientific surveys generally took months of planning that involved extensive consultations with the relevant literature, discussions among teams of researchers, and pretesting; followed by fieldwork lasting several months; and then a similar process before another survey went into the field. A second difference was that polls usually attempted to tap public opinion with only several questions or as few as one question, the responses to which were reported verbatim, and left to the public to interpret; whereas academic researchers at the time took seriously the advice of social psychologists who believed that attitudes underlying surface opinions could also be measured and should thus be examined with multiple, carefully tested questions from which attitude scales were constructed. Borrowing ideas from educational testing earlier in the century, and then progressing to the work of psychologist Gordon Allport in the 1930s, among others, the logic of attitude scaling emphasized deep-seated and relatively stable attitude formations rooted in personality dispositions and family backgrounds, as opposed to ephemeral opinions of the kind addressed in polls. By the late 1940s, the most notable effort to develop such scales and arguments was the *Authoritarian Personality* research conducted at the University of California at Berkeley.[5]

Academic studies of religious beliefs and activities in these years differed from both commercial polling and earlier community surveys by emphasizing the idea of underlying concepts that interested social psychologists. Instead of conducting large-scale surveys meant to represent national opinions, researchers conducted in-depth studies among smaller selected populations with an eye toward generating concepts and testing theories. University of Chicago psychometrician L. L. Thurstone and former Chicago Divinity School student E. J. Chave, for example, conducted studies in the 1920s arguing that effective religious education involved the shaping of underlying attitudes toward biblical creeds and doctrines, and presenting empirically tested scales to measure those attitudes.[6] At Harvard, Allport studied religious attitudes among students at several colleges and universities, drawing on William James's concepts of healthy-minded and sick-souled religious experience to develop measures of intrinsic and extrinsic religious orientations. Allport's research on religion, which began in the 1930s, culminated in the publication in 1950 of *The Individual and His Religion: A Psychological Interpretation.*[7]

The organizations founded in the early 1950s to promote social scientific studies of religion reflected these diverse disciplinary and institutional legacies. Early members besides Allport included Harvard psychologist Henry Murray and Middlebury College psychologist Walter H. Clark; Harvard anthropologist Clyde Kluckhohn and sociologists Talcott Parsons and Pitirim Sorokin; Harvard theologians Paul Tillich and James Luther Adams; University of Chicago ethicist Gibson Winter; and National Council of Churches researchers Lauris Whitman and Benson Y. Landis. With interests as wide-ranging as personality formation, attitudes, church policies, and grand theories of modernization, it was impossible for those involved to agree on much, but agree they did, at least on the idea that the study of religion could be advanced through the various perspectives of social science (and perhaps through natural science as well, although those relationships never transpired). As the decade progressed, annual meetings continued, and in 1959 the Religious Research Association founded the *Review of Religious Research*, the Society for the Scientific Study of Religion founded the *Journal for the Scientific Study of Religion* in 1961, and the Catholic Sociological Society in 1963 broadened and renamed its journal as *Sociological Analysis*.[8]

Landmark Studies

Were it of interest in the early 1950s to know what the American public thought about religion, it would have seemed preferable to consult national poll results, which were reproduced routinely in the *Public Opinion Quarterly*, or to draw inferences from qualitative studies such as *The Lonely Crowd*. Whether the public thought a person could be a good Christian and join the Communist Party, for example, or whether they considered it important for colleges to sponsor courses about religious prejudice could be ascertained from polls. Already in 1943, Cantril had argued that polling data could be a particularly useful source for social scientists interested in religion, examining an analysis of some fourteen thousand responses to Gallup polls asking how Catholics and Protestants compared in educational attainment, taking account of differences in income levels and region.[9] In the early 1950s, a few other studies, such as Samuel A. Stouffer's *Communism, Conformity, and Civil Liberties*, would also provide glimpses of religion's role in American life, along with topics such as race, gender, region, and political affiliation. It was hardly necessary to consult the work of scholars associated with the new specialty organizations studying religion. That was not because they were doing inferior work. It was rather that much of the work had to be done with sparse information drawn for the most part from churches, historical sources, and theoretical discussions.

With resources severely limited, the few researchers who succeeded in securing sufficient funding to conduct expensive surveys gained considerable influence in shaping the discussions within their various fields of academic inquiry. Surveys that dealt extensively with religion were rare enough that the results generated books as well as articles, which elevated the standards for conducting smaller-scale studies and provided information for textbooks and lectures. Like other scholarly endeavors, surveys were labor intensive, but the tasks involved also varied from ones requiring specialized computing and statistical skills to others better performed by graduate and undergraduate students or by hired assistants doing nontechnical work. Although individual faculty members and their students conducted quantitative studies, the most ambitious studies eventuated increasingly from large universities with survey research centers and PhD programs in the social sciences.

The Dynamics of a City Church, published in 1951 by Reverend Joseph H. Fichter, a Harvard-trained Jesuit social scientist who joined Loyola University in New Orleans in 1947 as chair of the sociology department, was arguably the first major post–World War II study to employ systematic survey methods and, in that respect, was unusual by virtue of the institution from which it was conducted. Using questionnaires combined with interviews and archival materials, Fichter investigated the characteristics of religious belief and practice among Catholics in New Orleans, documenting not only the extent of active involvement in the church (about a third were inactive) but also their views toward the church, relationships with clergy, and attitudes about race. The book received immediate acclaim from sociologists as a major work demonstrating the possibilities of advancing understandings of religion through intensive empirical research. University of Chicago religion scholar Joachim Wach, for example, considered it "infinitely more important" than any "general survey," leaving ambiguous whether the latter referred to nonempirical textbook overviews or to the general impressions of religion currently available in polls. It was the kind of study, Wach observed, that demonstrated the value of statistical methods while avoiding broad generalizations and focusing on concrete social relationships and organizational features as well as attitudes. The book received praise as well for bringing ideas to bear on the research about the contours of contemporary culture from theorists such as Parsons, Sorokin, and Kluckhohn.[10]

However, Fichter's research also revealed the difficulties of studying religion in ways that depended to such an extent on the cooperation of religious authorities. According to historian R. Bentley Anderson, the study "created such a furor in the archdiocese of New Orleans that publication of [Fichter's anticipated] multi-volume study was halted in 1951."[11] Among other things, the study riled church leaders who felt it portrayed them as poor leaders harboring pejorative attitudes toward African Americans. It did not help that in his role as Jesuit priest Fichter also gave homilies calling on the church to mend its attitudes and wrote articles in Catholic publications suggesting a re-examination of the concept and image of the parish priest. Although Fichter's dual roles complicated the issues, the controversy presaged ones that would plague religion researchers in the years ahead. When funding and access depended on cooperation from religious organizations, results that put those organizations in a bad light were difficult to present without repercussions for future funding and access.

Two years after Fichter's book, a major survey that also focused on church members—in this case, Episcopalians—took place, although it received little attention until 1966 when a book-length report of its findings appeared. The study was conducted at Columbia's Bureau of Applied Social Research by sociologist Charles Y. Glock, whom Lazarsfeld had recruited in 1951 to direct the organization. Glock was a founding member of the Society for the Scientific Study of Religion and an early recruit into the Religious Research Association. In her authoritative history of survey research, Jean M. Converse described him as a "'working' scholar who conducted his own research into religion as well as a 'worrying' scholar who was concerned about the overall Bureau agenda, trying to match people who could work together and get the reports out to sponsors and clients."[12]

A chance encounter with one of Lazarsfeld's assistants in 1941 resulted in Glock meeting Lazarsfeld and being offered a Rockefeller fellowship in conjunction with the radio project, only to be interrupted five months later when Glock was drafted into the army. After completing his military service, Glock returned to Columbia, where he finished a PhD in sociology and resumed working at the bureau. The Episcopal study originated when the denomination's Director of Christian Social Relations, Reverend M. Moran Weston, approached Glock, who besides directing the bureau was teaching a course in sociology of religion, and asked if a study could be done to see if parishioners' views in any way conformed to the denomination's statements on social policy. With the $3,000 Weston made available, Glock enlisted the help of several students, selected a sample of Episcopal parishes, and sent questionnaires to a sample of members within each parish, as well as to priests and bishops, and tabulated the results. Two articles and the eventual book showed the extent to which parishioners deviated conservatively from clergy and denominational positions on social and political topics, and developed an argument about congregations' roles in providing comfort for those in particular need of such support. Glock and several of the students associated with the project would continue to conduct surveys about religion in coming years.[13]

At the same time that Glock's study was in the field, Gerhard E. Lenski, a sociologist at the University of Michigan, was one of several faculty members invited to participate in the first Detroit Area Study, which was a practicum for graduate students in survey research and administered by the university's Survey Research Center. Like Glock, Lenski was from a Lutheran background and was interested in sociology of religion, among other things, and had recently examined the relationships of gender, marriage, and fertility on religious participation, drawing on a community survey conducted in Indianapolis in 1941.[14] The Detroit Area projects were unique in that they took place every year or two and, by virtue of using graduate students to conduct interviews in one city, were able to include relatively large numbers of interviews with only minimal additional funding from the university or in some cases from the Ford Foundation. In 1958 Lenski directed the Detroit Area Study, focusing the questions on religion and examining variations among white Protestants, black Protestants, Catholics, and Jews in religious patterns as well as the impact of religious training on political and economic attitudes. Lenski's graduate students interviewed a randomly selected sample of 656 people and, like Glock's project, included interviews with 127 clergy as well. A book-length summary of the results appeared in 1961 as *The Religious Factor: A Sociological Study of the Impact of Religion on Politics, Economics, and Family Life.*[15]

Despite, or perhaps because of, the extensive data on which the book was based, it received mixed reviews. Glock, conceding that it was a "major contribution," considered the arguments unconvincing because of unexamined effects of gender and age, variations among Protestant denominations that were not fully dealt with, and possibilities that the presumed effects of religion were more likely the result of differences in religious heritage than in beliefs and practices. In contrast, sociologist of religion Peter Berger praised the effort as "one of the most important sociological studies of American religion in recent years," noting its contributions to understanding religious pluralism and how religion related to discussions of urbanism.[16] For his part, Lenski turned to other topics, never to produce another book-length study of religion, but *The Religious Factor*'s discussion of Protestant–Catholic differences in economic and educational attainment, rooted as they were in Max Weber's arguments about the Protestant ethic and the spirit of capitalism, inspired numerous subsequent studies and discussions reconsidering Weber's thesis.

In 1964, an article summarizing research to date by psychologists and sociologists in which some attempt had been made to collect or analyze empirical data about religion identified 130 such studies, but only twenty-five included individual interviews either in surveys or clinical settings.[17] Several of the publications involved further analysis of Lenski's Detroit data. Others examined results made possible by the inclusion of a question or two about religion in surveys of high school, college, and graduate students. Clearly, survey research was beginning to take hold but had a long way to go both in popularity and topics covered. In comparison, hundreds of Gallup polls about religion had been conducted by that time. Poll results, moreover, received immediate publicity in press releases, whereas, with the possible exception of Lenski's book, which reached beyond academic readers, hardly anyone in the general public was likely to have heard about academic surveys of religion. The exception was college students, and yet, text materials at the time devoted as much attention, if not more, to conceptual and theoretical ideas as to research.

Although the researchers undoubtedly believed they were contributing valuably to knowledge, those who thought about what exactly they were contributing identified accomplishments that contrasted sharply from the ones that may have been seen in polls. It was true that none of the academic surveys produced results generalizable to the American public. It was also true that none of them capably documented trends. If anything could be said by way of generalization about "American religion," it had to be from polls, not from a modest study of New Orleans or Detroit or among Episcopalians. The academic studies, though, were intent not on generalizing descriptively about a population but on generating ideas about how religion worked and why. The arguments focused on relationships among attitudes and behavior, on the roots of religious orientations in personalities, and on the organizations in which religious practices occurred. How priests and parishioners related to one another was at issue as were questions about why some people participated more actively in congregations than others.

At the time, all that made sense to the academic researchers studying religion. Although the idea that something appropriately termed American religion was gaining prominence in public discourse, the time had not yet come when polling conceptions of American religion would supersede almost anything else that survey researchers might have to offer. Polling about religion and academic studies of religion remained almost in separate worlds. They were not completely separate, though, because academic researchers produced information that complicated the conclusions drawn from polls, and most academic researchers were drawn to poll results as well since data, after all, was researchers' holy grail, no matter where it was found.

Complicating the Polls

With rare exceptions, Gallup polls asked only a few questions about religion, and the most common questions were ones that had been asked before. Asking them again provided material with which to discuss trends, but the questions tended to be simple, squeezed into polls regarding opinions about public officials and household products, and for that reason gave only the most general impression of what religion in America was like. When Herberg concluded that religion in America was widespread but superficial, the complaint about superficiality could have been directed at how the polls were conducted, perhaps more credibly than to the polls' results. The notion that American religion was superficial, after all, was a trope that Gallup emphasized to render interesting the fact that far more of those polled believed in God than attended church regularly. The charge was about all that could be inferred from the questions polls asked, rather than reflecting any knowledge of how else religion might be deeply meaningful. The academic surveys, in contrast, had the advantage of being able to pose more nuanced questions, include a larger number of them, and produce results examining more complex relationships among the various topics and measures.

While the landmark academic surveys did not purport to offer generalizations about "American religion," they occurred in the context in which that rubric was increasingly being used (as in Berger describing Lenski's study as a contribution to "studies of American religion"). To the extent that American religion was at issue, though, the academic surveys implicitly criticized the polling results by showing that religion was more nuanced than usually captured in polls. Fichter's and Glock's surveys showed that religion was not a kind of disembodied aggregated aspect of national opinion but was located in parishes and shaped by the relationships parishioners experienced with priests and homilies and church teachings. Lenski operationalized concepts such as "orthodoxy," "devotionalism," and "communalism" that linked survey questions to broader understandings of religion, and, most significantly, showed that Herberg's tripartite division of Protestants, Catholics, and Jews needed, at least, to further distinguish white and black Protestants, and that conjectures about immigrant adaptation, Americanization, and the effects of urbanization were better understood through an in-depth examination of beliefs and attitudes in an actual city than through facile generalizations from national polls.

One of the clearest ways in which academic surveys complicated the picture of American religion from polls was evident in a survey of Northern California church members conducted under Glock's direction in 1964. Having migrated to the University of California at Berkeley in 1958 to start and direct its Survey Research Center, Glock became the principal investigator in 1962 of a half-million-dollar grant from the Anti-Defamation League (ADL) of B'nai B'rith to produce a series of studies examining anti-Semitism and other forms of prejudice in the United States. One phase of the research dealt with the possible effects of particularistic Christian beliefs, such as affirming that only Christians are saved, in reinforcing negative attitudes toward Jews. The survey of church members provided an opportunity not only to ask detailed questions about those possible relationships but also to probe other dimensions of religious commitment, including beliefs, experiences, church participation, and devotional activities. In a report of the results, published with coauthor Rodney Stark, Glock showed that members of different Protestant denominations differed dramatically on many of these characteristics, with Congregationalists and Episcopalians expressing greater doubts and exhibiting lower levels of commitment than Lutherans and American Baptists, who, in turn, showed less orthodox beliefs and practices than Southern Baptists and members of smaller evangelical denominations. Although Gallup reports typically distinguished Catholics from Protestants, the California data demonstrated the importance of denominational differences and, indeed, suggested that it was nonsensical to lump all Protestants together.[18]

Other surveys complicated polling inferences by showing that American religion was more than the opinion of an undifferentiated mass public in which each person's responses weighed equally with every other person's. Implicitly, the picture of American religion from polls pertained mostly to white Protestants and Catholics. Because the typical poll included relatively few African Americans and even fewer Jews or members of small denominations or atheists, American religion appeared mostly as a kind of white-bread homogenizing cultural phenomenon, rather than the highly diverse mosaic it actually was. Academic surveys illuminated that diversity. One of the ADL surveys under Glock's supervision, for example, sampled African Americans in Southern cities to explore how religious participation related to attitudes toward civil rights militancy, and another study combined survey results with analysis of publications to explore the political role of far-right religious activist groups such as Billy James Hargis's Christian Crusade and Fred Schwarz's Christian Anti-Communism Crusade. Other surveys examined the beliefs, practices, and changing identities of Jews.[19]

Following Lazarsfeld's work on radio as a possible influence on public opinion, researchers trained in that tradition supplemented poll results by examining how other public opinion leaders might be shaping religious beliefs and practices. Surveys such as Fichter's, Glock's, and Lenski's that included clergy obviously did this, but so did surveys of scientists and college faculty and mental health professionals, as well as studies in which urban, younger, and better-educated populations were taken to be bellwethers of emerging ideas.[20]

With polls focusing on large issues of general interest, academic surveys carved out another distinctive niche by examining religion's relationship to issues of particular relevance to particular subpopulations. To know how religion might be related to attitudes toward childbearing and birth control, for example, it made more sense to survey women of childbearing age than to present poll figures drawn from a sample representing the entire public. Similarly, the possible relation of religion to drug use or juvenile delinquency was better studied in populations particularly at risk for those activities.[21]

In addition to studying specialized populations and topics, academic studies continued to differ from polls about religion by developing scales and complex indicators of attitudes and beliefs instead of relying on single questions. Social psychologists paid particular attention to these tasks, focusing further on Allport's scales of religious orientations and developing measures of religion within larger scales of values. Other studies used multiple survey questions to identify and measure such concepts as dogmatism, consensual religion, and religious meaning systems.[22]

The major limitation of academic surveys was that they rarely provided descriptions of religion generalizable to the American public. That remained the special purview of polls. If it was of interest to know how many Americans were Protestants or Catholics and what proportion attended worship services, the answer was to be found in polls, rather than in academic surveys, which in most instances were conducted in particular communities, on college campuses, or among the members of one denomination. With limited capacity to produce results generalizable to the population, academic researchers took as their mandate the idea of generating "scientific" generalizations. That meant identifying causal patterns and other regularities in limited contexts that nevertheless could be tested and replicated in other settings.

Causal generalizations about religion came in two varieties. They were statements about the sources of variation in religion or statements about the consequences of that variation. From the start, social scientists were interested in both. They considered the idea that particular kinds of religion were caused by different locations in the class structure, by gender and race, and by psychological trauma and deprivation. Interesting as those ideas were, they paled compared with questions about the consequences of religion. Did religion encourage people to work harder and move up in the world? Did it help them to be happier and healthier? Were they better able to face bereavement and death? If not, there was little reason to be interested in it. Even the ideas about sources of religion merged into arguments about its consequences. Its presumed sources could perhaps be understood as clues to the functions it performed, such as helping the poor cope with their problems or the sick with theirs.

The possibility that generalizations about the causes and consequences of religion could be identified was perhaps the clearest way in which academic social scientists' understanding of science differed from pollsters'. But the hope of identifying such generalizations diminished almost in direct proportion to the number of actual studies. The idea that people who were deprived of earthly rewards would be more religious because of promised rewards in an afterlife, for example, was nice in theory, but in practice proved harder and harder to justify when evidence showed that middle-class Americans were just as religious in some ways as lower-class people, and even when multiple kinds of deprivation were posited—people could be psychologically deprived or perhaps ethically deprived because their values were not respected—the connection with religion proved tenuous. The idea that generalizations about religion's consequences could be identified—greater happiness, more friends, and longer lives, for example—lasted longer but also proved to increasingly depend on particular circumstances.

The difficulties in finding scientific generalizations about religion, then, perhaps ironically, shifted the center of gravity among academic researchers closer again to how pollsters viewed science. In a word, a kind of empiricism prevailed in both, an empiricism intent on presenting results from data collected in systematic ways and assumed generalizable to a population within a specific geographic and temporal context. Hypotheses drawn from theoretical arguments would serve less as ideas to be tested and more as hunches about what might be happening in particular places and times.

Embracing the Polls

With relatively few sources of quantitative data available but with growing interest in statistical analysis, social scientists of religion turned increasingly to the material available from polls. So many national polls were being done, and they were receiving such attention in the media, that it seemed a shame not to make greater use of them. Especially if poll data were increasingly being taken for granted as an apt characterization of American religion, then it made sense to statistically oriented social scientists to mine the data for additional results.

Gallup and Roper data were being archived in electronic form at the Roper Center at the University of Connecticut. Academic researchers faced two difficulties. The data were embargoed for two years, which meant that further analysis could never compete with or question the conclusions pollsters published in their own reports or in the newspapers. The other difficulty was that the pollsters' reports rarely presented results in detail other than for standard categories such as gender, region, and several categories of age and education. That difficulty posed the greatest opportunity for researchers interested in examining the results in greater detail using more sophisticated statistical methods.

Just as Cantril had done earlier, researchers analyzed poll data to provide a richer picture of American religion. A 1971 article in the *Journal for the Scientific Study of Religion*, for example, examined Gallup polls from 1965 and 1969 to elaborate on arguments about denominational differences in church attendance and to address the questions Lenski posed in Detroit about educational differences between Protestants and Catholics. The logic now was that national data were better than local data, especially if the national data offered a few new possibilities, such as showing that church attendance increased with length of residence but apparently not with larger numbers of children.[23]

Besides its availability, poll data attracted academic researchers convinced by the social and political turmoil of the 1960s that social change was perhaps more important to document and examine than static generalizations about religion. "Is God Dead?" *Time's* April 8, 1966, cover asked, prompting social scientists and pollsters alike to imagine that the question surely could be answered with trend data from polls and surveys. Harvey Cox theorized that secularization was certainly a feature of urbanization, and Peter Berger associated it with pluralism undermining the plausibility of taken-for-granted beliefs; but Daniel Bell, whose writing also focused on broad trends in postindustrial societies, declared, "If one looks at survey data about the beliefs and religious conduct of the ordinary American, there is little evidence to sustain the argument about a crisis of faith or a loss of institutional strength of the churches."[24]

In 1972 the *Journal for the Scientific Study of Religion* signaled what was emerging as a rapprochement between academic researchers and pollsters by initiating a "review of the polls" as a regular feature. A year later, sociologists Jackson W. Carroll and David A. Roozen published an essay in the journal in which they argued that national polls available through the Roper Center for Public Opinion Research could be "used profitably by students of religion to a much greater extent than they have been used in the past."[25] From issue to issue, subsequent review articles summarized and presented additional analyses of Gallup polls in which one or more questions about religion had been asked. The essays considered variations in church attendance and religious beliefs, related these variations to social class and size of community, and examined how religious factors were involved in attitudes toward birth control, civil liberties, nonmarital sex, homosexuality, and altruism. Between 1960 and 1965, only about seventy articles and reviews in all sociology journals mentioned Gallup polls in the context of discussing religion, but from 1970 to 1975 that number jumped to nearly a hundred and fifty. Little noted at the time, that convergence would influence how academic surveys of religion were conducted in the coming years while polling about religion became increasingly influential. As information from academic surveys and commercial polls became more abundantly available, the criteria guiding them and the standards by which they were judged would remain different, but there would be a preference for national data capable of describing American religion.

The Religious Connection

The scientific norms governing academic research stipulated that social scientists were to be objective, dispassionate, and impersonal. They were to avoid being influenced in any way by personal backgrounds and idiosyncratic perspectives. Yet, those were textbook ideals, seldom fully realized in practice. It mattered in subtle ways that social scientists were men or women, black or white, raised in the heartland or in cities, young or old, immigrants or native born, and from affluent or working-class backgrounds. That was true among researchers studying religion as well. They frequently had personal interests in religion stemming from positive or negative experiences with religious organizations. It mattered, too, that religious organizations were often the sponsors of research projects or provided the populations among whom the research was done.

A 1974 *Review of Religious Research* essay, examining some five hundred articles about religion in social science journals since the 1890s, reported that a quarter of the ones produced in the 1960s were by clergy or authors affiliated in other ways with religious institutions, seminaries, or divinity schools, and argued that scientific studies of religion were hindered by the sizable proportion of researchers "torn between their scientific and religious commitments."[26] Whether that was actually the case was hard to know, although instances such as Fichter's difficulties in New Orleans certainly provided anecdotal evidence. The Religious Research Association in the early 1970s remained true to its founding vision of facilitating research of value to churches and church leaders, publishing articles and reviews about church planning, the theological views of grassroots members and clergy, and surveys examining patterns of church attendance. Numerous articles in the *Journal for the Scientific Study of Religion* focused on those topics as well.

Unsurprisingly, researchers expressed ambivalence about their work's connections with religious organizations, arguing, as earlier generations had, that research was beneficial to religious leaders, appreciating the opportunities to conduct such research, but at the same time noting the potential difficulties. If it was possible that studies of religion were hindered by the involvement of scholars with religious affiliations, there was also a kind of faith among researchers that more was better, perhaps especially when the resulting knowledge created the opportunity, as one researcher put it, "to subvert the sanctioned beliefs and undermine the existing order of [the] religious establishment."[27]

The ADL project at Berkeley illustrated how these practical considerations might intersect with research. Why the ADL decided to locate the project at Berkeley appears to have been largely the result of its leaders having known and worked with some of the recipients, especially Glock while at Columbia, but, under university auspices, the project undoubtedly benefited from the prestige of being conducted at a leading research institution rather than done by a polling firm with less transparency and still subject to misgivings among some of the public. By all indications, the sponsoring agency provided funding and approved the recipients' general research plan but did not interfere in any way with the research itself. The research was, however, put to practical use almost immediately because the Second Vatican Council was in session, and the ADL representative in Rome wanted to make sure the research, suggesting that Christian beliefs did contribute to anti-Semitism, was considered. Glock produced an eight-page summary and dispatched it to Rome. "We learned that the ADL representative had arranged to have it translated and reproduced," he later recalled. "A copy in their native language was made available to all the Cardinals in attendance at the Council a day or two before a proposed statement on the Jews was to be considered." The document was in fact mentioned, and the statement cautioning against anti-Semitism was adopted. "We never learned whether our report had any influence on the decision," Glock observed. "We found ourselves, nevertheless, hoping that it did."[28]

But was there solid evidence that Christian beliefs encouraged anti-Semitism? And if so, what exactly was the connection? Subsequent analysis of the data by Glock's team and others and follow-up studies suggested that the connection was tenuous. Not as popularly believed in some quarters was Christian fundamentalism or even the view that only Christians went to heaven sufficient as a source of anti-Semitism. The connection was hardly present at all unless Christians held the theolog-ically uninformed view that Jesus should have lived and reigned had it not been for Christ-killing Jews, as well as other negative views, which were almost indistinguishable in the survey from how anti-Semitism was measured. Years later, Glock remembered the criticisms in detail, dis-counting most of them but also recalling tense meetings with church leaders who either disbelieved the results or inadvertently revealed their own anti-Semitism.[29]

Differences of interpretation did not in that instance undermine the integrity of the project, but religion research was always suscep-tible to questions about the biases that might be present because of funding sources, intended applications, and researchers' own religious backgrounds and beliefs. Andrew Greeley, who, like Fichter, doubled as priest and academic researcher, felt and vocalized the concerns perhaps more clearly than any other social scientist of religion. Upon publi-cation of *The Church and the Suburbs* in 1959, Greeley found himself unenviably criticized for bringing either too little or too much research into his work. With a PhD in sociology from the University of Chicago a few years later, his work moved decidedly in an empirical direction, using survey results to show in almost every way possible that Weber's and more recently Lenski's arguments about the superiority of Protes-tant over Catholic achievements were wrong. Career plans, educational attainment, exposure to Catholic schools, and results in other stud-ies all suggested, as he argued in a much-discussed 1964 article, for a moratorium on the Protestant ethic thesis.[30]

Through his affiliation with Chicago's National Opinion Research Center, Greeley made full use of the surveys that included questions about religion. His *Religion and Career: A Study of College Graduates*, published in 1963, examined survey data from forty thousand 1961 graduates at 135 colleges.[31] A subsequent volume, *The Education of Catholic Americans*, published in 1966 with coauthor Peter H. Rossi, presented data from a national sample of more than three thousand Catholics and additional data from Catholic teenagers showing generally powerful and positive ef-fects on teens' academic behavior from families' religious involvement.[32] By 1970, Greeley's books, articles, and reviews had established his reputa-tion as one of the nation's premier sociologists of religion. And over the next few years, he would further solidify that reputation with new sur-veys and books challenging the idea of secularization and documenting in greater detail and with more statistical sophistication than any poll the characteristics of American Catholics' beliefs, practices, and relationships to the Church.

Greeley nevertheless continued to be at odds with both the Church and academic social science. Critical of Church policies from the start of his career as a priest, he conducted a national study at the request of the US bishops in 1972 that displeased many Catholic leaders by showing the extent of parishioners' dissatisfaction with the Church and disagreement with its policies, especially on birth control. About the same time, he was also denied tenure at the University of Chicago. Staying as an untenured researcher at the National Opinion Research Center, he continued to produce research published in the most respected academic journals, but Greeley increasingly turned to writing novels, which by the 1980s earned sufficient royalties to pay the cost of conducting additional surveys about religion, as well as establishing a chair in Roman Catholic studies at the University of Chicago.

Greeley's unique talents as social scientist, writer, theologian, and priest demonstrated the possibilities but also the challenges of combining multiple roles. While possessing the kind of faith in survey research that pollsters shared, he unceasingly kept an eye on topics of particular interest to the Church and at the same time wrestled with questions about theology, the religious imagination, and narrative accounts of religious experience that could not be studied with statistical methods. As he explained to an interviewer in the late 1990s, there was a disturbing lack of empirical evidence in some of the most respected works of social science, but, despite being called a naive empiricist, he also found that even survey data analysis could be a form of poetic expression.[33]

Two Cultures or Three

By the 1970s, social scientists were clearly divided in how they viewed religion in relation to their scholarly work. The ones who regarded themselves most seriously as scientists favored the use of statistical methods and quantitative data. Others, who took a humanistic approach, felt more at home with theory, history, and ethnography. Those were the clearest alternatives. But there was a third perspective as well. It regarded science more as a tool with which to achieve practical ends, rather than as an end in itself or as a distinctly superior form of knowledge. This third perspective was particularly important because it, more than the other two, inadvertently facilitated a perspective that made polling all the more acceptable in the coming years.

The approach that privileged science drew inspiration from the early to mid-twentieth-century faith that science itself was the driving force in human betterment, bringing a clearer understanding of the world that would ultimately shape culture and behavior and public policy into its reason-based image. To apply that understanding to religion was, of course, awkward because the logical implication of faith in science was that religion itself was backward thinking that needed to be replaced. The understanding of science that guided social science investigations followed that logic to the point of suggesting that modernization rooted in science would in fact diminish the importance of religion and, while it thus might be interesting to monitor religion's decline, better uses of scarce resources could be found in studies of other topics, such as population trends, economic behavior, and inequality.

A more appreciative approach to religion, still from a scientific perspective, held that social scientific studies should aim toward cumulative theoretical knowledge, driven not by practical implications but by better concepts, arguments, and empirical evidence. To that end, researchers making use of survey data offered the prospect of testing and improving on Weber's arguments, for example, as Lenski's study did, or by conceptualizing religion into "dimensions," such as belief, knowledge, and experience, as Glock's contributions suggested. The ideal, in this regard, was to weave understandings of religion into broader social science debates as well. For example, evidence about religion might contribute to arguments about the pervasiveness of relative deprivation or status inconsistency in shaping human behavior.

The difficulty in advancing academic studies of religion as contributions to science lay especially in the lack of relevant data. Small, poorly funded studies among college students or church members or studies based on a question or two about religion squeezed into surveys about other topics could go only so far. Keeping religion officially separate from government in the United States meant that questions about it were not included in the census or in surveys conducted by government agencies or, for that matter, in projects supported by the National Science Foundation. The most significant breakthrough of that barrier came in the late 1960s when social scientists from the leading survey research centers at Chicago, Michigan, and Berkeley proposed a plan to measure and monitor social indicators. The plan called, first, for assembling what was known (mostly from polls and government data) about topics ranging from family patterns and employment to racial attitudes and views toward government policies, and then to conduct annual surveys in which new questions would be asked about these topics and repeated from year to year. With funding from the National Science Foundation, the General Social Survey, which asked questions of a representative sample of the American public, commenced in 1972.

The General Social Survey included questions about religion and became the most respected nonpolling source of information about American religion. As the surveys were repeated, at first every year and then every other year, the information provided opportunities to monitor trends and to relate religion to other topics, such as marital status, family background, and attitudes about civil liberties and government spending. With no particular applied agendas, and with the imprimatur of highly respected academic institutions, the information was particularly conducive to the perspective in which cumulative scientific contributions were the purpose of conducting research. However, reflecting the limited questions about religion that had been asked in polls, as well as the constraint of covering numerous other topics, the surveys typically included only a few questions about religion. To the extent that conclusions could be drawn about American religion, the information was still mostly about denominational affiliations among Christians, church attendance, and a few other topics, such as prayer and belief in an afterlife.

The humanistic approach considered it hardly worth the bother to pay much attention to studies that reduced religion to such simplified measures and chose instead to emphasize richer and more detailed questions arising from history, theology, and comparisons among religions across traditions and cultures. Peter Berger's *The Sacred Canopy: Elements of a Sociological Theory of Religion*, published in 1967, exemplified, and indeed significantly shaped, the approach to religion that largely eschewed quantification. Berger had taught for five years at Hartford Theological Seminary and written a popular book, *The Noise of Solemn Assemblies*, criticizing contemporary church teachings. His approach to the sociology of religion drew from phenomenology, which emphasized questions about meaning and the cultural construction of reality, as well as from Weber, Durkheim, and Marx. Subsequent work discussed what he termed signals of transcendence, the relationship of play to religion, and broad questions about long-term trends in modern societies. Although his work was widely read among scholars both outside and within the social sciences as a treatment of American religion, its contributions lay more in the development of general concepts about what religion was, why it existed in human societies at all, and how it conformed to changing cultural conditions. Neither particularly critical of nor interested in polls and surveys, he drew from a rich tradition of metadata that included theology and literature as well as sociological theory, and the scholars who followed most closely in his tradition produced studies that favored qualitative more than quantitative approaches.[34]

Like Berger, Robert Bellah's contributions in the 1960s shaped what would become known as the cultural turn in studies of religion, particularly by focusing on the roles of symbolism in religious traditions and the potential importance of symbols in shaping the meaning of individual lives and of human existence writ large. Best known for his work on Japanese religion, Bellah's efforts through the early 1960s dealt with large comparative and historical questions about religion in modernizing societies. Scholars interested in American religion gravitated to his 1967 essay on civil religion, which Bellah followed with a series of lectures in 1971 (published as *The Broken Covenant* in 1975) and to which he later returned in his most widely read book, coauthored in 1985, *Habits of the Heart*. However, by the mid-1960s Bellah was reaching beyond Weber, Durkheim, and Tocqueville for inspiration from theologians Paul Tillich and Herbert Richardson, philosopher of language Suzanne Langer, anthropologist Mircea Eliade, poets Robinson Jeffers and Wallace Stevens, and theorists Philip Rieff and Herbert Fingarette. From these and other writers, Bellah challenged the positivist agenda of mainstream social science and argued for an approach to religion that normatively and ethically privileged the search for holistic meaning and criticized societal trends that he believed were antithetical to this quest. In rare passing references to polls and surveys, he implied that they were limited at best and probably not to be taken as serious evidence of large cultural meanings and trends. He observed, in writing about religion in 1964, "the subject does not lend itself well to investigation via questionnaires and brief interviews."[35]

The cultural turn that shaped studies of religion in the 1960s included significant contributions by anthropologist Clifford Geertz, especially in relating religion to ideas about worldviews and ritual; anthropologists Mary Douglas and Victor Turner, for work on rituals and cultural classification; and from writers as diverse as comparative religion scholar Wilfred Cantwell Smith and philosopher Michel Foucault. The cultural turn gained traction in conjunction with the global protests that peaked between 1968 and 1972 against the Vietnam War, colonialism, and what critical theorist Herbert Marcuse termed the one-dimensional culture of late industrial capitalism. In addition to drawing on theoretical traditions featuring cultural complexity and power, the cultural turn explicitly rejected the positivist social science to which survey research was indebted, favoring inquiries instead that probed more deeply into the meanings and sources of cultural interpretation. While American culture and thus American religion lay in the background as a foil for cultural criticism, the cultural turn more specifically directed attention away from simplistic generalizations about American religion toward a larger critique of late capitalism and an interest in nonmainstream or, indeed, subversive developments, including new religious movements and efforts focusing on racial and gender equality and empowerment.

Academic studies of religion that emphasized surveys were neither fish nor fowl. On the one hand, they differed from the pure science approach in being as concerned with topics of practical interest to churches. On the other hand, they were too wedded to positivist social science to be of particular interest to scholars of religion influenced by the cultural turn. And yet the 1960s represented for social scientific studies of religion what eighteenth-century England did for industrial development—a takeoff period in which the organizational and intellectual conditions for subsequent growth came significantly together. As aspirations for generalizable scientific laws of human behavior failed to be realized, a more modest understanding of science implicitly came to be the operating principle for research, emphasizing empirical information collected through rigorous replicable methods and presented transparently for review and critique by knowledgeable peers. Ideas from the humanistic side filtered into the research in small ways, including closer attention to worldviews and the construction of meaning and studies focusing on nonmainstream religions and questions about gender and racial equality. Despite the ambivalence social scientists of religion expressed toward the church-based tradition of practical research, that tradition provided the most distinctive template going forward, for it emphasized research's applied potential for the world beyond academe, whether for church leaders or to criticize church policies and to address questions about the relationship of religious beliefs and practices to social, moral, and political issues.

But those emphases also meant that academic surveys of religion occurred in the same context as nonacademic polls of religion, functioning as contenders for scarce resources and as competitors in the increasingly common proclivity for American religion to be defined by polls and sur-veys. Coming from related but different traditions and having been shaped by different institutional locations, the two would remain distinct and yet were concerned with similar topics and interested in being relevant to larger discussions about the public role of religion in the United States. When the cultural turbulence of the 1960s ended and when conservative mainstream religion began exercising its influence in national politics, those larger discussions looked to polls and surveys for evidence with which to interpret what was happening. The relation of academic surveys and nonacademic polls then became harder to define and more difficult to distinguish. Polling firms would continue to have greater access to the media and greater ability to produce timely information about the latest developments. Academic surveys would continue to carve out specialized research niches by studying smaller populations and by bringing longer-term perspectives to bear on the results. It would also increasingly fall to academic researchers to challenge the validity of poll results and the interpretation of those results.

When social scientists of religion reflected on what they had and had not accomplished, as they periodically did over the years, the one thing on which they almost always agreed was that they felt marginal—under-appreciated by colleagues in the social sciences and humanities alike, and not quite able to understand why. The most commonly cited reason for this lack of appreciation was that somehow the scholarly world did not understand or respect religion itself, both as a meaningful aspect of personal life and as a legitimate topic of investigation, and if so, either nothing could be done or an entirely new intellectual path needed to be taken. That may have been the case, but as social scientists they probably pondered the complex institutional dynamics affecting their work as well. If the cultural perspective taught one thing, it was that religion's symbols, meanings, and rituals were hardly the subject matter that could be readily measured with survey questions about church attendance and belief in God. And yet the proliferation of polls in which American religion was defined in precisely such ways beckoned academic social scientists to take account of that definition and work to refine it. Going forward, the question was whether academic efforts to complicate and further refine that approach would matter much to discussions of American religion or whether those discussions would be guided by the media's interest in polling results.

5

Pollsters as Pundits

IN 1976 NOBODY expected Jimmy Carter to prevail in the Democratic primaries, let alone go on to win in the general election. It was odd enough that Carter was a plainspoken peanut farmer from the Deep South. The fact that he claimed to be a born-again evangelical Christian seemed not to be in his favor either. As far as anyone knew, evangelical Christians disliked politics, disproportionately steered clear of political activities, focused on personal salvation, and looked forward to an afterlife in heaven.

Carter's victory forced major media pundits who had little knowledge of grassroots religion to scramble. It was not unheard of for someone to be described as an evangelical. But what did that mean? Were there really people in the heartland who considered themselves born again? If so, how many? And were they capable of becoming a significant factor in American politics?

The best answers to these questions, had they been asked earlier, would have been from preachers and organizations that embraced the rubric of evangelicalism as their own. Born again was gospel shorthand for having turned over a new leaf, asking Jesus into one's heart as redeemer and personal savior. Evangelicalism was popularly associated with evangelistic services, revival meetings, and calls for repentance. It connoted distinct views of the Bible and heaven and end times, although the precise wording in which these views were expressed varied. Evangelicalism was the kind of teaching that preachers hoped would persuade hearts, save wayward souls, and pull people toward their denominations.

That approach did not deter numerical assessments. When delegates met in Chicago in 1943 to draw up plans for a National Association of Evangelicals, news reports indicated that the groups represented totaled about two million members. It was a significant number, twice that of the

fledgling American Council of Christian Churches organized by fundamentalist Carl McIntire, but miniscule compared to the sixty to seventy
million Christians represented by the Federal Council of Churches. By
all accounts, size was a function of denominational affiliations. In 1953,
when President Eisenhower signed a Freedom Declaration sponsored by
the National Association of Evangelicals, urging Americans to cherish
their faith in God, the organization's leaders claimed they represented ten
million of the nation's Christians. But nobody knew if the number was
correct.

Well into the 1960s, the scope of evangelicalism remained indetermi-
nate. The forty-odd denominations affiliated with the National Association of Evangelicals were small. To the extent that evangelicals could be
considered a definable category, its public persona inhered in occasional
conferences, evangelical colleges, and the appearances of prominent
preachers. Billy Graham was its face more than anyone else.

Graham's influence broadened the variety of denominations that pundits lumped under the evangelical umbrella. Because he was one, Southern Baptists came to be seen as evangelicals in addition to the smaller
denominations located mostly in the North. They were united at least in
having opposed Roman Catholic John F. Kennedy for president in 1960.
By the late 1960s, the National Association of Evangelicals still claimed
only about two million members in formally affiliated denominations.
But when Southern Baptists, Missouri Synod Lutherans, and various
Pentecostals, fundamentalists, and nondenominational Protestants were
combined, it was possible to imagine that some twenty million Americans were evangelicals.[1]

Against that backdrop, the polling that took place in connection with
Carter's election dramatically redefined the face of American evangelicalism. Instead of twenty to twenty-five million, Gallup put the number
closer to fifty million. More than a third of the eligible electorate were
evangelicals who shared the born-again religious experience that Carter
described, George Gallup Jr. told a gathering in Minneapolis six weeks
before the election. There were more evangelicals than Catholics, which
meant that religion could shape the turnout for Carter just as it had for
Kennedy. Evangelicalism was a "built-in power base," Gallup said. It was
currently the "hot movement" in American Christianity.[2]

Carter's election catapulted evangelicals into national prominence.
Newsweek's cover story by religion writer Kenneth L. Woodward the week
before the election was "Born Again!" Woodward visited Carter's Baptist

church in Plains, Georgia, attended the men's Bible class led by a Carter cousin, and concluded that evangelicalism was potentially a decisive force in American politics. "According to a recent Gallup survey based on personal interviews with 1,553 Americans of voting age," Woodward observed, "half of all Protestants—and a third of all Americans—say that they have been 'born again.' That figure comes to nearly fifty million adult Americans who claim to have experienced a turning point in their lives by making a personal commitment to Jesus Christ as their Savior." The same poll showed that 37 percent considered the Bible "the actual word of God" and thought it should be "taken literally, word for word." An even larger number—47 percent—said they had "tried to encourage someone to believe in Jesus Christ or to accept Him as his or her Savior."[3] *Time* reported the same figures, quoting Gallup that this was the "Year of the Evangelical."[4]

Could it be that twice as many people were evangelicals as previously thought? Journalists presented anecdotes suggesting that Gallup was right. Billy Graham's book *Angels* had just sold a million copies. Former Nixon aide Charles Colson's *Born Again* was on its way to selling 300,000 copies. Former Black Panther leader Eldridge Cleaver announced his conversion to Christianity. The "death of God" movement of the 1960s, they concluded, was surely over.

Evangelical leaders were naturally elated. *Christianity Today* editor and prominent evangelical author Carl F. H. Henry later recalled that the "year of the evangelical" was indeed a time of noteworthy spiritual growth and remarkable evangelical resurgence, evidenced by an unprecedented number of students at evangelical colleges and seminaries, attendance at evangelical conferences, international evangelistic outreach, and the growth of radio and television ministries. The high regard in which evangelicals were held did not last, he remembered, but for a while the term "evangelical" became so popular that Christians across the spectrum seemed to embrace it.[5]

With evangelicals' prominence, polling about religion also gained heightened visibility. If evangelicalism was part of a broader resurgence of interest in religion, commentators wanted to know more. Gallup figures were in high demand. The *Boston Globe* reported that church attendance in Gallup polls had stabilized after a decade of decline among young people in the 1960s. *New York Times* religion correspondent Kenneth Briggs reported that Gallup polls in sixty countries showed the United States to be more religious than any other major industrialized society. Lewis Lapham in *Harper's* drew on Gallup polls to put the American public in a less favorable light, arguing that Americans might be religious but were sadly ill informed. In the *Washington Post*, Seymour Martin Lipset observed that Carter's support among churchgoing conservative Protestants was also evident in a variety of polls.[6]

The year of the evangelical was the most notable instance to date in which polling played a major role in defining a significant feature of the religious landscape. Religion was already becoming a topic of greater interest in polls and among journalists. A new generation of pollsters was also coming onto the scene. As religion moved more prominently into the White House and as religious leaders organized themselves to be a force in decisions about abortion and homosexuality, pollsters were positioned to become an increasingly important voice in public discussions about religion as well.

In many ways, polling about religion during the last quarter of the twentieth century represented a crescendo in the frequency with which polls were conducted, the topics included, and the media's coverage of the results. In other ways, heightened interest in polling about religion recast the topics that came to characterize the public face of American religion. Although the academic study of religion flourished as well, its role in shaping broader public understandings continued to be eclipsed by the nonacademic polling community. That community was undergoing a significant restructuring that increased its public presence and at the same time set the stage for a subsequent erosion of confidence in polling. Understanding these changes requires starting with the polling community as it existed in the early 1970s and tracing the developments that occurred at the two organizations most involved in polling about religion.

Expanding Interest—and Concern

Interest in religion among the polling community had been steadily expanding well before Carter's campaign. Kennedy's entry and subsequent victory in the 1960 election prompted polling about attitudes toward Catholics in public office, differences in political preferences among Protestants and Catholics, tensions between the two, and federal aid for Catholic schools. The Second Vatican Council from 1962 to 1965 sparked interest in polls about birth control, ecumenism, and attitudes toward clergy. In 1965 the Gallup Organization conducted a major study comparing the attitudes of youth ages fifteen to nineteen with adults on a wide variety of issues, including birth control, sex, television, and religion. Later that year, *Catholic Digest* commissioned a Gallup study of religion in American life asking questions about religious training, funding for religious schools, birth control, divorce, relations among Christians and Jews, prayer, the Bible, and beliefs about Jesus and God.[7]

Polling about religion was part of the more general expansion of interest in public opinion research that took place during the 1960s. That interest was evident in the coverage that major newspapers devoted to polling results. During the 1950s the *New York Times*, for example, mentioned Gallup polls approximately two hundred times, but during the 1960s that number jumped to more than nine hundred.

By the late 1960s, polls were being conducted by Harris and Roper and for *Newsweek* as well as by Gallup on topics ranging from celibacy among Catholic priests to churches' teachings against abortion to the role of priests and pastors in the civil rights movement. Other topics included attitudes toward clergy, views about religion's influence, beliefs about heaven and hell, and perceived threats from opponents of religion. In conjunction with the Watergate hearings in 1973, a Senate committee commissioned a Harris poll asking about confidence in the nation's leaders and institutions, including religion.[8]

The Harris poll did not ask about confidence in polls, but a congressional committee a year earlier had become sufficiently interested in the growing influence of polls that it convened a hearing at which the major pollsters were called to testify. The hearing on September 19, 20, and 21, 1972, chaired by Democratic Congressman Lucien N. Nedzi of Michigan, included testimony by George Gallup Sr., Mervin Field, Louis Harris, Burns Roper, and several other pollsters and academic researchers about the possible costs and benefits of legislation requiring more detailed reporting of the methods used in conducting public opinion polls.[9]

The concerns that led to the hearing included complaints from Hubert Humphrey about the negative effects of early polls during his campaign against Richard Nixon in 1968 as well as complaints from candidates in several statewide and municipal elections. Nedzi's proposed legislation gained no traction in 1969 or 1970. It failed again in 1971 and 1972. But the hearing elicited exceptionally frank disclosures from pollsters not only about their methods but also about the strengths and weaknesses they perceived. None of the testimony dealt with questions about religion. It nevertheless identified a number of issues that would have been relevant to polling about religion, had anyone been interested at the time, and that would eventually be asked as polling became more common.

The legislation Nedzi proposed would have required that information about every poll be deposited within a specified period at the Library of Congress. That information would include the name of the sponsoring organization, when the poll was conducted, how many people were interviewed, the method of sampling, the response rate, and a copy of the questions asked. Gallup's remarks about the idea were the most forthcoming, indicating that he had been in favor of the proposed legislation from the start because he thought it would deter upstart polling efforts by political candidates and should apply to the polling recently being done by television networks. He said the Gallup procedures were already in compliance. There was one exception, he acknowledged. That was the point about response rates. In attempting to secure responses from a probability sample, he said, there would always be a large number of people who could not be contacted or who refused to cooperate. He did not view that as an important matter, though, because the probability method was accurate down to the block level and after that contacting neighbors according to various criteria provided substitutions. Besides, any demographic categories that appeared to be under-represented would be weighted to compensate for the problem.

At the hearing, the question of response rates went without further scrutiny. It was a topic of great interest among academic survey researchers, however. Those who felt the commercial pollsters were doing as well as could be expected based their conclusions largely on the pollsters' ability to make accurate electoral predictions. Others remained unconvinced. They worried that low response rates yielded potentially misleading results, especially if the persons who did respond happened to be different from persons who did not—more outgoing, for example, more likely to be at home, or more trusting of a stranger knocking at their door wanting to conduct a survey.

A second line of questioning focused on how pollsters determined the likelihood of a person voting. That was crucial to making accurate predictions. Gallup replied that this had been a matter of considerable effort over the past three decades. He said it was not sufficient simply to ask if a person was registered to vote. Asking it that way made it too easy for people to say they were, when perhaps they were not. It was necessary to ask several additional questions, including whether the registration book at their place of voting included their name. Pressed further about how he knew if people who said they were going to vote actually had voted, he explained that people interviewed were contacted again after the election and asked if they had voted. The follow-up was particularly useful because it also permitted weights to be developed that could be applied next time around.

Polling firms' reputation depended on accurately predicting elections. That fact made it necessary to obtain valid information about who registered to vote and who voted. The same uncertainties could have been raised about church membership and attendance at worship services. If people were asked simply if they were members and had attended, there was as much chance of over-reporting as there was about being registered to vote and voting. Because an election happened, the accuracy of the poll could be checked. No independent measures of church attendance occurred, and if membership estimates happened to disagree with denominations' figures, it was anyone's guess as to which numbers should be believed.

Another topic at the hearing focused on the use of forced-choice questions. The specific concern was whether people who were undecided but leaned slightly toward one candidate or another were forced to make a decision and then were reported as having a more solid preference than they in fact did. Gallup's reply was measured. He acknowledged the importance of knowing how firm a preference was and at the same time being convinced that people really did have clearer preferences than they were sometimes willing to admit. Harris noted that the real value of polls was in assessing preferences not only about candidates but also about more complex issues, such as abortion and school desegregation. The same might have been said about religious topics, such as belief in God and views about life after death. These, too, were complex issues, and yet the tendency to use forced-choice questions applied to them as well.

Yet another topic came up indirectly. That was whether the responses to a particular question might be influenced by the questions immediately preceding it. The possibility was evident in Gallup's reply to a question about polling by telephone. He was dubious that telephone polling could ever be as effective as in-person surveys. The reason was that the framework of a question could not be described as fully or as clearly by phone. In response to a question about polling related to commercial products, he acknowledged that most of his polls included questions about such products but that these were asked after the ones about political issues. That reply also showed that the order in which questions were asked mattered.

By implication, it would likely have mattered when questions about religious beliefs and practices were asked.

The larger topic on the minds of those at the hearing was the possibility of polls producing a bandwagon effect. The concern was that polls influenced the outcome of elections because people who were otherwise undecided would vote for the candidate who was ahead in the polls. The evidence was mixed. There were enough examples of that not happening to undercut the argument that polls gave an additional edge to the leading candidate.

It was less clear if a bandwagon effect might also apply to social issues, such as people becoming more favorable toward abortion if they thought a majority of the public was already favorable. Nor was the hearing the occasion to raise similar questions about the possible effect of polling on religion. If it were public knowledge that a large share of the public attended religious services, for example, would that encourage others to attend or at least to say they attended? Could the same be said about belief in God or prayer or life after death? Nobody knew or seemed to care.

The Nedzi hearing was rare for the candor it evoked about the complexities of polling. None of these was a concern with which the leading pollsters and academic researchers were unfamiliar. Two years later, the American Statistical Association revisited the same issues. Response rates were not what they were, the inquiry suggested, poll questions were becoming so humdrum that people were probably giving thoughtless answers, and, in any case, the responses to questions about views of marriage and belief in God were hard to interpret.[10] The criticism prompted a pollster in Britain to remark that polling was "the most stupid job you can ever take up, no matter how hard you try to find a worse one." Gallup felt compelled to write an essay explaining yet again how the predictions in 1948 had gone wrong and arguing that pollsters were doing the best they could to accurately report public opinion.[11]

Difficulties became of increasing concern in the 1990s as polls proliferated and response rates declined. Meanwhile, polling was to enjoy a period of steadily rising interest and national visibility. Polling provided information on nearly all aspects of American life, including religion. In the process, pollsters became leading interpreters of the nation's religious beliefs, practices, and trends. Columnist George Will might have been voicing an emerging undercurrent of distrust in 1977 when he wrote, "Opinion data often measure impulses so soft, volatile and fleeting that they barely exist."[12] But if he was, the polling business seemed undeterred.

A Born-Again Episcopalian

It was noteworthy that *Newsweek* and *Time* not only cited Gallup statistics but also quoted Gallup Jr. and credited him with the idea that 1976 was the year of the evangelical. It was equally notable that news coverage described him in terms of his own religious beliefs. He considered himself an evangelical. He was a born again Episcopalian.

The younger Gallup had grown up in the shadow of his father's national prominence, attended the Episcopal church in Princeton, and then gone to Princeton University, graduating in 1953. As a religion major, he imagined going to seminary after college and becoming an Episcopal priest. But a summer of research during which he conducted a kind of survey about religion for his senior thesis deepened his interest in polling and, following a brief stint as an intern at a church in Galveston, he joined the Gallup Organization in 1954.[13]

By the early 1970s, the marketing side of the Gallup Organization had expanded to the point that additional managerial staff could be hired, including Andrew Kohut, who was to become the firm's president in 1979, allowing Gallup Jr. to devote the major share of his time to polling about religion, spirituality, and related topics. With coauthor John O. Davies III, he published a handbook in 1971 telling clergy how to conduct surveys within their congregations. And with Catholic Sister Dr. Miriam Murphy, he founded the Princeton Religion Research Center in 1977 and began a monthly newsletter about religion called *Emerging Trends*.[14]

The timing was good. As director of Gallup's youth surveys, Gallup Jr. was in command of data that brought invitations to speak at denominational conferences about how churches could better meet the spiritual needs of young people. At a meeting of United Methodist Church agencies in Dayton, Ohio, for example, he advised church leaders to downplay denominational traditions and devise new ways of helping youth transcend materialistic interests.[15] With polls documenting sharp declines in Mass participation among young adults, Gallup also found an audience among Catholic leaders. Other topics tapped developments on the edges of mainstream religion. The same poll that documented the extent of born-again experiences, for example, showed that 2.7 percent of the public was practicing yoga and 4.2 percent was involved with Transcendental Meditation.

The timing introduced circumstantial elements, though, that shaped how polling about religion was done, and even more so, how the results were interpreted. The Nedzi hearing had focused on possible biases within the polling community, including how the questions were asked, when the results were released, and whether the data were scientifically valid. But pollsters had limited ability to control what the media did with polling results once those results were released. Standard practice, which reflected the arrangement worked out by Gallup Sr. in the 1930s, was to produce press releases, which appeared as columns under a pollster's own byline or that provided most of the words for a separate article. That practice was already being altered by 1976, and it changed dramatically with the publicity surrounding Carter and the year of the evangelical.

Two different relationships between the media and polling about religion became evident in 1976 and continued to be prominent over the next decade. Gallup Jr. was the clearest example of the first, because he was a pollster who did not speak on behalf of polling in general, like Gallup Sr. did, but who brought specific interests and expertise in polling about religion. The other relationship was best illustrated by Woodward of *Newsweek* and Briggs of the *New York Times*. They were correspondents employed at leading national publications who had training and expertise in writing about religion and whose job it was to cover stories about religion.

These twin features of media coverage worked hand in glove at times to give polling about religion greater publicity than it otherwise may have had. Religion correspondents on the staff of major national publications increased the chances that those publications would print stories in which poll results about religion were discussed. At the same time, competition existed between the pollsters and the correspondents over who offered the most authoritative interpretation. Pollsters provided their own spin, usually emphasizing the numbers, while correspondents brought in other evidence that sometimes challenged the numbers. This competition was important in the 1970s and early 1980s as a corrective lens through which polling about religion was interpreted. But, by the 1990s, as pollsters increasingly became pundits, that dynamic shifted.

The 1976 year-of-the-evangelical publicity illustrated these emerging relationships between polling about religion and journalism. The fact that Gallup Jr. was the source of the polling information reflected the increasing role he had begun to play since the start of the decade as a pollster with special interests and expertise in religion. The gathering in Minneapolis at which he made the remarks about fifty million Americans being born again was the national convention of the Episcopal Church. Gallup was there as a lay Episcopalian whose polling was of interest to the assembled delegates. His comments were recorded and publicized nationally because journalists were also present. National newspapers usually carried brief stories about the conferences of major denominations, and this one was of particular interest because the Episcopal Church was embroiled in controversy about ordaining women as priests. Reporters from the *Baltimore Sun, Los Angeles Times*, and *New York Times* were on hand to cover the story.

As the source of polling about evangelicals, Gallup Jr.'s visibility instantly increased. News reports described it as his survey and included the human-interest angle that he was born again. Other media such as *U.S. News and World Report* and the *Washington Post* turned to him for interviews and commentary. He was the person to ask not only about evangelicalism and the election but also about the spiritual health of the nation. The coverage differed from standard Gallup Poll releases, especially by including more speculation about how evangelicals might influence the election and, more broadly, about who they were, whether their numbers were growing, and whether they were energizing the nation.

The role that religion correspondents played in interpreting poll results was best illustrated in Woodward's *Newsweek* cover story. During 1976, ten of the nation's leading newspapers carried more than a thousand articles mentioning Gallup polls, but less than 1 percent mentioned anything about religion.[16] Had it not been for *Newsweek*'s article, the Gallup results about evangelicals could easily have been missed or quickly forgotten. Woodward was a graduate of the University of Notre Dame and had been responsible for *Newsweek*'s religion coverage since 1964. Raised Catholic, he had been interested in religion's influence on Kennedy's election in 1960. He saw parallels with evangelicals' possible role in 1976. Woodward knew the importance of born-again experiences, having attended Billy Graham meetings, but figured journalists covering the election had little understanding of the phenomenon.

The *Newsweek* story quoted Gallup and presented the numbers from the Gallup Poll, but it also provided nuances about evangelicalism that put the poll into perspective. Woodward described the theological meaning of being born again, discussed the various organizations and denominations that embraced literal interpretations of the Bible, and pointed out that both candidates in the presidential race claimed to be born-again Christians. The article quoted Reverend W. A. Criswell of Dallas, who pastored the largest Southern Baptist church in the country, saying that he was for Ford instead of Carter, and quoted Reverend Foy Valentine, a theologically moderate Southern Baptist, who favored Carter but preferred terms other than evangelical.

Using but not fully accepting poll results was the approach adopted by church leaders most interested in the kind of evangelical beliefs that polling about Carter represented. "We are looking more and more to the pollsters to tell us what we need to know," a professor at an evangelical seminary remarked. Another leader went further, stating, "Listening to social science can be godly." But there were also concerns. *Christianity Today*, which served almost as a house organ of the National Association of Evangelicals, was critical of the way the questions were framed that led to the conclusion that 34 percent of the public was born again.[17]

In 1978 the editors of *Christianity Today* worked with Gallup Jr. to conduct a national survey to learn in greater detail how many of the public shared evangelicals' beliefs and teachings. The study differed from previous Gallup polls both in asking more detailed questions and in the implicit intent of the questions. To date, the most commonly asked Gallup questions reflected an underlying view of religion as a belief and practice that everyone shared or could share. The fact that nearly everyone believed in God was the clearest example. Church attendance was something that involved only a fraction of the public on a regular basis, but nearly everyone attended once in a while, and polling rarely dealt with the varied theological and doctrinal topics church members heard about when they did attend.

The *Christianity Today* questions were different. They drew boundaries. They reflected the divisions that evangelical leaders fought about—differences in interpretations of the Bible and especially about the charismatic gifts that Pentecostal and Holiness Churches favored and denominations in the Reformed tradition did not. Although the study showed, for example, that 94 percent of those polled believed in God, it divided people into the 42 percent who believed the Bible "is the word of God and is not mistaken in its statements and teachings" and those who thought it contained errors or was not the word of God at all. It separated the 44 percent who believed in getting to heaven only though a personal faith in Jesus from those who held other views about heaven. It showed that 20 percent of the public considered themselves Pentecostal or Charismatic Christians and that 18 percent had spoken in tongues. More to the point, the questions provided the basis with which to sort out the minority of the population that truly conformed to the most important evangelical teachings from the ones who might only give lip service to some of those practices. Instead of identifying evangelicals as anyone who claimed to have been born again, it included adherence to important evangelical teachings about the inerrancy of the Bible, belief in Jesus for salvation, and active church participation.[18]

The result of emphasizing these distinctions was that estimates of the number of evangelicals had to be revised dramatically downward. In a 1982 publication, Gallup reported that evangelicals constituted 18 percent of the public rather than 34 percent, meaning that the number was less than thirty million rather than fifty million.[19] The *Christianity Today* study demonstrated that religious leaders saw sufficient value in polling to be worried about publicity that defined religion in ways that did not correspond to their own teachings and practices. Gallup polls that merely reported on belief in God or churchgoing or being born again might be of general interest, but if better numbers were to be found, it might be necessary to sponsor different polls.

That it was important to not rely on polls alone became evident soon after when sociologist James Davison Hunter reanalyzed the Gallup data in relation to more extensive information about the history of evangelicalism and its current manifestations in book titles and among evangelical leaders. Instead of the large undifferentiated block of evangelical votes that Gallup described, Hunter found important regional differences, variations in political affiliations, and considerable ambivalence toward traditional creedal beliefs. Evangelicalism might be on the ascendancy, but if it was, Hunter's analysis revealed that it was more complicated and more culturally conditioned than polls suggested.[20]

Gallup's sensitivity to clergy interests nevertheless elevated his credibility and that of the Gallup Organization in interpreting the shape of American religion. From 1977 to 1982, Gallup's Princeton Religion Research Center conducted major studies on topics ranging from Catholic teachings about divorce and birth control; to views of the Latin Mass and miracles; to speaking in tongues; alienation from religion; why people quit going to church; the attitudes of teens toward sex and marriage; parenting; crime; alcoholism; religious books and religious television; and what it meant to be a mature Christian. The studies were paid for by the Catholic Press Association, the Episcopal Church, *McCall's* magazine, the National Council of Churches, the Southern Baptist Convention, and several other denominations, as well as from internal funds.

Gallup Jr. was to religious polling what his father had been to political polling. Like his father, he traveled the country giving lectures—only the audiences were now church conferences and meetings of clergy. The monthly newsletter included summaries of lectures, charts, and tables showing trends and the results of recent studies. Booklet-length reports provided details on particular studies and presented overviews of religion in America. The reports were the most detailed sources of information for academics, as well as for clergy and journalists, about trends in church attendance and religious belief and on special topics, such as comparisons of Protestants and Catholics, the unchurched, and how religious observance varied by race, region, and gender. Gallup Jr. cultivated his relationships with academics through presentations at scholarly conferences and by enlisting consultants such as prominent scholars of religion Dean Hoge, Wade Clark Roof, and David Roozen.

Gallup polling on religion reached a new high in 1983. Following an appeal by President Reagan at the National Association of Evangelicals convention, the organization commissioned Gallup to conduct a study comparing opinions among evangelicals and nonevangelicals toward nuclear arms. The US Conference of Catholic Bishops drew on Gallup research to warn against declining Mass attendance. The Year of the Bible project, directed by Campus Crusade for Christ leader Bill Bright and endorsed by Reagan, repeated earlier Gallup polls showing the extent to which Americans read the Bible. Writing for *Newsweek*, Woodward again put the poll in context, showing the Bible's diminishing role in public education. And when the World Council of Churches published a major statement about ecumenism, Gallup figures about common beliefs and practices were there to support the effort.[21]

John Dart, religion correspondent for the *Los Angeles Times*, observed in 1984 that Gallup Jr. was the single most influential interpreter of American religion. Dart wrote, "Who is the most listened-to figure in organized religion today? Pope John Paul II, Billy Graham, Jerry Falwell and Chicago's Cardinal Joseph Bernardin would no doubt top any public opinion survey. But the most accurate answer right now would probably be Gallup himself." Church leaders across the spectrum, Dart argued, were looking to Gallup to tell them what was happening. *Emerging Trends* was circulating monthly to more than 1,700 church leaders and seminaries. News releases about Gallup polls were regular features in religious periodicals. The information was compelling, Dart thought, because it was objective and because Gallup himself was an active churchgoer who cared deeply about the churches and about faith.

Dart had been writing about religion for the *Los Angeles Times* since 1967 and was well aware of the rising role that polls were playing in describing the spiritual state of the nation. But Dart's reporting rarely took poll results at face value. He enjoyed doing the background research that went into the stories he wrote and paid close attention to what religious leaders and scholars were saying. It was as common for his reporting to highlight an argument from scholars, such as Robert Lifton or Thomas Luckmann or Martin Marty, as it was to mention a poll. It was from considering these broader perspectives that Dart pondered—appreciatively but also critically—how Gallup's work was shaping public discussions of religion.

"Surveys are a very important tool in God's work," Gallup told Dart. They were of practical value in the same way that information about public opinion was to business leaders and public officials. But Dart had an additional theory about why Gallup was influential. No matter what the issue was, Gallup's interpretation was nearly always upbeat. Spiritual renewal was just around the corner. Better days were ahead. The trends were going in the right direction. Church leaders, Dart believed, warmed to that kind of encouragement.[22]

Much of the polling Gallup conducted through his research center focused on topics of value to congregations and denominational leaders. It was of interest to the churches to know, for example, what problems were facing teenagers and parents and to have national statistics against which to compare local exhortations about Bible reading. Clergy could take heart that religious television was not eroding attendance at Sunday services. They could tell their congregations that the American public overwhelmingly wanted more emphasis on family values and morality, and inform them that active churchgoers in Gallup polls had higher ethical standards than nominal Christians did.[23]

As the Religious Right through the efforts of Jerry Falwell and Pat Robertson drew churches into politics, Gallup polls also became a weapon in these endeavors. They did so in most instances not by enlisting Gallup Jr. directly, but by defining the agendas that led to polling and then selectively interpreting the results to support those agendas. In a speech to four thousand members of the National Religious Broadcasters Association in 1984, Reagan quoted Robertson and Gallup Jr. in the same breath, agreeing with Robertson that the nation needed spiritual revival and citing Gallup to the effect that one had been happening during Reagan's first term.[24] Falwell extrapolated from Gallup figures that there were thirty million Bible believers who could be mobilized for conservative candidates. That spring, the issue Religious Right leaders cared most about was a constitutional amendment in support of prayer in public schools. In an appearance on Robertson's *700 Club* television program, Republican Senator Howard Baker observed that Gallup figures showed overwhelming support for the amendment. That was the same point fundraiser Richard A. Viguerie had been making for the past several years in arguing that opposition to school prayer was only the position of a "small elite minority."[25]

Other clergy found it useful to cite the latest polls. "In a Gallup study in America a decade ago," W. A. Criswell explained to his audience in Dallas, "41 percent of our people in America were unchurched. Today it is 44 percent. America is increasingly becoming secular." The polls persuaded him that Christians needed to be all the more active in opposing the powers of darkness. "We face an increasingly unbelieving, antagonistic, and secular civilization."[26] Reverend D. James Kennedy, a Presbyterian pastor in Fort Lauderdale, Florida, who had a national television audience and was an outspoken supporter of conservative political activism, viewed the data differently but drew the same conclusion. "George Gallup has said America is in the midst of a religious renaissance in our time," Kennedy observed, arguing that liberal groups wanting to keep religion out of politics were out of step with public opinion.[27]

Activists on all sides understood that polling was a tool they could use to their advantage. One of the more interesting examples was a small congregation of about one hundred fifty members in Virginia that favored the sixteenth-century Latin Mass, which the Second Vatican Council banned from general use in the mid-1960s. Besides lobbying at meetings of the National Conference of Catholic Bishops and taking out advertisements in church newspapers, the congregation hired Gallup Jr. to conduct a national poll of Catholics to see if they favored the Latin Mass being offered as an alternative.[28]

Gallup Jr. was called on increasingly to make personal appearances on behalf of polls and for the Gallup Organization. He gave speeches at meetings of Christian fundraisers, spoke at denominational conventions, participated in government hearings about families and schools, and appeared on newscasts and religious television. On at least one occasion Robertson's Christian Broadcasting Network paid Gallup to conduct a national poll about attitudes toward school prayer, abortion, and feminism. Gallup appeared on the *700 Club* with Robertson to discuss the results, which Robertson argued were in line with conservatives' efforts. Another Robertson venture was a program about God and prayer based on a nationwide Gallup poll. In anticipation of Robertson's bid for the Republican presidential nomination in 1988, yet another Christian Broadcasting Network poll conducted by Gallup asked questions about God speaking to people and people receiving guidance from God. Robert Schuller's *Hour of Power* telecasts from the Crystal Cathedral in California typically avoided hot-button political issues, but Schuller routinely invited celebrities to make brief appearances on the program and offer words of inspiration. Gallup put in appearances on several occasions. Schuller also funded several Gallup studies, including a poll about Jesus and one on self-esteem, which was a favorite topic of Schuller's and gave him ammunition for arguing that people with low esteem could benefit from his message of "possibility" thinking.[29]

Poll results were one of the ways in which Religious Right leaders could measure their success in reaching the public. Other ways, such as donations and legislative victories and attendance at rallies, were probably more meaningful in terms of the goals they wished to accomplish, but it did not hurt to know and see reports in the media that more of the public was aware of what they were doing and favorable toward it. Indeed, polling was about the only way to do that if a leader was interested in promoting something beyond a single congregation or community. Polling was how to demonstrate a person's celebrity status. It went hand in hand with an understanding of religion as somehow more legitimate if a large number of people approved of it.

Billy Graham's celebrity status had been the focus of earlier polls, but now the polls that the news media found interesting to report were about leaders like Falwell and Robertson. Polls tracked familiarity with the Moral Majority, showing that 55 percent of the public was aware of it in 1982, up from only 40 percent two years earlier, but that unfavorability outnumbered favorability by two to one. Falwell himself, though, evoked positive responses from 35 percent of the public compared with negative ones from 29 percent. Robertson left less to chance, commissioning Gallup on two occasions to conduct name recognition polls prior to entering the 1988 presidential race.[30]

Although the Religious Right found many Gallup results to its liking, Gallup's reputation for objectivity brought in business from groups on the left and in the middle as well. In 1984 the National Council of Churches included a Gallup survey in a large multimethod study of

religious television, which, among other things, cast doubt on the influence of Falwell, Robertson, and fellow televangelists. The same year,
Planned Parenthood commissioned a Gallup poll about abortion, which
challenged the views held by conservative Catholic and Protestant leaders that the public was antichoice. The nonpartisan Joint Center for Political Studies commissioned another Gallup poll to examine attitudes
toward politics, social issues, and religion among African Americans.
Observing the growing divide between liberal and conservative leaders
at some of the religious conferences he attended, Gallup Jr. initiated another study that examined the extent of differences and how each side
perceived the other.[31]

Gallup watchers like Dart noted that Gallup polls seemed to show that
religion nearly always had favorable consequences, a view that Gallup
embraced in his personal appearances. It strengthened the family, kept
people from addictions, and raised their self-esteem. That message fit
well with the various strands of American revivalism preached by Billy
Graham and Norman Vincent Peale and Robert Schuller. Although it did
not have the sharp political edge of Falwell or Robertson, it reflected the
Religious Right's sentiment that America did need religion to save it from
perdition. "I'm sufficiently convinced that our society is heading in a dan-
gerous direction," Gallup declared in a 1984 publication, "that I feel compelled to sound a note of extreme urgency." He was a kind of prophet, one
observer remarked, "a man who really likes America [and] writes with an
almost Old Testament fervor."[32]

By the late 1980s, what had begun in the 1970s as polling concerned
with religious identities that happened to connect with politics evolved
into polling that defined religion to a much greater extent in terms
of its positions on political issues. Gallup polls still monitored trends
about church attendance and Bible reading, and they tracked what
percentage of the public could be described as bona fide evangelical
Christians. But the interest in those topics focused less on what they
meant to clergy and congregations than on how they played in political
campaigns. Gallup Sr.'s death in 1984 put Gallup Jr. in the spotlight as
spokesperson for the nation's best-known and most respected polling
results. It was a role that seemed to fit uneasily with Gallup's pastoral
style of embracing diverse points of view, but it was in high demand
and there were other spokespersons waiting in the wings, eager to
provide their own interpretations of what was happening in American
religion.

The Christian Pollster

In 1984 George Barna, a twenty-nine-year-old church consultant, founded the Barna Research Group, variously described as a polling and marketing firm, and began conducting national polls. Barna had been a Boston University sociology major and done graduate work at Rutgers University. Unlike Gallup, he was raised in the Catholic Church, but like Gallup was currently a Protestant who described himself as a born-again evangelical. By 1990, Barna had become Gallup's leading rival for polling about American religion.

Barna's entry into polling reflected several of the broader developments shaping the polling community. Barna used random digit sampling and telephone interviewing, which saved money, and provided little enough information about response rates that observers sometimes wondered what the response rates were. As the major polling firms, including Gallup, shifted attention toward social and political issues, Barna carved out a niche that specifically focused on topics of practical concern to church leaders. And unlike pollsters whose publicity depended mostly on newspapers and other media, Barna wrote books. A prolific author with an ability to capture the practical significance of poll results, he wrote books with titles such as *Vital Signs, Marketing the Church*, and *The Frog in the Kettle* that sold widely to clergy and lay leaders. Like Gallup, Barna also published newsletters and produced annual reports about American religion.

The polls Barna conducted were of greater interest to evangelicals than to other Protestants or Catholics. They described how many Americans were evangelicals by various criteria, told what they believed and practiced, and presented conclusions that church leaders could use to make their churches grow. If Gallup's results about evangelicals shaped public understandings, Barna's did too and in similar ways, including headlines about numbers and trends. Barna's emphasis on evangelicals did not prevent his reports from offering broader generalizations about the contours of American religion. To some extent, though, Barna may have had a greater impact on evangelicals' understanding of themselves than Gallup did. They saw him as one of their own, more so than Gallup. If anyone could be trusted to provide numbers of use to evangelical churches, it was Barna.

Barna used different criteria for identifying evangelicals than Gallup did. What mattered was not saying that one was evangelical or having had a born-again experience but believing in Jesus as the only way to get to heaven. By that measure, Barna found even more evangelicals than Gallup: 34 percent of the public, Barna said in 1990, were evangelicals, which with population increase amounted to sixty million people. It might even be more than that and was undoubtedly growing, according to another poll that showed evangelicals increasing from 33 percent of the public in 1988 to 38 percent in 1990. Those were impressive numbers. They appealed to advertisers and booksellers and radio stations intent on reaching a market of that size. There was money to be made selling Christian music and guitars and drum sets and folding chairs and architectural designs. "The Christian market is a paradise," the head of an advertising agency in Houston observed.[33]

The media loved the idea. The year of the evangelical, Carter-style, was long forgotten. The trend now was savvy church growth driven by a new generation of leaders who knew what appealed to young people and families in the suburbs. ABC World News anchor Peter Jennings drew the nation's attention to this kind of religion the day after Easter in 1991. Saddam Hussein was slaughtering Kurdish rebels in Iraq, but in the Chicago suburbs and on the outskirts of Houston, Americans were worshipping in plush auditoriums with theater-style seating, listening to new-style discussions of the Bible, and drifting off to the church cafeteria and bookstore when the service was over. Historian Martin Marty ridiculed the trend, calling it a religion in which "people tell the polltaker [what] they would like" and receive something superficial in return. But Barna commended the new-style leaders: "They are the ones who are understanding the new lifestyle in America, which is that convenience is king."[34]

The less public side of Barna's research, shielded like other proprietary work conducted for commercial clients, included studies for organizations as diverse as the Disney Channel and VISA and about topics ranging from media consumption to household expenditures. Barna's rising stature among religious organizations included surveys for Robertson's Christian Broadcasting Network, the Billy Graham Evangelical Association, Compassion International, the Christian and Missionary Alliance denomination, and Focus on the Family, as well as lectures about Americans' religious attitudes to the Christian Booksellers' convention, the International Bible Society, and gatherings of church growth consultants.

Barna walked a fine line between describing his work as Christian marketing and emphasizing its relevance to saving souls. To large independent megachurches, the distinction probably did not matter, but he considered it important to retain credibility to old-style churches at the same time. He strived for balance between touting the size of the evangelical market and warning evangelical leaders that they should be doing better. Evangelicalism might be holding steady as a percentage and growing as the population did, he cautioned, but broader interest in religion seemed to be waning. People were looking too much to themselves instead of to Jesus. Churches were spending too small a share of their budgets on evangelism.

Notably, Barna and Gallup rarely asked exactly the same questions, which meant that any discrepancies that might have been found seldom received comment. In 1992, for example, Barna concluded that three-fourths of Americans believed the Bible is the word of God and is totally accurate in all that it teaches. That was an astounding figure, suggesting that the number of biblical fundamentalists was nearly twice the size of any estimate from Gallup polls. News stories reported the result as factual evidence without noting the discrepancy. The general impression of American religion from the two polling organizations, though, was much the same. Most Americans prayed regularly and considered religion important, but the number who spent much time on it was small. Biblical knowledge was limited, some Americans were diehard believers in particular doctrines, but the majority was tolerant of other faiths. People were busy, distracted with material pursuits and family obligations, good-hearted but also selfish. Church leaders needed to be more innovative and work harder if much was to change.

Barna rendered his major diagnosis of American culture in *The Frog in the Kettle*, published in 1990. Like the frog that fails to realize the water is getting hotter until it is too late, Barna warned that the culture was shifting in ways that church leaders had yet to recognize. Americans were becoming more materialistic, focused on wealth, and seduced by technology. Families were spending less time together and more on individual leisure activities. Baby boomers especially were at fault, but Barna claimed the trends were endemic to all society.

The skepticism that critics voiced periodically toward polls seemed not to register when Barna's results were presented. The standard method of presentation was to mention the number of people polled and the sampling error and, on occasion, the exact wording of the questions. More often than not, the exact wording was not included. Response rates, weighting procedures, the number of callback attempts, and the specific days during which the polls were conducted did not receive attention.

The academic literature on religion did not engage with Barna's polls, either positively or negatively, perhaps because of uncertainty about the methods used and the information's quality. Between 1984 and 1993, only three articles in sociology journals referred to Barna's polls compared to more than six hundred that mentioned Gallup polls. But in other quarters, Barna's work appeared to be highly respected. Pastors and church periodicals cited his polls as evidence that Americans either believed the Bible but were not following it or did not believe the Bible as much as they used to and needed to repent. Media accounts described him as the world's foremost expert on church marketing, as president of one of the nation's leading polling organizations about religion, and simply as the Christian pollster.

From Print to Television

During the 1970s and early 1980s, much of the publicity that polling received was still in newspapers, just as it had been when Gallup Sr. began producing syndicated columns in the 1930s. The generational transition that took place at the Gallup Organization in 1984 was accompanied by several changes in how polling was conducted and the results were publicized. In 1985 the Times Mirror Group, which owned the *Los Angeles Times, Baltimore Sun, Newsday,* and *National Journal,* commissioned Gallup to conduct a study of what it perceived to be a credibility crisis for news media. The project led to a continuing relationship involving regular Times Mirror surveys conducted by Gallup president Andrew Kohut and publicized in Times Mirror newspapers under the rubric, "The People, the Press, and Politics." A second development was that Gallup Jr. joined with religion correspondent Jim Castelli to coauthor a book about American Catholics and to publish regular columns in the *Los Angeles Times.* Telephone polls, which lowered the cost and produced results more quickly, facilitated these developments. Following the death of Mrs. George Gallup Sr. in 1988, the family sold the Gallup Organization to a firm in Nebraska but continued to handle some of its business from the Princeton office. By that time, the firm had also contracted to conduct polls and publicize results in cooperation with television stations.

These shifts at Gallup were part of a larger expansion in the polling industry involving more organizations sponsoring polls, polls being conducted more often, closer ties between polls and news organizations, and more regular reporting of polls on network and cable television. Polls were cheaper to conduct than in the past, and the publicity they received in national media played an important role in the leading companies' ability to capture the lucrative market for polling about consumer products and advertising.

Not surprisingly, the greater visibility of polling renewed some of the criticisms that had been present from the beginning. "Every time we turn around, we trip over another survey on some burning issue," one commentator complained, "It's a wonder how this nation survived before Gallup, Harris, and the rest burst onto the scene. How did Columbus have the nerve to sail west without polling his crew? Would George Washington have crossed the icy Delaware River, standing up in a boat, no less, if he had taken a random sampling of his troops?" But the writer's main complaint was not that too many polls were being done, but that his opinions were never asked. How disappointing it would be, he remarked, to step out for a few minutes and miss that important call from Gallup.[35]

Time magazine tried to reassure its readers that polls were generally trustworthy even if they sometimes erred. Polling, it explained, was based on a branch of mathematics called probability theory. It was always subject to a statistical margin of error. Besides that, the questions asked were sometimes ambiguous, interviewers did not always ask the questions the same way or correctly, and maybe the people being interviewed had been talking about the polls and those conversations somehow biased their responses. But for all that, *Time* contended, polls were so much a part of the news business that editors rarely met a poll they didn't like. For the public, the better part of wisdom when seeing numbers and percentages was to remember that polls were a blunt instrument at best. "Proceed at your own risk," the essay advised.[36]

For polling about religion, the changes at Gallup involved several significant developments. The *Los Angeles Times* columns with Castelli again put religion results in general circulation but did so in truncated form that presented the numbers but provided little in the way of commentary or interpretation. The Times Mirror surveys included a few basic questions about religion and suggested that religion was important. But it did so with a new typology of the electorate that relegated the salience of religion to a relatively small number of people and dealt with religion only as a factor in predicting opinions about issues influencing how people voted. The most significant development was that a portion of the revenue from the sale of the Gallup Organization went to the creation and support of a new nonprofit entity directed by George Gallup Jr.

The George H. Gallup International Institute, as it was called, was a nonprofit survey organization that aimed to carry on Gallup Sr.'s interest in social reform. With input from a board of advisors and resident fellows, it saw as its mission discovering new ideas, testing those ideas, and disseminating the results. It planned to conduct studies of practical value to leaders especially in the areas of religion, education, and environmental policy. Between 1988 and the end of the century, the institute continued the work of its predecessor, the Princeton Religion Research Center, by publishing periodic reports about religion, and it conducted studies of attitudes toward environmental conservation, aging, disability, charitable giving, and participation in small fellowship groups. However, the institute's funding from the start was meager enough that unless other support could be raised, few studies could be done. Apart from studies conducted from time to time for religious organizations or with foundation support, most of the results about religion continued to be standard questions about attendance, religious preferences, and a few other topics included in regular Gallup polls.

Poll results continued to appear in newspapers, but polling organizations found it increasingly necessary to work with network and cable television. CBS began sponsoring occasional polls jointly with the *New York Times* in 1976. The Harris Survey organization began polling for ABC the same year and formalized the arrangement in 1979 under the rubric of ABC News Harris Surveys. NBC teamed with the Associated Press and began conducting its own polls in 1977. In 1986 CNN and *U.S. News and World Report* contracted with the Roper organization to conduct regular polls. In 1989, the contract shifted to the Yankelovich organization. To stay competitive, the Gallup Organization installed a small broadcast center at its Princeton office, and in 1992 succeeded in securing a contract with CNN and *USA Today*.

Pollsters' personal appearances on television news reports were rare in the 1970s. Gallup Sr.'s dozen or so appearances on evening news broadcasts occurred mostly during the 1972 and 1976 presidential campaigns. Daniel Yankelovich made a rare television appearance as an invited guest in 1978 on a PBS special program about the presidency. Louis Harris was the most regular guest, making periodic cameo appearances on ABC. That pattern continued through the 1980s despite more frequent references to poll results. The 1990s, in contrast, saw a significant expansion of personal appearances as pollsters provided commentary on evening news programs and filled time on morning programs and round-the-clock cable news. Andrew Kohut became a frequent guest discussing the latest results from Times Mirror polls. Political scientist Frank M. Newport, Kohut's successor at Gallup, played a similar role. Gallup Jr.'s television appearances ranged from panel discussions on local Sunday morning telecasts to guest interviews on Robertson's and Schuller's programs. His most widely viewed appearance was on the nationally televised 1997 "People's Choice Awards," which included a short presentation about how the Gallup Organization conducted the poll for selecting the awardees.

The frequency of pollsters' appearances picked up considerably at the turn of the century. During the 2000 presidential campaign Kohut made regular appearances. Newport's poll discussions on CNN appeared as often as three times a day. Both continued to offer regular polling results about current events, including the nation's reactions to the September 11, 2001, attacks and attitudes toward US military intervention in Afghanistan and Iraq. In 2004 Newport discussed the presidential campaign and other topics on CNN more than two hundred times. Kohut was a guest on CBS, NBC, ABC, CNN, and PBS.

Although most of the discussions were about politics, the telecasts called on pollsters to interpret religion as well. After the 9/11 attacks, for example, Kohut explained that the apparent revival of interest in religion was short-lived. Newport's discussions ranged from support for school prayer to religion's relationship with views about gay marriage to holiday shopping to respect for the Catholic Church. In addition to the personal appearances, the results described by Newport and Kohut and less-prominent pollsters were picked up on hundreds of other telecasts. The topics were usually brief and presented as authoritative facts about the American public. Americans were said to be religious, generally satisfied with religion, tolerant of religious diversity, but intolerant of atheists. They were also divided along religious lines when it came to politics and social issues.

The shift from print to television effected another change in how polling results about religion were communicated. The major national newspapers published articles written by full-time religion correspondents who cited polls but located them in a larger interpretive context, just as Woodward did in the 1976 *Newsweek* essay about evangelicals. Kenneth Briggs's articles in the *New York Times*, for example, quoted theologians and other scholars of religion such as Robert Bellah, Harvey Cox, Richard

John Neuhaus, Mark A. Noll, and Max Stackhouse and drew on Briggs's extensive familiarity with the Catholic Church. In essays that sometimes ran to two thousand words or more, Briggs was able to include information from denominational reports, provide historical perspective, and show how religious leaders from various traditions were tackling issues of the day. Those additional perspectives were especially important in suggesting to readers how poll results should be interpreted. As Briggs noted in one essay, the polls seemed to indicate that interest in religion was increasing, but the "quality and meaning" of that apparent awakening was "much debated." Bringing in multiple perspectives had the additional effect of putting Gallup and other pollsters in the position of having to acknowledge that the numbers were subject to varying interpretations.[37]

Briggs was by no means the only example. E. J. Dionne Jr. wrote lengthy articles putting poll results about Catholic teachings on birth control, divorce, and male priests into context with information from church history and interviews with Catholic theologians. Woodward penned dozens of articles for *Newsweek*. Other correspondents who provided regular coverage of religion included Ari L. Goldman for the *New York Times*, Jeffery L. Sheler for *U.S. News and World Report*, David E. Anderson for United Press International, Helen Parmley for the *Dallas Morning News*, and George W. Cornell for the Associated Press.

The shift to television coverage of polls—this in the late 1980s and early 1990s before poll data were distributed via the Internet—had the consequence of reducing the informed commentary that put numbers in a larger context, as the better religion correspondents writing for major news media had done. Poll data were reported more often simply as straightforward numbers without the larger context, or pollsters provided the interpretations through short clips or news releases, or as guests on news programs.

The coverage both in print and on television focused on topics media managers and editors deemed newsworthy. The simple release of a new poll was less often newsworthy, especially if it revealed for the nth year in a row that the same percentages were going to church and believing in God. To be of interest, it helped if controversy was present. That meant linking religion to controversies about abortion and homosexuality or controversial statements made by religious leaders or politicians. Polling in the 1990s rarely reported, as it had in earlier decades, that nearly everyone believed in God or that most Americans practiced religion in ways that had nothing to do with hot-button issues or that as many people honed to the middle on social issues as veered to the far right or far left.

It was true that polling about religion reflected the times. Had there been no culture wars, polls that attracted wide publicity would not have portrayed religion as a deeply contentious cultural arena. Polling never- theless did more than simply register the opinions that would have been there anyway. It added an aura of facticity to the conflicts, putting num- bers to them and suggesting that they were characteristic of the general public and not merely the views of activist groups.

As polling about religion focused on hot-button issues, the chances of it being of interest to the news media probably increased, and yet the danger for pollsters was that their credibility as sources of objec- tive, nonpartisan opinion results would be diminished. It would suffer because people on the various sides of controversial issues would claim the polls were biased or that the other side was using the polls for par- tisan purposes. A case in point occurred in April 1990 in conjunction with heightened efforts by conservative Protestant and Catholic groups to oppose abortion. Dan Rather on the CBS Evening News, which crit- ics said leaned to the left but which claimed to be ideologically neutral, opened the broadcast on April 6 stating: "In the week-to-week, state- by-state battle over abortion policy in this country, new and escalating tactics are emerging. Among the latest, the nation's Roman Catholic bishops will now go beyond the biblical text and start using advertising from high-priced consultants and pollsters to promote anti-abortion views." The report mentioned a $5 million public relations campaign and several boycotts of Planned Parenthood and companies supporting Planned Parenthood. It said nothing more about the role that pollsters were to play, but viewers might have assumed that polling results were going to be shaped by church money.[38]

The discussions on CNN from time to time registered possible skepti- cism as well. During a discussion of religion mixing with politics, for example, the host of a CNN program presented the results of polls on the topic conducted by Gallup, *Newsweek*, ABC, and the *New York Times*, showing possibilities for widely discrepant interpretations. Asked to ex- plain, a representative from the American Association of Public Opinion Research argued that the differences were due to different wordings and possibly reflected sampling error. But the host remained unconvinced. "I must admit that when you look at those numbers it kind of makes me sit back and think," she replied, "I can't really trust any of these polls if they're all asking different questions [and] getting such different responses [and] yet we're supposed to believe that these polls are very scientific."[39]

As pollsters became the voice of statistical observations about American religion, academic social scientists produced survey-based research in increasing volume as well but faced significant limitations in doing so. A list of twenty-two major ongoing national survey projects at the end of the century that were funded by the federal government and carried out by agencies such as the US Census Bureau, Centers for Disease Control, and National Institutes of Health did not include a single study in which anything about religion was asked besides an occasional question about religious preference. Nineteen other recurring national surveys partially funded by government grants and conducted by academic organizations such as the National Opinion Research Center and the University of Michigan included only two in which questions about religion were regularly included. The American National Election Studies included questions about religion only to the extent that religious identities and activities might be helpful for understanding elections. The General Social Survey's emphasis on documenting trends limited its questions about religion except on several occasions to ones about religious preference, attendance, and a few other items.[40]

For social scientists interested in understanding religion, the best academic surveys with the best data based on the best methods pushed research in the direction of considering religion simply as a variable, like race and gender. Religion as a variable meant comparing respondents who attended religious services frequently with those who attended less frequently and examining the possible differences between Protestants and Catholics. That focus provided plenty to do. The social science of religion, insofar as social science meant quantification, involved correlating these few basic religion variables with other topics, such as levels of education, gender, race, voting, and participation in civic organizations.

The contrast between opportunities for statistical studies of religion and statistical studies of other topics was striking. Whereas demography flourished on the basis of opportunities to analyze census data and to work with government-funded surveys about fertility and health, the Census Bureau's decision earlier in the century to exclude questions about religion excluded similar possibilities for social scientists of religion. Ample opportunities existed for social scientists to study other topics as well, including education and schooling, housing and segregation, family incomes and status attainment, gender, and employment patterns.

It fell to religious organizations and foundations to fund anything social scientists might do quantitatively that examined religion in greater depth than merely as a variable. Through the 1980s, denominations that conducted research did so mostly by focusing on topics of particular practical interest to church leaders and by limiting the research to surveys based on samples of clergy and laity. Only in the 1990s did foundations with mission statements that included religion direct some of their attention to funding survey research. The Indianapolis-based Lilly Endowment, which focused on the needs of Christian congregations and clergy, was the principal source of foundation funding for religion.

The result for broader understandings of religion was mixed. On the positive side, overall growth in higher education, including the social sciences, created opportunities for academic studies of religion that did not depend on large-scale funding for large-scale surveys. The 1980s and 1990s produced a wealth of ethnographic, historical, and text-based studies of religion. A few of those studies had a wide impact on public discussions of religion. But discussions based on evidence that purported to explain what Americans really believed necessarily reflected the work of pollsters more than anyone else.

Pushback

By the turn of the millennium, then, anyone casually familiar with polls about religion would have known at least three indisputable facts. First, evangelicals, more so than mainline Protestants or Catholics, were the most dynamic and interesting sector of American religion. Second, they composed anywhere from 25 to 40 percent of the population. And third, they were solidly active on conservative social issues and reliably in the Republicans' camp.

The way a casual observer would have known this is that polls overwhelmingly, consistently, and repeatedly said so. Evangelicals were dynamic and interesting because poll after poll featured them, and those polls indicated that their numbers were growing. They made up 25 to 40 percent of the public because polls agreed on those numbers—25 percent if evangelicals were counted on the basis of denominational affiliation, and up to 40 percent if everyone was included who said they were when asked if they were born again or evangelical. And what was mostly known was that evangelicals considered it important to be involved in politics, wanted their churches to speak out, were adamantly opposed to abortion and homosexuality, and voted Republican. Those were the prevailing characterizations of American public religion.

If anything demonstrated the power of polls to define reality, this was it. Evangelicals were no longer a hodgepodge of congregations and denominations with distinctive worship styles and organizations and histories. They were now a unified voting bloc, recognizable as a well-defined category in polls in the same way that African Americans or women or Hispanics or Republicans were. Pollsters could report confidently that this or that many evangelicals existed and that these evangelicals believed such and such. Journalists and political operatives could take that information to the bank. Or so it seemed.

The things that are real in daily life fairly often seem that way because it is more convenient to agree and to take them for granted than to quibble. Americans agree to measure distance in inches and feet rather than in centimeters and meters. We agree to set our clocks backward or forward each fall and spring. It would be inconvenient to contest these agreements.

Polls create reality by evoking agreement as well. When the true test is their ability to predict an election, there is a collective sense of confidence in polling if most of the polls come within a few percentage points of offering a correct prediction. When there is no external reference number of that kind, confidence that the polls are producing a true representation of reality hinges mostly on whether they agree with one another. If they mostly agree that evangelicals make up a quarter of the public and generally vote Republican, that agreement buttresses the view that pollsters' way of thinking about evangelicals is correct. The same could be said about pollsters' representation of Catholics and Jews or of other groups.

But evangelicals were a particularly interesting test case of pollsters' ability to define reality. Evangelicalism certainly became a well-defined category in the polling community's language about religion. And yet, there were continuing disputes about what evangelicalism was and how it should be considered, which provided a clear indication that polling could shape public understandings of religion but was incapable of getting everyone on board.

An important indication that not everyone agreed was from the evangelical community itself. The National Association of Evangelicals included in its doctrinal affirmations and mission statements having had a born-again experience as only one of several criteria for defining evangelicalism. In addition, it considered important having a life-long process of following Jesus, expressing the gospel through missionary and social reform efforts, holding the Bible in high regard, and emphasizing Jesus

Christ's sacrifice on the cross as making possible the redemption of humanity. The organization emphasized other criteria as well that pollsters rarely considered, including belief in the virgin birth of Jesus, the ministry and indwelling of the Holy Spirit, and the spiritual unity of all believers in Christ. Holding to theological tenets rendered through long discussion within the churches, it was not surprising that religious leaders sometimes found it distressing to consider the criteria pollsters used.[41]

Pushback came from academic researchers as well. Their contention was not that polls needed to include extensive theologically refined questions, but that even the frequently included questions yielded quite different assessments of the numbers and characteristics of evangelicals. The numbers varied from as few as 5 percent to as many as 50 percent of the population, depending on the use of questions about the Bible, church attendance, denomination, born-again experiences, and self-perceptions. How important evangelicals were in broader considerations about social issues and politics necessarily varied as well.[42]

Further scrutiny would have suggested additional quandaries. Few results about evangelicals were quoted in the media as often as Gallup polls showing the percentage of the public claiming to be born again or evangelical. But there were peculiarities in the results. In March 1994, for example, 45 percent said yes when asked, "Would you describe yourself as a 'born-again' or evangelical Christian?" But three months later, only 39 percent did. In December 1995, 43 percent claimed to be born again, but six months later only 35 percent did. These were in polls having a statistical margin of error of only plus or minus 2 percent. A different pattern emerged in 1996. In July 36 percent were born again but in September 42 percent were. And fluctuations of that kind continued, including a 5-point drop in less than three months in 2003 and a 5-point gain within six months in 2005. It wasn't that everything was volatile. The percentage who said they were Republicans deviated by more than a point from year to year only once. But it was hard to imagine that the number of born-again evangelicals was really that unstable—unless the polls were not as accurate as they claimed to be.[43]

Other results that muddied the clarity with which pollsters spoke about evangelicals came from studies in which comparisons among different kinds of evangelicals could be made. Polls that lumped all evangelicals together neglected the significant differences in teachings and styles of worship that separated charismatics from other evangelicals. A national study of congregations, for example, showed that among congregations classified as white evangelical churches, 31 percent included services in which speaking in tongues took place while 69 percent did not. Another study documented sharp theological differences with respect to understandings of the Bible among evangelicals and even within the largest evangelical denomination—the Southern Baptist Convention. Yet another study revealed large differences among evangelicals in attitudes about churches being involved in politics. The proportions that thought churches should express their views on day-to-day social and political questions ranged from only 43 percent among Missouri Synod Lutherans, to 52 percent among Southern Baptists, to 79 percent among Assemblies of God members.[44]

A study of attitudes toward abortion produced interesting results for a different reason. In 1997 demographer Larry L. Bumpass published a report addressing the important question of how the American public was currently thinking about abortion. Drawing on data from the General Social Survey, which was well respected for its sampling design and had a high response rate, the report showed that attitudes toward abortion among the public at large had been remarkably stable since 1975. But were attitudes really that stable? To find out, Bumpass varied how the questions were asked in 1994. In one version, the first question asked about abortion for any reason. In the other version, that question followed a series of questions in which particular reasons were given, such as not wanting any more children or having been raped. The experiment produced large differences. When the question about abortion for any reason was asked first, significantly larger percentages agreed that abortion was acceptable than when that question was asked last. Among Baptists, 42 percent agreed in the first version and only 37 percent agreed in the second. Among Catholics, 61 percent agreed in the first but only 41 percent in the second. Clearly, it mattered how particular questions were asked—a fact that pollsters and journalists sometimes acknowledged but that news reports about religion rarely mentioned.[45]

Among pollsters, disagreement about how to characterize evangelicals became evident most clearly in Barna's work. Unlike most of the polling firms that produced polls about social issues and elections, Barna's primary audience were evangelical clergy and evangelical lay leaders. Barna turned toward categorizing evangelicals based on questions about theological beliefs and practices, rather than relying on the standard question about denominational affiliation or considering oneself born again. By the turn of the century, Barna's classification required evangelicals not only to say they were born again but also to assert that their faith is very important, accept responsibility for sharing their faith about Christ, believe that Satan exists, believe that eternal salvation comes from grace rather than works, believe that Jesus Christ lived a sinless life, accept the inerrancy of the Bible, and consider God as the all-knowing and all-powerful creator of the universe. Using those criteria, Barna estimated the number of evangelicals to be approximately eighteen million adults or about 8 percent of the population, dramatically lower than his earlier estimates of sixty million.[46]

Barna's work illustrated an important point about the power of polling. The way to push back against polling with which one disagreed was through additional polling. Barna's polls consistently showed evangelicals to be more active in their churches and more oriented toward spirituality in their personal lives than other polls did. If that put evangelicals in a good light, it also provided opportunities to present evidence that evangelical leaders could use, knowing that it pertained more particularly to their churches than the results of broader polls.

This way of pushing back against mainstream polling was clearly illustrated in a 2012 debate about premarital sex. A widely discussed poll reported that, contrary to evangelical teachings, 80 percent of unmarried evangelicals in their twenties were sexually active. This was hardly welcome news among evangelical leaders. It suggested that evangelicals were losing their grip on the younger generation and failing to be as distinctive from the rest of society as they claimed to be. One response, which some leaders embraced, was to redouble the churches' teachings about chastity. The other response was to fight unwelcome numbers with numbers. The National Association of Evangelicals commissioned its own poll. The results were much better. Instead of 80 percent, only 44 percent in their twenties were having premarital sex.

How was it possible that the two polls showed such different results? The first one used the standard polling method that categorized upward of a quarter of the public as evangelical. The latter used a different method that categorized people as evangelical only if they attended worship services at a Protestant church at least once a month, accepted Jesus Christ as their savior, believed they were going to heaven, thought eternal salvation was possible only through Jesus Christ, considered the Bible inerrant, and felt they had a personal responsibility to share their faith. By those criteria, only 10 percent of the public was evangelical.[47]

On balance, polling about religion had come a long way since the 1970s when Jimmy Carter made it imperative for pollsters to look closely at how many members of the public were born again. It had followed the rise of televangelism and the Religious Right and had documented the tensions between religious conservatives and liberals and among Catholics. Pollsters had become leading interpreters of what was happening in American religion. Their ability to shape public discussions was considerable, but by no means universally accepted. Going forward, the question was whether the polling community's work was mostly to be trusted or whether the level of trust polling had achieved was beginning to erode.

6

In Polls We Trust?

POLLSTERS HAVE ALWAYS depended on the goodwill of the public. It matters if the public trusts the results enough to consider them worthy of interest. It matters that people believe in the value of polls enough to participate in them when asked.

A person whose dinner is interrupted by a pesky phone call from a polling company wanting an unspecified amount of time may consider it a civic duty to participate or even find the process mildly enjoyable. But that person is more likely to be annoyed if this is the tenth time the pollster has called and if the results are unlikely to be credible.

In the 1980s, several polling firms conducted studies to see how the public felt about polls. The results were reassuring. Most of those who answered the questions expressed positive opinions. Seventy-five percent thought opinion polls "work for the best interests of the general public." The same proportion thought pollsters were almost always or usually honest about their polls. Eighty percent believed pollsters mostly interviewed typical, representative people. And nearly everyone thought the people interviewed usually told the truth.[1]

Of course the views of people who refused to answer the pollsters' questions may have been less positive. But on the whole, there was little reason to think the public's mood toward polling was negative. Nor was it trending in that direction. Comparisons of responses from the late 1970s to the mid-1980s showed no change in the proportions that felt polls were useful and enjoyable.[2]

Two decades later, the picture was quite different. When a national sample was asked in 2006 if they would "generally trust each of the following types of people to tell you the truth or not," the five kinds of professionals receiving the most favorable responses were doctors, teachers, scientists, police officers, and professors—all considered trustworthy by at least three-quarters of the public—while the five kinds receiving the least favorable responses were pollsters, trade union leaders, stockbrokers, lawyers, and actors. Only 34 percent thought pollsters could be trusted to tell the truth. That was a percentage point fewer than the number who thought members of Congress could be trusted.[3]

Not only was the response toward pollsters alarmingly low, but it had also declined precipitously since 1998. In that year, 55 percent of the public thought pollsters could be trusted to tell the truth. The 21-percentage-point decline between 1998 and 2006 was the largest decline for any of the twenty-three kinds of professionals listed.

Other responses indicated serious erosion in views toward polling as well. In contrast to the 86 percent who thought "the survey research industry serves a useful purpose" as recently as 1995, only 54 percent felt that way in 2006. Over the same period, the proportion that considered answering questions in polls an interesting experience declined from 54 percent to 36 percent. Similarly, the proportion that felt that answering polls and survey questions was in their best interest dropped from 65 percent to only 33 percent. And these were the responses of people who were still interested enough to respond at all.

Why the public was losing confidence in polls was unclear. It did not appear to reflect concern that polls were failing to predict election results. Opinions about that were stable and mostly favorable. Nor was it likely attributable to people disbelieving that small samples could accurately depict the sentiments of millions. Most people did disbelieve, but that proportion had not increased. The most likely reasons were that significant numbers of people doubted that polling was based on sound scientific practices, thought it did not accurately reflect public opinion, felt that pollsters did not ask the right questions, and worried that poll results could easily be twisted. These concerns were as common among people with higher levels of education as among people with less education.[4]

The most curious result was that the erosion of confidence was taking place at the same time that larger numbers of people were being polled. Between 1982 and 2003, the proportion who said they had previously participated in a poll or survey during their lifetime increased from 54 percent to 82 percent. And the proportion that had participated in a previous survey in the past year grew from 23 percent to 51 percent.[5]

But if more of the public had personal experience participating in surveys, more were also refusing to participate. In 1982, only 15 percent said they had refused to participate in a survey in the past year; in 2003, that proportion was 47 percent.

It was likely that the erosion of trust in polls had more to do with polls about political issues than anything else. Those were the topics most frequently reported in the media. But polls asking about religion were conducted by the same firms and discussed in the media as well. In addition, polls about religion came under increasing scrutiny at the same time that broader concerns about the truthfulness and value of poll results were becoming more common.

The scrutiny directed toward polls about religion came from several quarters and was directed at particular studies and questions. It ranged from scrutiny challenging the validity of some of the most frequently reported questions about religion to considerations about what questions were being asked and how to interpret the results. The most serious challenges began in the early 1990s and they continued well into the twenty-first century. They did nothing to diminish the number of polls that asked questions about religion. But they did contribute to the growing unease with which the results were received.

Frontal Assault

As near as anyone could tell, public confidence in opinion polls was still relatively high in the early 1990s. News media routinely reported poll results about religion along with other topics. Social scientists may have believed that their own surveys were better than those of commercial pollsters. But academic studies of religion included frequent references to poll results.

It was thus of considerable importance that a team of social scientists published a major study in 1993 arguing that some of the most highly respected and frequently reported poll results about religion were wrong. The study set off a debate that challenged the credibility of polling about religion at a level beyond which even its authors intended. At issue was whether poll results about relatively simple, straightforward activities could be believed or whether polling itself somehow encouraged the public to give responses that could not be believed.[6]

Published in the *American Sociological Review*, the discipline's flagship journal, the study's lead author was C. Kirk Hadaway, who headed the research office of the United Church of Christ's Board for Homeland Ministries. The study's coauthors were Penny Long Marler and Mark Chaves, sociologists respectively on the faculty at Samford University and the University of Notre Dame. Besides their credentials as well-regarded sociologists of religion, it was significant that the authors' affiliations linked them not only with academia but also with mainline and conservative Protestant and Roman Catholic institutions, and that the study received funding from the Lilly Endowment as well as the Board for Homeland Ministries. The study was of immediate interest to church officials as well as to academics.

The topic was church attendance. Had it been about almost anything else, it could have been argued about on grounds that different words or concepts should have been used. But church attendance was as basic as anything polling had ever tried to measure. If polling was incapable of getting that right—if it suggested that tens of millions of Americans were attending religious services when that was not the case—could polls about religion be trusted at all?

Hadaway and his coauthors were concerned about more than the accuracy or inaccuracy of polls. They were also troubled by social scientists' uncritical acceptance of poll results. The relatively high percentages of Americans claiming to attend religious services and the remarkable stability of these percentages, they contended, played a prominent role in social scientists' arguments that secularization was not happening. But if those percentages could not be trusted, the arguments against secularization were not as solid as they might appear.

The figures at issue were from Gallup polls. For brevity's sake, Hadaway and his colleagues mentioned several of the most recent polls reported by Gallup's Princeton Religion Research Center, noting that the results were "extraordinarily stable." Had space permitted, they might have observed that Gallup polls had asked the exact same question—"Did you, yourself, happen to attend church or synagogue in the last seven days?"—more than one hundred fifty times since the early 1950s.

It was a simple question that could be asked quickly, eliciting a yes-or-no response about an activity recent enough that people could be presumed to remember it and answer truthfully. It was not the only question, either: other ways of asking about religious participation produced considerable agreement. For example, two Gallup polls conducted in 1978, the first in late April and the second in early November, illustrated this level of agreement. The first asked people if they had attended religious services at all in the past six months and then asked those who had about how often they had attended. Among all those polled, 34 percent said they had attended at least once a week. The second poll asked simply, "About how often do you attend church or religious services?" In this poll, 35 percent said they attended weekly or more than once a week. If that many attended every week, adding the ones who attended occasionally would have increased the number present in any given week to at least 40 percent.[7]

Was it credible that some 40 percent of Americans attended church or synagogue in any given week? Gallup polls with different questions suggested the proportion might even be higher. A national poll conducted in 1990 by the Gallup Organization for the World Values Study Group, for example, reported that 43 percent of the public claimed to attend religious services at least once a week, which would have put them at church or synagogue during the past seven days, and that figure would have increased to at least 47 percent if a fraction of those claiming to attend once a month were included.[8]

The Gallup figures seemed consistent with other firms' results. A 1990 Gordon Black poll showed 40 percent attending once a week or more and 14 percent attending once or twice a month. A 1991 Yankelovich poll concluded that 38 percent of the public attended at least once a week and 18 percent attended once or twice a month. And a 1992 Marttila and Kiley poll showed 40 percent of the public attending once a week or more, with another 8 percent attending at least once a month.[9]

But other surveys suggested that the Gallup figures were high. The General Social Surveys, which asked, "How often do you attend religious services?" consistently produced lower estimates. In 1978 when Gallup reported 34 to 35 percent attending weekly, for instance, the comparable General Social Survey figure was 28 percent, and that remained the case in the early 1990s, when commercial polls were reporting 38 to 40 percent.[10]

The General Social Surveys were conducted in person, drew from carefully selected national samples, and had high response rates, whereas the commercial polls were conducted by telephone and generally included fewer respondents. Was it possible that the commercial poll results were inflated? And if they were, what difference did it make? The General Social Survey figures suggested that fifty-three million Americans age eighteen and older attended religious services weekly. The Gallup figures put the number between seventy-five and eighty million.

The Hadaway study suggested that even an estimate of fifty-three million might be high. It drew that conclusion by triangulating the results from different methods of data collection in a single community in Ohio. The methods included attendance records provided by all churches in the county, an independent count of cars in church parking lots, and a survey in which detailed questions were asked about which services persons attended. The study supplemented the Ohio data with information about attendance from eighteen Catholic dioceses. The conclusion: "Protestant and Catholic church attendance is roughly one-half the levels reported by Gallup"—in other words, forty million at most, not seventy-five to eighty million.[11]

If that were true, the General Social Survey estimate was too high as well. And social scientists that had been citing polls about church attendance to argue that secularization was not happening might be wrong. The debate widened. It was now about more than a minor disagreement in how to think about the numbers. Researchers convinced that religion was stable and strong defended the high numbers from polls while researchers contending that religion was weak or weakening argued that the high numbers could not be trusted.

In 1998 the *American Sociological Review* published a symposium about surveys of US church attendance. The symposium included the results of further analysis of existing data, information from other surveys, and evidence from a new national study conducted as part of the General Social Survey to examine closely what could possibly explain the discrepant results. The conclusions varied. One report examined General Social Survey results, argued that the Hadaway team's evidence was flawed, and suggested that church attendance was at least 90 percent as high as the General Social Survey claimed. Another report examined data from time-use diaries and suggested that church attendance might indeed be much lower than reported in surveys. There was no disagreement that the Gallup figures were too high.[12]

The investigation left social scientists of religion with two conclusions. First, the figures pollsters reported about church attendance could not be trusted. They might be off by as little as a few percentage points or by a factor of two, but they were clearly inflated—most likely because people queried in polls felt it desirable to say they attended every week even if they did not. Second, better estimates of church attendance required alternative methods and more sophisticated statistical analysis than pollsters supplied. The alternatives included time-use diaries, data from religious organizations, and estimates drawn from sampling congregations.[13]

An experiment conducted as part of the General Social Survey in 1996 proved that the addition of one or two simple questions to the standard question in polls could be an effective way of attaining a more accurate estimate of how many Americans attended religious services in any given week. Adding, "On what day or days did you attend religious services during the last seven days?" yielded a result of about 30 percent—7 to 10 percent lower than the standard question—who were able to recall a specific day or days on which they had attended. And that number ranged from 27 percent to 29 percent when the phrases "attend a regular, weekly worship service at a church or synagogue" and "don't include watching a service on TV or listening to one on the radio" were added.[14]

The debate filtered more broadly into the periodicals that religious leaders read. *Christian Century* published an essay by Hadaway and Marler summarizing their research and underscoring its implications. "Clearly, poll data should not be taken at face value," they argued. "Why does it matter? Because the image of religion in America as exceptionally strong and stable has been at least partially supported by poll data. Our research raises doubts about that image."[15] *Christianity Today* also picked up the story, observing that "when asked directly about attending church, people tend to over report their presence in the pews" and noting that evidence from time-use diaries put the figure attending in any given week at 25 percent instead of 40 percent.[16] Similarly, a popular online source for church leaders discussed the "disparate picture" of attendance from polls and concluded that the actual number was probably "less than half of the 40 percent the pollsters report."[17]

In a strongly worded essay, managing editor of *Religion in the News* Andrew Walsh warned journalists writing for the nation's major news media to be more cautious about polling data as well. Citing recent examples from the *Washington Post, USA Today,* and NBC's *Nightly News,* among others, in which prominent journalists reported on poll results about church attendance with no mention of the criticisms, Walsh considered it high time for journalists to be better informed.[18]

But the broadside from Hadaway and his coauthors did little to deter the polling community from using the same questions about religious participation and interpreting the results in the same ways. In the decade after 1993, more than thirty Gallup polls asked the standard question about attendance during the last seven days. During the following decade, the question continued to be asked twice a year, ostensibly for the sake of tracking long-term trends. None of the polling firms conducted experiments to learn why interviewees might be overreporting attendance, although extrapolations from alternative questions asking how often people attended religious services also suggested that 40 percent or more of the public attended weekly. In 2007, Gallup president Frank Newport explained on the organization's website that social scientists had questioned the firm's data about attendance but asserted that "the self-reported data give us a useful measure to trend over time," adding, "we find that it's remarkably stable."[19] In 2013, a reporter for the Religion News Service asked Newport why Gallup used worship attendance as a key barometer of religiosity when studies showed that Americans overstate how often they attend religious services. Newport conceded that people overstate how often they go to church but insisted that people who say they attend "are in fact more religious than others, even if they don't actually attend services as often as they say they do."[20]

Uncertainty about how many people actually attended religious services left considerable doubt about how to interpret polls purporting to document trends. Academic researchers emphasized the difficulty in taking self-reports at face value. Instead of drawing conclusions from comparisons of overall annual figures, they used statistical models to examine trends within cohorts and emphasized demographic patterns affecting attendance, especially the declining proportion of young adults who were married and had children.[21] In contrast, the major polling firms reported annual figures derived from overall samples and emphasized either the absence of trends or small changes from year to year. In 2010, for example, Newport reported that 43.1 percent of respondents in Gallup's daily tracking polls were frequent churchgoers, up from 42.8 percent in 2009. Noting that consumer confidence had also improved, Newport suggested that "instead of church attendance rising when economic times get bad, as some theorize, the opposite pattern may be occurring."[22]

As pollsters continued to report on trends about church attendance, though, religious leaders recognized the limitations of such information. National trends might be of passing interest but were less meaningful than local information. What might be evident among the public at large could be radically different, say, in a suburb of Dallas, a low-income neighborhood of Detroit, or a small town in Nebraska. The percentages attending or not attending were less important than local population trends. It mattered mostly to clergy to know if attendance at their own congregations was increasing, decreasing, or stable. A study of randomly selected congregations in 2006 in which pastors were asked about changes in the number of regularly participating adults, for example, found that participation in 36 percent of the congregations had remained about the same over the past two years, declined in 15 percent, and increased in 49 percent.[23]

The response from social scientists was to emphasize that estimates of attendance were too high but generally to agree with pollsters that variation in attendance still provided a good measure of variation in religiosity. However, that view was also limited. Social scientists were interested not only in overall patterns but also in differences in attendance, such as between men and women and among people with different levels of education. The difficulty in drawing conclusions about those differences was evident in Pew polls conducted in 2006, 2007, and 2008. Weekly attendance at religious services was 39 to 40 percent in all three polls. But among pollees who had not gone to college, one poll showed that women were only 2 percentage points more likely to attend weekly than men (statistically insignificant), while in the second poll they were 12 points more likely and in the third, 18 points more likely. Why?[24]

The differences stemmed from priming. Priming occurs when responses to a particular question are influenced (primed) by the topics asked about in previous questions. The poll in which women and men without college educations gave similar responses was a poll about economic issues. The other two polls were about religion and politics. In the poll about economic issues, men more often gave positive responses and women more often said "don't know" or "does not apply" to the questions preceding the one about religious attendance. In the polls about religion and politics, women more often gave positive responses to preceding questions on topics such as beliefs about God and the role of religious teachings in their lives.

At best, the polling information about attendance provided crude indications of religious involvement. If it had ever been believable that polling provided an accurate estimate of the churchgoing population, the possibility that estimates could vary by tens of millions raised serious doubts. The doubts did not mean that polling about attendance would cease, only that it would be harder to know how to think about the results.

Stirring the Pot

The assault on polling's credibility about religious attendance was specific, some might even have said narrowly conceived to the point of being of interest mostly to specialists, however wide ranging its implications may have been. In contrast, a second debate emerged in which religion was hardly central at all, and yet, the discussion posed broad questions about the meanings and uses of survey data—questions that eventually focused squarely on religion.

Since at least Tocqueville, if not before, observers periodically warned that Americans were so individualistic, so self-interested, that their sense of community obligations was in danger. David Riesman's *Lonely Crowd*, which was widely read in the 1950s, argued that Americans desperately wanted to fit in and enjoy the time-worn benefits of having good neighbors but were functioning more like anonymous faces in the crowd. A generation later, the 1980s became known as the decade of greed, characterized by what historian Christopher Lasch termed a "culture of narcissism." *Habits of the Heart*, published in 1985, gained nearly as wide an audience as Riesman's book had. In the book's chapter about religion, the authors introduced an interviewee they called Sheila Larson who typified a kind of religion cut off from tradition, absent of social ties and focused inward on her private thoughts, feelings, and insecurities. "Sheilaism" became the popular term for describing this kind of religion.

Habits of the Heart was not based on polls or surveys. Although it mentioned poll results several times in passing, the evidence was from in-depth qualitative interviews and aimed to show not what percentages believed this or that but the logics and symbols and discourse through which ordinary middle-class people defended their lifestyles and values. The book's success encouraged other studies to be conducted using similar methods. But the book's importance as a widely read critique of American culture also prompted criticism. Critics argued that it focused too narrowly on the white middle class and that it painted too gloomy a picture of Americans' self-interested individualism. Critics especially considered it flawed because it did not include statistical information from polls and surveys.

At face value, the reaction of mainstream social scientists to *Habits of the Heart* suggested that polls and surveys, at least if they were done properly, were to be taken more seriously than evidence from qualitative interviews. In a strongly worded critique, for example, Andrew M. Greeley chided Bellah and his coauthors for positing arguments without data to back them up and suggested that many of the arguments did not stand the scrutiny of rigorous data.[25] There might be value in qualitative information and it might be appealing to the wider public, but it was no substitute for solid numbers. Several important studies were conducted, in fact, to provide those numbers.

In 1993, sociologist Wade Clark Roof published a path-breaking book that demonstrated the value of adding a carefully conducted survey to the kind of qualitative interviews on which *Habits of the Heart* was based. Roof's *A Generation of Seekers: The Spiritual Journeys of the Baby Boom Generation* demonstrated that the self-interested individualism described in *Habits* could be more clearly understood by locating it specifically among the generation of young adults who came of age during the 1960s and 1970s. Building on the previous quantitative research he had conducted among mainline Protestants and extending results about denominational switching, Roof compared the characteristics of young adults who were seeking spirituality outside of organized religion with those who had remained conventionally religious and yet another group who returned to organized religion after having been religiously unaffiliated.[26]

Two years later, political scientist Robert D. Putnam published an article tackling the broad question of declining community attachments from a different angle. Mustering evidence from numerous polls and surveys, Putnam argued that the extent to which Americans were involved in civic activities such as voting and participating in political campaign activities, as well as their connections with one another through memberships in voluntary associations and visits with friends and neighbors, was significantly lower than it had been fifteen to twenty-five years earlier.

Although the article appeared in a relatively obscure journal, it became an instant sensation. Its author was a former dean of Harvard's distinguished Kennedy School of Government and was well known for a book about the role of civic associations in facilitating democracy in Italy. The article's strong claims and the solid statistical evidence it presented sparked interest among social scientists, community leaders, foundation officers, and public officials. Five years later, Putnam published a much-expanded version of the argument. *Bowling Alone: The Collapse and Revival of American Community* became one of the most widely read books by a social scientist of all time.[27]

Bowling Alone's relevance to religion most immediately stemmed from the fact that the book included an extensive chapter about religion. The book's broader relevance to religious leaders was its claim that community involvement was in serious decline—something that clergy and lay leaders in congregations could imagine themselves doing something to counteract. With coauthor David Campbell, Putnam went on to conduct a major study of religious attitudes and activities, published in 2010 as *American Grace: How Religion Divides and Unites Us.*[28]

If the credibility of polls was under siege, the popularity of *Bowling Alone* would appear to have gone a considerable distance toward restoring that credibility. The book presented dozens of tables and charts based on polls and surveys. It drew extensively from the results of the General Social Surveys and the American National Election Surveys. It included material from Roper polls about political participation and from Gallup polls about church attendance. Putnam also tracked down a previously unavailable trove of marketing polls from which trends about various kinds of social interaction could be inferred. With foundation support and funding from dozens of other sources, he conducted an original nationally representative survey and surveys in local communities. And the book with Campbell about religion presented data from another large-scale original survey.

But understanding the effects of *Bowling Alone* simply as reinforcement for the credibility of polls was not the whole story. Because of its bold claims and the attention it received, the 1995 article and the subsequent book generated discussions about the meaning and value of polling and survey research far exceeding the usual. These discussions included questions about religion specifically but framed those questions in larger terms that connected them with debates about methods, social networks, and political participation. At least three major topics of discussion surfaced.

The first was conceptual. The concept at issue was social capital. Social capital meant friendships, acquaintances, personal networks, and ties to social organizations that individuals and groups could exploit to get what they wanted. The notion in one form or another had been around for a long time. It was akin to the adage that who you knew was more important than what you knew.

Religion could be thought of as a kind of social capital. It put people in contact with kindred spirits in their congregations and cemented social ties that arguably redounded to the individual's benefit. A child from a Catholic family who went to a parochial school and whose parents knew the teachers and the local priest might benefit, for example. Similarly, a merchant in New York's diamond district might conduct business with greater ease because of interacting with the other merchants on Jewish holidays.[29]

The argument was relatively straightforward and easily tested. If polls erroneously estimated the number of churchgoers, it was still possible to compare the ones who attended regularly with the ones who did not.

The comparisons could show if regular attendance served as a kind of social capital. Was it related to health and happiness? Did it facilitate volunteering and voting? Questions like this provided reasons to be interested in studying religious participation apart from knowing if more people or fewer were attending this year than last. Religious participation maybe was beneficial not only to religious organizations but also to the participants.

But there was more to it than that. Discussions of social capital upped the ante. The argument was not only that social capital was good for individuals. It was that social capital was good for the society as well—especially if the society was a democracy. Social capital encouraged people to think about social issues, discuss them with their neighbors, send letters to public officials, and vote. Social capital, the argument went, promoted trust, which in turn encouraged people to be neighborly and more supportive of their communities' common good.

Like participation in other networks and organizations, religion could be thought of in these ways. If it encouraged volunteering and voting and discussions of social issues, those were benefits to the community as well as to the individual. And it was good when people, religious or not, interacted with their friends and neighbors. That encouraged them to get along with one another, trust one another, and overcome whatever differences they might have. These were ideas that could be tested with information from polls and surveys.

The difficulty was that social capital, conceived this way, was too much of a good thing. In praising its virtues, proponents put themselves at risk of arguments from critics who took a different view of social capital. Was it not the case that social capital could also have negative effects? Al-Qaeda probably relied on social capital to plan terrorist attacks. Fundamentalists perhaps cultivated such strong in-group ties that they reinforced dogmatic ideas rather than becoming more tolerant of others.[30]

Another difficulty was that social capital was hardly the essential ingredient for a well-functioning democracy. It might help. But social capital alone did not reduce wealth inequality or ensure that different ethnic and racial groups would get along. Churchgoers and members of other voluntary associations could do only so much to provide a safety net for the poor or to manage the complex health and insurance needs of a democratic society. A strong system of laws and courts upholding constitutional guarantees was needed to restrain the self-interests of those in power or claiming to speak for the majority.

Polls and surveys asking about the attitudes and activities of individuals tended to miss the complexity of these conceptual issues. None of this was particularly new. Arguments about the social role of religion had never been limited to ones that could be tested with information from polls and surveys about the beliefs and practices of individuals. But the debate about social capital brought the question squarely to the surface. It did so in a way that few other topics did because much of the information about civic involvement and its apparent decline was drawn from polls and surveys.

The second topic concerned the specific questions available in polls and surveys. In order to chart a decline in social capital, it was necessary to use questions that had been asked periodically for several decades. That meant using questions that reflected the habits and social norms of the 1950s, 1960s, or early 1970s, but that perhaps no longer captured how people interacted with one another. Questions about hosting dinner parties for friends and neighbors, participating in bowling leagues, mailing letters to public officials, and holding membership in Kiwanis, for example, might suggest that civic involvement was in serious decline. But the story might be different if questions were asked about newer forms of participation, such as having lunch together with friends and coworkers, participating in meet-up groups, e-mailing public officials, and doing volunteer work with Habitat for Humanity.

The discussion of which questions to ask and how to interpret them had implications for polls and surveys about religion. Was it any more appropriate to measure religious involvement only with a question about attendance at worship services than it was assessing social capital with questions about dinner parties and bowling leagues? Studying religion that way suggested that it was one-dimensional. People were more religious or less religious. But the discussion about social capital suggested that it was multidimensional. There were different kinds of social capital, different ways of connecting with other people, and different results from those connections. The same might be true of religion. As the contexts in which people expressed themselves religiously and spiritually changed, the questions also needed to change, rather than merely tracking time-worn trends. Besides worship services, participation might include home fellowship groups, meet-up groups, online chat groups, learning yoga or centering prayer, and doing volunteer work at a soup kitchen or homeless shelter.

The third topic involved the statistical methods deemed appropriate for inferring conclusions from polls and surveys. With critics on the lookout for miscues of analysis and interpretation, the debate about social capital encouraged researchers to employ the best statistical methods available. Surprisingly, the reports issued by commercial polling firms seldom employed any statistical analysis at all, other than percentages and estimates of overall sampling error. In contrast, the academic literature on social capital used multivariate statistical analysis, cohort analysis, methods of trend smoothing, and estimates of error terms. The use of these methods aimed to increase the confidence that could be placed on conclusions drawn from quantitative data, but it also suggested that academic researchers were becoming less confident about the raw information being produced by polling firms.

Whether, on balance, *Bowling Alone* and *American Grace* restored or further undermined confidence in public opinion polls is impossible to say. For those who already considered quantitative data ill informed, the books undoubtedly did little to alter their opinion, while they may have strengthened others' conviction that social science was best served by statistics.

A more nuanced appraisal, though, suggests several other possibilities. The critical scrutiny that Putnam's 1995 article received led to the inclusion and close analysis of a wider variety of quantitative data in the book that came five years later. Unlike polling companies under pressure to produce new information on a regular basis, Putnam's academic location made it possible to spend time assembling available information from multiple sources and analyzing it, not only to document trends but also to examine the possible sources and consequences of those trends.

Critics of *Bowling Alone*, like critics of Gallup church attendance reports, demonstrated the value of considering alternative measures and concepts. Despite the considerable attention it received, *Bowling Alone* did not have a monopoly over the available information. The ensuing debate showed the importance of researchers conducting separate studies that measured civic involvement in new ways rather than merely repeating outdated questions.

Along the way, Putnam's research moved a step in the direction of *Habits of the Heart* by including information from sources other than surveys. *Better Together* presented qualitative information about congregations that appeared to be resisting the general decline in civic participation.[31] *American Grace* included information from in-depth interviews to add richness to the statistical data.

The wider discussion prompted by *Bowling Alone* about democracy and civil society underscored the need for information beyond what polls

could provide. Social capital could work against as well as in favor of democracy. Laws mattered. Government mattered. *American Grace* provided an alternative to the evidence available from polling companies.
Instead of reporting overall national trends or the absence of trends, it
located those in a discussion of major social, cultural, and demographic
transitions. It further demonstrated the importance of considering topics
largely neglected in polls, such as social networks. But *American Grace*
did not appear until 2010, and, although it was widely read and discussed,
it did not lend itself to the brief headlines and quick sound bites that polling results did. Meanwhile, polling expanded and polling about religion
shifted substantially to a new location.

Taking Center Stage

By the mid-1990s, the Gallup Organization's prominence in polling about
religion was challenged not only by Barna but also by the Times Mirror
Center for the People and the Press under the direction of former Gallup
president Andrew Kohut. As the 1994–1995 president of the American
Association of Public Opinion Research and a frequent guest on television
panels, Kohut was poised to play an increasing role in monitoring and
interpreting public opinion about religion.

The opportunity to play that role came through a shift in funding priorities at the Pew Charitable Trusts. As one of the nation's largest foundations, distributing about $140 million in grants annually, Pew was well
positioned in the 1980s to play important roles in funding the arts, community development, and research. Its interest in religion stemmed from
its founder, J. Howard Pew, whose life as an entrepreneur and president
of Sun Oil had included extensive involvement in theologically conservative activities within and beyond the Presbyterian Church. By the late
1980s, the foundation supported an expanding array of projects focusing
on evangelicalism, including efforts to promote evangelical scholarship
and research about evangelicalism, funded through grants to religious
organizations and universities.[32] The projects were supported quietly,
as a reporter in Philadelphia where the foundation was located noted in
1990, reflecting "the family's religious conviction that charity needed no
rewards."[33] But that was about to change.

During the 1990s, the Pew board moved decisively in the direction of having a larger and more visible social impact. It funded programs to promote energy conservation and biodiversity, restore historic

buildings, finance computer science training and ballet performances, improve the quality of public schools, help low-income families with health and social services, and facilitate economic and democratic reforms in Eastern Europe. These efforts significantly raised the foundation's public profile. Coverage in major newspapers of Pew-funded initiatives was nearly five times greater in the 1990s as in the 1980s.[34] The foundation also funded fellowships and research about religion but focused more of its attention on the social and political impact of religion, partnered with other philanthropic organizations, and expanded its focus beyond evangelicalism.[35]

In 1994 a study of network television religion coverage conducted by the Media Research Center caught the attention of Pew staff. The study suggested that network television was essentially inept at reporting on religion. The study cited familiar polling evidence estimating the number of Americans attending worship services every week at more than one hundred million and argued that a nation so thoroughly religious was ill served by prime-time television news and entertainment. That was evident, the study concluded, from the fact that only 212 out of approximately 18,000 evening news stories during the previous year dealt with religion.[36] Unlike the major newspapers, television networks rarely hired trained reporters capable of handling the nuances of religion and understanding its social significance. "Things that really go deep with people and that strike at their ultimate concerns often have religious dimensions to them," Pew religion director Joel Carpenter observed. "You can't understand [the] whole complex of values and cultures without understanding the role religions play in it."[37] By the end of the decade, Pew's funding of research on religion was increasingly directed at playing a role in the news coverage that religion received.

With more than $4 billion in assets and annual expenditures now in excess of $200 million, Pew launched major initiatives in the late 1990s directed at specific topics of national concern, including global warming, civic journalism, and campaign finance reform. One of its initiatives was broadly defined as cultural policy, which included the arts, media, polling, and religion. Among its efforts to inform cultural policy, the foundation initiated the Pew Center for Civic Journalism in 1994, which aimed at stimulating citizen involvement in community issues through the news media, and the Pew Research Center for the People and the Press in 1996, which it had helped support since 1990 as the Times Mirror Center for the People and the Press.

The Times Mirror Center had grown from the efforts in the mid-1980s under the auspices of the Times Mirror Company to conduct opinion polls in cooperation with the Gallup Organization. In 1990, Kohut became the founding director of surveys for the center and in 1993 became its director. Pew's absorption of the center in 1996 ensured its capacity to conduct polls on a regular basis on a wider variety of issues. A study in June 1996, which drew widespread media attention, showed that evangelical Christians were an active and cohesive force in American politics.[38] In 1997, the Pew Center conducted ten national polls covering topics ranging from motherhood and Social Security to AIDS and global warming and, in 1998, eighteen national polls.

Then in 2003, Pew announced that plans initiated several years earlier for a major restructuring had been finalized and would take effect the following year. Henceforth, the foundation would function as a public charity, which meant that its operations could include raising money from donors and other foundations, lobbying, and engaging in activities otherwise prohibited or closely regulated for private foundations. Under the restructuring, the Pew Research Center for the People and the Press and six other centers and projects the foundation had initiated were consolidated within a single administrative framework.[39]

The shift had two significant implications for research about religion. In anticipation of becoming a public charity and focusing more of its attention on public policy, Pew initiated ten "centers of excellence" located at top-ranked universities to encourage academic studies of religion. Each center received start-up support to supplement funds provided by its university for activities such as conferences, planning events, interim staffing, and administrative costs. The centers varied in focus from emphasis on religion and media, professions, and civic culture, to religion and democracy, urban society, and world affairs. The locations included Boston University, Notre Dame, New York University, Princeton, University of Southern California, University of Virginia, and Yale. Each of the universities was expected to house its center at a prominent location on campus or otherwise emphasize its visibility, and each was required to develop or designate resources of its own to ensure the long-term viability of the center.[40]

The other implication was that research conducted directly by Pew would be done through the Pew Research Center and publicized through the Pew Forum on Religion and Public Life, founded in 2000. Having concluded its funding of university-based centers, Pew's support for

research about religion enabled the Pew Forum to be the most prominent organization through which polling about religion was done, and
the Pew Forum, in turn, located in Washington, DC, provided a central
location for journalists and policymakers to discuss the public role of religion. Polls including questions about religion were conducted at a rate
of approximately one a month, and special polls examined the relation of
religion to politics and social issues in greater depth.

Pew's rising influence in polling about religion was evident in small
details—such as the wording of basic questions. Through the early 1990s,
the most commonly asked question about religious service attendance—
the one Hadaway and company criticized—was the Gallup question
asking pollees if they had attended in the past seven days. The wording
of alternative questions asking about frequency of attendance varied from
poll to poll. Some of the questions asked respondents to exclude certain
times when they might have attended for special reasons. For example,
the 1988 Gallup survey of unchurched Americans asked when people had
last attended, apart from "weddings, funerals, or special holidays such
as Christmas, Easter, or Yom Kippur." Similarly, World Values Surveys,
American National Election Surveys, and General Social Surveys in the
early 1990s included phrases exempting weddings, funerals, christen-
ings, and baptisms. But there was no agreement on the exact wording.

In May 1996, a survey conducted by the Pew Research Center introduced the question that set the standard for subsequent polling about religious service attendance. It asked, "Aside from weddings and funerals,
how often do you attend religious services . . . more than once a week,
once a week, once or twice a month, a few times a year, seldom, or never?"
In that survey, 14 percent of the 1,975 people contacted by telephone said
they attended more than once a week, 25 percent said once a week, 17
percent said once or twice a month, 21 percent said a few times a year, 13
percent said seldom, 9 percent said never, and 1 percent said they didn't
know or refused to answer. Pew repeated the question five months later
and again in June and November 1997 with essentially the same results.

Over the next five years, Pew polls incorporated the same question in
studies of politics, news interest, and issues pertaining to gender, health,
Hispanics, the Internet, the millennium, and social values. By the end
of 2005, more than fifty Pew polls had included the question. The same
wording was being used in polls conducted for ABC News, the Kaiser
Foundation, *Religion and Ethics Newsweekly*, and the *Washington Post*, and
Gallup polls had adopted nearly the same wording.

As polling expanded, it made sense for new polling efforts to borrow the Pew question. By 2010, the Pew wording was being used by the Associated Press, NBC, the Public Religion Research Institute, *Time*, and numerous other polling firms, including Gfk Roper, KRC Research, Marttila Strategies, Opinion Access, Princeton Survey Research Associates, and SRBI, among others.[41]

The clearest evidence of Pew's prominence in polling about religion was the number of mentions it received in the nation's newspapers and periodicals. The number of mentions increased from approximately 1,800 in the 1990s to more than 11,000 between 2000 and 2010. In 2008 alone, Pew results about religion were mentioned more often than during the entire decade of the 1990s.[42]

That did not mean Pew was the only source of polling about religion; Gallup polls received numerous mentions as well. But Pew conducted more polls specifically about a variety of religious issues of public interest and hosted events at which the results were discussed. In 2008, media mentions of Pew results about religion exceeded Gallup mentions by more than two to one.

By all indications, Pew had become the name to trust for polling about religion as far as the media were concerned. Results about religion from the academically based General Social Survey received less than one-sixth the number of media mentions between 2000 and 2010 as Pew results did.

The picture was somewhat different when only citations in scholarly journals were considered. But Pew results about religion were still mentioned more often in those contexts than General Social Survey results. Between 2000 and 2010, Pew citations exceeded General Social Survey citations in scholarly journals by two to one.

If it appeared that Pew's prominence in polling about religion increased the level of trust in poll results overall, though, the widespread interest in these results prompted scrutiny, just as Gallup reports about church attendance and the discussions associated with *Bowling Alone* did. Some of the scrutiny came from Pew itself, as questions about response rates and the wording and interpretation of polls were raised. Pew's practice of making the data sets available to the public following a brief embargo also resulted in academic journal articles based on further analysis of the data.

Earlier differences in styles and interests between polling and academic research remained evident. Pew reports presented descriptive results about religion, included trends in responses to basic questions, and dealt with topics of immediate interest, such as how people with different religious orientations were planning to vote or what the public felt about Muslims. It was thus important that the polls be conducted and the results reported quickly. The General Social Survey, in contrast, was conducted once every two years, took months to complete, and included more than basic questions about religion only on rare occasions. Other academically based surveys that focused specifically on religion also took longer to complete, and the results that were published in scholarly journals and as books rarely received media attention. They typically situated statistical results with information about previous studies and historical contexts.

To the extent that academic researchers may have been critical of Pew results, the criticisms were more often implicit than explicit. If Pew data were worth mentioning as descriptive evidence, it appeared to be of less value for probing deeply into issues that required more extensive data and better statistical analysis. Academic studies drew on other data and followed in the tradition of looking for causal explanations rather than providing descriptive evidence. They surveyed populations that national polls did not include, such as teenagers, and targeted groups of special interest, such as religious leaders and immigrant congregations. Implicit criticisms emphasized the value of ethnographic research rather than statistical data as well. For example, it noted that polls showed how often people prayed but said nothing about where they prayed. It argued that polls were ill equipped to examine the dynamics of decision making in small groups or the narratives that shaped individuals' spiritual identities.

Explicit criticisms that questioned pollsters' methods and the conclusions they and the media drew occasionally focused on Pew results. One example was a sharp attack in *Foreign Policy* by Middle East specialist Fouad Ajami against Pew's international polls about attitudes toward the United States in Muslim countries. "The reports are one dimensional and filled with panic," Ajami argued. Instead of listening to pollsters "brandishing their findings," he urged that the public should understand the complexities of modernization and foreign intervention in Muslim countries. Another example was a critique by sociologist of religion Darren Sherkat questioning the value of commercial polling in general. "Polling is conducted by whores who violate every scientific convention that social scientists developed to make sure that polling would indeed produce high quality results," Sherkat complained, adding, "Worse yet, indifference towards high quality data is infiltrating the social sciences."[43]

What to Make of the Nones

Most indications through the first decade of the twenty-first century suggested that polling about religion, just as polling about other topics, was flourishing, on the one hand, but perhaps evoking closer scrutiny and criticism from academic social scientists, on the other hand. An exception—the topic on which everyone in the polling world and social science seemed to agree—was the discussion of what came to be known as the "nones." Nones were people who said in polls and surveys that they had no religion. They were of interest because their numbers were growing.

In 1987, Norval D. Glenn, a distinguished social scientist at the University of Texas, with the support of a grant from the National Science Foundation, published a report examining the trend of people in polls saying they had no religion. The report covered more than a hundred national polls from the late 1950s through the early 1980s. It showed that the percentages saying they had no religion were trending steadily upward but had recently leveled off. It further demonstrated that the trend involved persons from all religious backgrounds.[44]

Subsequent polls and surveys found that the proportions of respondents claiming to be without religion had indeed stabilized. General Social Surveys, for example, showed that 7 percent had no religion in 1974 and that in 1991, 7 percent had no religion. Furthermore, there was hardly any variation in the percentages from year to year—6 percent in 1977 and 1987 and a high of 8 percent in 1988, 1989, and 1990.

But then things changed. From 7 percent in 1991, the proportion with no religion rose to 9 percent in 1993, 11 percent in 1996, 14 percent in 1998, 16 percent in 2006, 18 percent in 2010, and 20 percent in 2012.[45]

Results from polling firms showed a similar trend. Pew classified 15 percent of its respondents in 2007 as "unaffiliated," and that proportion rose to 20 percent in 2012. Gallup reported an increase from 15 percent in 2008 to 18 percent in 2012. Like church attendance, there was some quibbling about the numbers, but for the most part the various studies seemed to point in the same direction.[46]

Finding any change in anything about religion was so unusual that the phenomenon of rising nones attracted wide interest in the media. The Associated Press, *Dallas Morning News*, Huffington Post, *New York Times*, USA Today, Washington Post, television stations, and news services across the nation carried stories. Headlines ranged from "Godless America" and "America's Fast Track to Secularization" to "Religion Important in U.S." and "Spirituality Soars." Commentators speculated that nones would soon be driving the nation's elections, proposed ways the churches could retrieve the nones, and argued about who the nones were and what they represented about America.

Under the apparent agreement that religious nones were an interesting and growing phenomenon, there was as much uncertainty about what to make of this phenomenon as there was consensus. The potential significance of large numbers of Americans claiming to be devoid of religion put the spotlight on polls and surveys providing this information. There was no consensus, as there was for the information about church attendance, that it was simply wrong. Hardly anyone disagreed that the number of nones was increasing. But there was agreement that a trend of this magnitude required further discussion and empirical scrutiny. In that respect, it resembled the debate about declining community prompted by *Bowling Alone.*

The first order of business was to figure out if any particular part of the population was driving the trend. True to form, academics and pollsters tackled the question in different ways. The most widely cited academic analysis included charts showing confidence intervals adjusted for survey sampling effects, a spline function that smoothed fluctuations from year to year attributable to sampling, and estimated the statistical significance of multiple regression models examining variations among age cohorts and people from different religious traditions.[47] Another study reexamined the data to look more closely at who was becoming nonreligious from the various traditions and to extrapolate what the long-term effects of those shifts might be.[48] The Pew Forum produced a report with charts and percentage tables showing descriptive evidence about the proportions of people in various subcategories of the population between 2007 and 2012 who were religiously unaffiliated. The varying approaches yielded conclusions that younger people were more likely than older people to be nonreligious, that baby boomers had also become somewhat more likely to be nonreligious, and that the trend among white non-Hispanics was probably more pronounced than among Hispanics and African Americans.[49]

The harder question to answer was what it meant to be a religious none. One possibility was that nones were people so exhausted with answering survey questions that they simply said they had no religion to avoid being asked additional questions. That was unlikely but impossible to rule out, especially in view of the rising number of people who said they had little confidence in polls. A second possibility was that no religion actually meant

multiple religious backgrounds or affinities or an unwillingness to be pi-
geonholed. That was more likely in the Pew surveys, which counted people
who said "nothing in particular" as nones, than in the General Social
Survey, which gave "no religion" as an option. It was difficult to know, although that possibility also did not seem to provide a major interpretation.

Better information came from cross-checking the no religion response
with responses to other questions. When asked if they were atheists, between 2 and 3 percent in most of the polls said they were, compared with
the much larger number classified as nones. When asked if they attended
religious services, about a quarter of the nones said they did once in a
while, suggesting that they were perhaps not completely negative toward
religion. A third said religion was at least somewhat important in their
life, four in ten said they were spiritual but not religious, and only a quarter said they did not believe in God.

The take-away message was that polls about religion were probably
useful and apparently could be trusted, but needed to be subjected to more
detailed analysis and perhaps include more detailed categories. Glenn's
study in 1987 concluded that dichotomizing the public into religious and
nonreligious was less useful than considering more nuanced gradations
in the extent to which people were involved in religious activities and considered themselves to be religious persons. The same was now evident in
inferring conclusions about religious nones. Some nones were skeptics
and disbelievers, some were interested in religion or spirituality but disaf-
filiated from religious institutions, and some were perhaps still involved
to an extent in organized religion but reluctant to identify with any particular organization or tradition.

Those possibilities did not undermine the extent to which polls could
be trusted. But there was another take-away message that posed a more
serious challenge. The implicit assumption in polling about religion had
from the start been that religion was basically a stable feature of society
characterized by a considerable amount of inertia. There were individuals who decided to quit going to church or who switched denominations.
But if 40 percent of the public went to church regularly and if 80 percent
had a religious affiliation and 90 percent believed in God, then that was
a characteristic that described the society. It somehow was how people
thought of themselves and thus was how the society could be characterized as well.

In those terms, religion was not fickle. It was not like public opinion
that could swing in different directions from day to day. People might

change their opinions about a political candidate if that candidate performed badly in a debate. But they would not say they were religious one week and nonreligious the next. They would not describe themselves as regular churchgoers and then a few months later say, no, they were not. Religious identities were more stable than that.

That was the basis for assuming that the responses people gave in polls about religion could be trusted. It was supported, or so it seemed, by the fact that week after week and year after year the proportions that said they attended church regularly and were born again or were affiliated with a religious tradition were nearly the same. The rising percentage of nones might signal a cultural shift, but it did not suggest that the answers people gave to pollsters were subject to happenstance differences in situations or changes in mood. One version of the argument went so far to suggest that survey responses were actually the best way to tap into these deep, enduring personal predispositions, even better than talking to people at greater length because the conversations were more easily influenced by the moment.[50]

All that made sense as long as polls from week to week or from year to year queried different people. But what if the people who were polled one year were polled again the next year or the year after? If the assumption about religious identities being deep-seated and enduring was true, the responses should be the same or very nearly so. Was that the case?

As part of their research for *American Grace*, Putnam and Campbell attempted to interview the people in their 2006 survey again in 2007. They were able to reach 62 percent. Only a year had elapsed between the first interview and the second. But during that year, 30 percent of the people who said their religious preference was "nothing in particular" in 2006 said something else in 2007. And about 30 percent of those who said "nothing in particular" in 2007 had said something different in 2006. An analysis of the data suggested that there were probably two kinds of religious nones rather than one. Ten percent of Americans could probably be described as stable or secular nones, while ten percent probably should be characterized as unstable or liminal nones, meaning that they were on the fence about their religious identity rather than truly nonreligious or perhaps were giving answers that did not reflect who they were.[51]

The inconsistency of responses in that instance appeared to be attributable to something particular to liminal nones. They did not appear to have shifted much during the year in terms of other beliefs or religious practices but were in a kind of betwixt-and-between status with respect to their religious identity. It made sense that they were unstable about how to describe their religious preference. They were more likely to give inconsistent responses for this reason.

But they were not the only ones who did. Among the people who fell into the "some other religion" category in 2006, only 35 percent were still in that category a year later. Among the ones who were not Protestant or Catholic but "another type of Christian," only 52 percent were still in that category a year later. Fourteen percent of the Protestants were no longer Protestants and even 9 percent of Jews were no longer Jews.

The results raised the question of whether the responses people gave to other religion questions in other surveys were stable. In 2010 the General Social Survey reinterviewed some of the people it had interviewed in 2008. The religious preference results were similar to the ones in Putnam and Campbell's study. About a quarter of the nones in 2008 were no longer nones in 2010, and a similar proportion of the nones in 2010 had not been nones two years earlier. The results for Protestants, Catholics, and Jews were more stable, but about 10 percent gave inconsistent responses.

On other questions, the levels of inconsistency were higher. Thirty-eight percent of the people who were weekly churchgoers at the first interview were not at the second, and 25 percent who were at the second were not at the first. And when asked if they were a religious person or not, 38 percent who said they were "very religious" in the first interview no longer said that in the second, and 33 percent of those who were "very religious" in the second had not been in the first.[52]

What exactly was going on was difficult to say. It had long been recognized that people did not give entirely consistent responses in surveys, even when similar questions were asked in the same survey. If most people gave the same response to questions about religion after two years, perhaps that was good enough. But it did raise doubts about how stable religious identities were, particularly on fine-grained survey questions and when the categories pollsters used might not capture how people regularly thought.

American religion had always been considered a matter of choice, unlike aspects of identity that might be constructed in various ways but were still rooted in phenotypical or ascribed characteristics, such as gender, race, and sexual orientation. In that respect, religion was more like a person's residence or occupation or political preference. It was possible to move. It was possible to pick and choose. Even if a person was born Catholic or Jewish or Muslim, the argument went, that person could freely identify with that tradition, embracing it as a personal choice, or reject it. But the question now was whether Americans were actually becoming less stable in how they thought of themselves religiously, and if that was the case, were polls that mostly reported stability failing to capture something important.

At minimum, Putnam and his coauthors argued, the instability they observed had serious implications for survey research. Religious affiliation, they suggested, might be better conceived as a "fuzzy set" rather than as a "crisp set" of mutually exclusive categories. Wouldn't it make sense, they asked, for pollsters to include a follow-up question or two to obtain a clearer idea of religious affiliation, just as was done for political party affiliation?[53]

The Missing Majority

Were it not enough that the accuracy of poll results about religion was facing questions, the polling community was experiencing increasing difficulty in conducting its work. The most serious difficulty was declining response rates. When pollsters called, fewer people were agreeing to be polled and fewer were answering the phone at all. What that meant for the results that pollsters reported and for the trends they hoped to document became a question of serious concern.

The congressional hearing about polling chaired by Representative Nedzi in 1972 had failed to secure an agreement from the major polling companies to release information about response rates. The pollsters agreed that high response rates were preferable to low ones. But, unlike academic surveys that generated precise numbers about the proportion of the original sample that responded or did not respond, the practice that some pollsters used of substituting neighbors with similar characteristics for nonrespondents made it difficult or at least embarrassing to say what the true response rate was.[54]

As polling shifted to phone interviews conducted on samples selected by random digit dialing, standards for determining response rates became possible. The rates achieved were generally lower than in academic studies, such as the General Social Survey, but when as many as ten to fifteen attempts were made to reach sampled phone numbers, response rates of around 60 percent could be achieved. That still meant that as many as 40 percent of the persons who should have been interviewed to provide representative information about the public were missing, so, to compensate for potential biases, the responses of people in categories who appeared to be underrepresented were given additional weight.

By the early 1990s, response rates in commercial polls had fallen on average from 60 percent to about 30 percent. The reasons were unclear but appeared to be the result in large measure of polling companies wanting to produce results quicker and thus expending less effort contacting difficult-to-reach persons and households. Instead of ten to fifteen attempts, as few as three or four attempts were made. The more attempts were made, the higher the response rate. Other factors seemed to be involved as well. Research showed that people were more likely to respond if they thought the topics were interesting and important and if they thought the results would serve a useful purpose. But it was becoming evident that fewer people thought polls were interesting and important and useful.

As response rates declined, journalists began to worry that the polling results they were reporting might be flawed. In 1992 National Public Radio aired a discussion on its "All Things Considered" program with journalist Daniel Schorr in which Schorr disclosed his concerns about the problem. Noting that fewer people were voting in primaries, Schorr observed, "Now comes an alarming new form of non-participation—more and more people failing to respond to opinion pollsters, and that can sometimes skew their conclusions." He added, "If you miss a significant number of people in your sample and you're not sure why they're being missed, then your conclusion may be thrown off."[55]

In 1996 at a panel discussion hosted by the Roper Center for Public Opinion Research in Connecticut, a frank exchange about declining response rates took place among three of the nation's leading pollsters, George Gallup Jr., Burns Roper, and Helen Crossley. Gallup attributed the problem to poor interviewing. Roper considered the shift from in-person to telephone polling the culprit. Crossley doubted that response rates would continue to fall. But all three acknowledged the problem. Roper was especially concerned about the practice of reporting that results from a sample of a certain size were accurate within a particular range, such as plus or minus 3.2 percent. "It's not true [that] you can tell within 3.2 percent what the American public thinks," he said. "Actually, you can tell within 3.2 percent what the *cooperating* American public says and that's different. Thirty percent of the public doesn't cooperate. You don't know much about them."[56] By implication, the problem would be that much greater if only 30 percent of the public *did* cooperate.

At Pew, Kohut took up the challenge of determining how much of a problem low response rates actually were. Kohut's concern was that low response rates could generate erroneous results in pre-election surveys if biases were unknown and thus uncompensated for through weighting schemes. Kohut compared "amenable" respondents who agreed to be interviewed when they were contacted with "reluctant" respondents who refused at first but then agreed after being contacted one or more additional times. The results suggested that easier-to-reach and harder-to-reach respondents were remarkably similar in terms of the percentages who were younger or older, men or women, and better educated or less educated. However, reluctant respondents who were white held significantly more negative attitudes toward blacks than the amenable respondents, suggesting a possible source of bias in predictions in closely contested biracial elections as well as possible differences in other opinions.[57]

In a second experiment, Kohut compared responses from a sample in which standard polling methods were used with responses in a sample subjected to more rigorous methods. The standard responses were obtained over a five-day period involving limited attempts to reach potential interviewees. The rigorous method involved unlimited attempts over a seven-week period as well as an advance letter in which a $2 bill was enclosed. The standard method achieved a 36 percent response rate, while the rigorous method achieved a 61 percent response rate.[58]

Although the study was designed for other purposes, a public release of the data made possible a comparison of the responses to several questions about religion in the two versions. The percentage of respondents who said they attended religious services weekly or more was essentially the same: 40 percent in the standard version and 41 percent in the rigorous version. That remained true when the data were weighted to account for possible differences in age, gender, level of education, and race. However, there were two exceptions to the general pattern. Among African Americans, 46 percent attended weekly or more in the standard version but 55 percent did in the rigorous version. Among young people age eighteen through twenty-nine, 30 percent attended weekly or more in the standard version but only 25 percent did in the rigorous version. There was some indication as well that studies with lower response rates overestimated the number of people who were born again and underestimated the number who were nonreligious.[59]

The Pew data left two questions unanswered. It did not address the possibility that polls in which 35 to 40 percent of the sample did not

respond might already be obtaining biased results. And it did not say what
the biases might be when response rates dropped below 30 to 35 percent,
as was increasingly the case. These questions were especially relevant
to reports about religion because those results, unlike predictions about
elections, did not have independent means of validation.

There was a way to partially answer the questions. In 1973 the General Social Survey adopted a new stratified random sampling design
that closely represented the US population. In the early 1970s, the response rate for the General Social Survey averaged around 75 percent.
The survey included a question about frequency of attendance at worship services. Among all respondents, 28 percent said they attended
worship services every week or several times a week. Among the 15 percent of respondents who were interviewed last, only 21 percent said they
attended that often. Had the fieldwork ended when even the best commercial polls with response rates of 60 percent did, those people who
attended in significantly smaller numbers would have been missed.
And among the first 15 percent to be interviewed, 33 percent said they
attended every week or several times a week. In other words, a 15 percent response rate similar to the ones commercial polls were attaining
in the early twenty-first century would have exaggerated attendance at
religious services.[60]

Those results suggested that conclusions about attendance at religious
services could vary considerably depending on how well or how poorly
the survey from which the conclusions were drawn achieved a high response rate. For broad comparisons between people who attended frequently and those who did not, the variation may not have mattered. For
example, frequent attendees would more likely have been women than
infrequent attendees no matter what the response rate was. But in other
ways, response rates mattered. A survey with a 15 percent response would
have overestimated the number of weekly religious attendees in 1973 by
approximately eight million, or nearly 20 percent, and if all else had remained the same, would have exaggerated weekly attendees by eleven
million in 2010. Errors of that magnitude would have been problematic
had they occurred in predictions about elections. In addition, the characteristics of infrequent attendees would have been difficult to assess accurately when hard-to-get respondents were excluded. Most of all, trends
in religious attendance would have been affected by declining response
rates, making it difficult to know if reports about trends were reasonably
accurate or inaccurate.

A decade after Kohut's comparison of standard and rigorous methods, Pew again conducted an experiment to determine how declining response rates might influence polling results. Replicating the earlier study, the new standard method produced only a 25 percent response rate and the new rigorous method yielded a 50 percent response rate. The standard rate was about what other Pew surveys were achieving at the time. Pollsters and journalists were justifiably worried. And yet, the Pew results produced a surprising conclusion: it didn't matter. The results from 25 percent were just as good as the ones from 50 percent. That was the case for seventy-seven of the eighty-four items the two versions compared.[61]

For the polling community, it was almost too good to be true, and, indeed, a more cautious assessment was published about the same time based on comparisons drawn from a large number of surveys. This study advised that low response rates did not necessarily indicate nonresponse biases—a point that pollsters recited in subsequent defenses of standard methods. But the study also argued that high response rates were still legitimately valued and contended that pollsters anticipate nonresponse bias and seek auxiliary data to reduce those effects.[62]

The possibility that low response rates sometimes did and sometimes did not affect results was evident in questions about religion. In 2005 a Pew survey with a 32 percent response rate estimated that 43 percent of the public attended religious services weekly or more. Had the survey made only three attempts to reach people in the sample, the response rate would have been 21 percent and the estimate of weekly attendance would have still been 43 percent. If only one attempt had been made, the response rate would have dropped to 9 percent and the weekly attendance estimate would have increased to 46 percent. In short, there seemed to be little harm in lower response rates. By the end of the decade, Pew was in fact reporting results from polls with response rates as low as 9 percent.

However, a drop in response rates from 60 percent in the early 1990s to 9 percent in 2010 could easily have affected inferences about trends. An apparent increase in weekly attendance from 40 percent to 43 or 46 percent could have occurred from declining response rates alone. Responses to other questions could have been affected in different ways. In the 2005 data, for example, the persons contacted first were 8 percentage points more likely to say they were born again than the persons contacted last. And among young adults, those contacted last were almost twice as likely to say they were nonreligious as those contacted first.[63]

With no single or easily defined metric for summarizing the possible effects of low and declining response rates, the major polling firms downplayed the importance of response rates. Whoever the public was that was now being captured by the 9 to 15 percent who responded to polls gave remarkably predictable answers to standard questions about religion. In 2008, for example, a Pew poll of 1,500 respondents with a response rate of around 24 percent showed that 41.8 percent attended religious services weekly or more. But if only the first seventy-five people had been surveyed, the result would have been off by less than a tenth of a percent. The estimate from those seventy-five people of how many were born again would have been off by less than 5 percent and the proportion nonreligious by less than 2 percent. By that measure, the polling firm was simply wasting its money contacting 1,500 people. It might as well have stopped with seventy-five. Or its audience might have assumed that response rates did not matter after all.

But other conclusions were clearly misleading. During the 2012 presidential election campaign, a writer for the *American Spectator*, a respected journal of conservative commentary, observed that a recent Pew poll showed 92 percent of Republicans never doubting the existence of God compared to only 77 percent of Democrats. In other words, nearly all Republicans were believers, while nearly a quarter of Democrats were not. Moreover, there appeared to have been a dramatic drop in belief among Democrats over the past quarter-century. However, Pew's overestimation of religiosity in churchgoing was evident in these responses as well. General Social Survey results in 2012 showed that only 67 percent of Republicans and 60 percent of Democrats had no doubts about God's existence and that Democrats were only 4 percentage points less likely to believe than they had been a quarter-century earlier. Had these results been used, the *American Spectator* story could still have noted the difference between Republicans and Democrats, but it would not have been correct to argue that nearly all Republicans firmly believed in God.[64]

What was the public to think? Judging from the frequency with which polls about religion were mentioned in newspapers, few readers seemed aware of declining response rates, or if they were, they seemed not to care. Roper's concern that reports of 3.2 percent margins of error were untrue seemed to have been forgotten. Never mind that errors of 8 to 10 percent were becoming common, not from sampling probabilities, but from low response rates. The fact that some results might be as accurate from seventy-five people as from twenty times that many could not be taken as proof that polling numbers were always accurate. Reports that 17 percent of Americans said this and 26 percent believed that seemed as factual as statistics about birth rates and gasoline prices. The truth was far different.

As response rates dropped, another strategy was to use alternative methods for drawing samples in the first place and weighting the results to approximate what a better response rate would have been. The method used to reduce nonresponse bias in telephone surveys was to weight the results by comparing the demographic characteristics of interviewees with the demographic characteristics of the adult US population as determined by the most recent census or population survey. These characteristics usually included gender, race, age, and level of educational attainment. If the poll failed to attain an adequate number of men or persons in their seventies or those with less than a high school diploma, the ones who did fall into those categories were simply given more weight to make up the difference. Sample matching took the idea a step further.

Surveys based on sample matching were conducted on the Internet instead of by phone. By 2006, a large majority of US households had Internet service. To compensate for the fact that some people did not have Internet access, better-funded government studies sometimes supplied Internet-connected devices. The more economical method was to use weighting formulae, just as with telephone surveys. The process involved setting up a website to which anyone interested could subscribe without charge and to encourage participation by promising to ask interesting questions, giving participants the results, and including various additional incentives, such as the possibility of being selected at random to win a small prize or being able to accrue points that could be redeemed for online merchandise. With hundreds of thousands of people participating, the responses could be selected and tallied only from respondents whose profile matched the profile of respondents in telephone surveys or census data.

Sample matching was just one of the techniques being experimented with to keep polling alive despite the growing challenges it faced. Another method relied on telephone calls but also circumvented the cost of hiring interviewers to conduct the calls. ASP, which stood for automated survey process, used digitally recorded survey questions fed into a calling program that placed calls to randomly selected phone numbers and then determined the order in which to ask the questions and included branching

options. With response rates deemed unproblematic, ASP could efficiently ring the phones in tens of thousands of homes, timing the calls at
the dinner hour when people were usually home or on weekends. Then
to compensate for biases due to who answered and who did not, the responses were weighted to reflect census information about age, race, and
gender. To produce accurate predictions when questions about elections
were asked, a computer program further tweaked the responses to take
account of previous elections and the results of other polls. "Automated
technology," one of the firms using the method explained, "insures that
every respondent hears exactly the same question, from the exact same
voice, asked with the exact same inflection every single time."[65]

Although ASP was designed to track daily preferences during elections, pollsters put it to use for other purposes as well, including questions about religion. "If it's in the news, it's in our polls," one of the
companies' websites advertised, inviting interested visitors to subscribe
for several dollars a month. Computerized branching made it easy to go
beyond standard questions about church attendance and belief in God. A
person interested in religion, for example, could learn that 42 percent of
Americans who do not believe in God think that those who do believe are
foolish. Only from close inspection of the fine print would it be evident
that this conclusion was drawn from only 120 people in an automated
survey with an unknown response rate.[66]

With ASP efficiency, polls shifted increasingly to specialized populations as well. Instead of asking the same questions to tens of thousands
of respondents and then reporting the results by congressional district or
state, they employed "hyper-local" polling to blitz local populations with
questions of presumed interest in local media markets. When media attention fell on several preachers' lavish lifestyles in 2007, for example, a
national polling company targeted respondents in Oklahoma City, finding that 75 percent thought preachers should live in modest homes. A
few weeks later the same company conducted a poll in New Hampshire,
the results of which were reported on a Boston television station, including the observation that 48 percent of registered voters who were born
again considered it important that a presidential candidate practice the
same religion as they did.[67] Like the poll about disbelievers in God, it was
again necessary to examine the fine print to interpret the results. The
New Hampshire poll was conducted among 675 registered voters, 401 of
whom said they belonged to an organized religion, and of whom fewer
than 100 said they were born again.

Summing Up

By the end of the first decade of the twenty-first century, then, the picture of polls about religion and polls in general was mixed. On the one hand, polls were cheaper, more efficiently administered, and more frequently conducted than ever before. The major news media's thirst for interesting poll results seemed unquenchable. Political campaigns that began almost as soon as one election was over provided revenue for polling companies and prompted public interest in the results. Religion was sufficiently relevant to the campaigns that most of the polls included something about religious preferences and participation. Social scientists, for their part, showed no decline in interest in polls and surveys, either. On the other hand, a large and growing share of the public thought polls could not be trusted. And fewer people were willing to answer when pollsters called.

Nobody suggested that polling was a waste of money or even that polls should be done differently, less often, or better. It would not have been overly cynical to suggest that pollsters had a vested interest in conducting business as usual. That was as true for questions about religion as it was for other topics. Having asked the same few questions about church attendance and religious preferences for years, it would have seemed irresponsible to abandon those questions. Erroneous estimates of church attendance could be blamed on the public as long as the problem was attributed to respondents' tendency to overreport how often they attended. No matter that they occasionally missed a service because they were sick. They still attended most of the time. People could be excused for overreporting because it was socially desirable to attend, pollsters claimed. Still, it was interesting that pollsters were able to ask the right questions to compensate for overreporting about voting and plans to vote, but felt it unnecessary to offer the same kind of evidence about religious behavior.

Less surprisingly, the different styles that had characterized commercial polling and academic survey research from the start continued. Polling presented descriptive results of what (it hoped) a representative sample of the American public presumably believed and did. The descriptions included comparisons with previous results and usually provided comparisons among a few standard categories of the population, such as men and women, young and old, and breakdowns by region and race. Poll results included the standard notation about sampling error but rarely said what the error was for less than the full sample or adjusted it for low response rates or for systematic errors from sources other than sampling.

Despite software readily available for statistical analysis, poll reports rarely included measures of statistical significance. They rarely included efforts to empirically test causal arguments or to go beyond speculative interpretations of trends. Academic social science distinguished itself by providing those statistical analyses, causal tests, and interpretations drawn from extensive knowledge of the relevant literature.

The point was not that one approach was necessarily preferable to the other. It was rather that commercial polling and academic survey research served different purposes. The litmus test for commercial polling was whether it could accurately predict elections. If polls happened to include information about other topics that might be newsworthy, such as religion, so much the better. It was hard to imagine that foundations and commercial polling agencies had a vested interest in describing religion in particular ways. But they did have a vested interest in producing information quickly and focusing on topics appealing to the general public. Academic surveys were not conducted on tight deadlines or to make headlines. They went beyond descriptive information, offering instead to develop and test explanations for what was happening. And the reports frequently included qualitative evidence that facilitated interpreting the statistical data.

But the worlds of commercial polling and academic surveys were never completely separate. They were frequently confused in journalistic write-ups and in popular books. They competed for public attention, for recognition, and for funding. Funding was especially a matter of contention. When funding went in large measure to one kind of research, less of it was available for the other. That was especially true when government agencies, foundations, and private sources funded polls because they were cheap and well publicized but failed to understand the significant differences between polls and academic research.

The larger question for religion was how the abundance of quantitative information from polls may have shaped the public's perception of what religion was. To be sure, people continued to think about the sacred in private ways. Some proportion worshipped regularly in congregations of their choice. But when public discussions of religion so often focused on who attended and who did not and on categories of the public who might be born again or have no religious preference, it was hard to imagine that those discussions were unimportant. Those were the more difficult questions to answer.

7

Talking Back

ALTHOUGH POLLING, FROM its inception, presented itself as a way of giving voice to the people—as an instrument in the service of vox populi—it left the public and pollsters alike wondering what people really thought about the issues, including polls themselves. Eventually the unsolicited letters, newspaper commentaries, and public appearances that provided early pollsters with feedback gave way to self-reflective polling questions in which pollees were asked their opinions of polls. The results of such polls in the 1990s that registered declining confidence in polls prompted additional efforts in which more refined questions were asked in hopes of determining more precisely what the public thought.

During the 2008 presidential campaign, a series of questions about polls seemed mostly to suggest that the public viewed polls favorably. A Pew poll conducted a month before the election showed that 50 percent of those who responded had heard a lot about what the latest polls were showing. An Associated Press poll reported that 25 percent of the public had been following polls about the election within the last month and that 62 percent had read or heard something from polls during the run-up to the election. In another poll, 7 percent said they had personally participated in a poll about the election and more than half of that number said they had participated more than once.[1]

As the nation anticipated the next election, pollsters continued to report that the public viewed their work favorably. Gallup reported, for example, that 68 percent of the public thought the nation would be better off if "leaders of our nation followed the views of public opinion polls more closely," while only 25 percent thought the nation would be worse off. A Harris poll followed suit, showing that a majority of the public (55 percent) thought opinion polls had too little influence on policymakers in Washington, while only a third (31 percent) thought they had too much.[2]

The difficulty with those results was that the questions could be interpreted as sentiment against Washington and in favor of public opinion instead of as support specifically for polls. Other polls showed that the vast majority of people responding to polls were still skeptical. Pollsters and commentators alike expressed doubts about the accuracy of polls and cautioned an already wary public to be careful about trusting polls.

Following the 2012 presidential election, the *National Journal* published a story about polling under the headline "Americans Don't Trust Polls" in which it observed, "if you're like 75 percent of Americans, you think the polling data presented in this article is biased."[3] The story was based on a national poll conducted by the Kantar data investment management organization showing that 59 percent of those polled would pay a great deal or fair amount of attention to consumer surveys when deciding on which consumer products to purchase, but that only 33 percent would do the same for public opinion polls when deciding about issues and candidates. When asked if they thought polls were biased or unbiased, only 19 percent said they were unbiased while 75 percent said they were biased. Only 20 percent held favorable overall impressions of pollsters. And even fewer—4 percent—said they placed a lot of trust in the results of polls conducted by polling companies. The only result that may have given encouragement to some of the best-known polling organizations was that more of the public—8 percent—said they would place a lot of trust in the results of polls conducted by nonpartisan foundations.[4]

Observers provided interpretations of why public confidence in polling was sinking. *National Journal*'s Steven Shepard argued that the days of accurate polling were numbered due to the proliferation of polls and the attendant difficulties of reaching people. Many of the polling companies, he feared, were abandoning the rigorous survey research methods used in the past. Huffington Post survey consultant Mark Blumenthal described the reality of polling as "they're all pretty ugly." Noting the increasing difficulty of distinguishing accurate research from "crap," he observed that the Pew Research Center, despite being regarded as doing "rigorous, expensive, high quality" surveys was "getting a typical response rate of 9 percent."[5]

None of the polls and commentaries about polls dealt specifically with polling about religion. The prevalence of polls about candidates and issues during presidential campaigns suggested that much of the concern was directed at polls focusing on those topics. And yet, many of the political polls included questions about religion and polls specifically about religion suffered from the same low response rates as other polls. Concerns previously discussed behind closed doors in academic seminars started to be aired in public.

"When I was a young sociologist at Berkeley's Survey Research Center," sociologist of religion Rodney Stark wrote in the *Wall Street Journal*, "it was assumed that any survey that failed to interview at least 85 percent of those originally drawn into the sample was not to be trusted." They were not to be trusted because nonrespondents were known to differ from respondents and, for those reasons, response rates should always be reported. However, he wrote, Pew was now reporting response rates of only 9 percent, and other firms were not disclosing their response rates at all. "Only one thing is really certain," he concluded: "those who take part in any survey are not a random selection of the population."[6]

Wall Street Journal "Numbers Guy" Carl Bialik, whose essays frequently emphasized journalists' misuses of polls, cautioned readers about the difficulties in interpreting religion polls as well. He was less concerned with low response rates than with question wording. "Questions remain," he wrote, "about how to count population by religion, and how to define those who have no religion. Different surveys use different question wording and definitions, which, combined with the huge variety of beliefs and practices, complicate researchers' work."[7]

As they had done in the past, religious organizations also questioned pollsters' results. When Pew announced that 57 percent of evangelicals thought many religions can lead to eternal life, evangelical leaders questioned the poll's validity, especially when journalists interpreted the poll as evidence that a majority of evangelicals now believed that anybody could get to heaven whether they believed in Jesus or not. To counter the misinformation, LifeWay Research, which conducted polls for Southern Baptists and evangelical organizations, asked instead whether a person could obtain eternal life through "religions other than Christianity," to which only 31 percent of Protestant churchgoers agreed. "The LifeWay Research finding adds quantifiable data to growing criticisms that the Pew survey was flawed," a columnist for *Religion Today* wrote, "in how it asked its questions and that poor wording caused the Pew's counterintuitive conclusions." Still, journalists and op-ed columnists continued to find grist in polls for sweeping conclusions about vast changes in American religion, including evangelicalism. As a writer in the *New York*

Times concluded, "Evangelicalism as we knew it in the 20th century is disintegrating."[8]

Speculation of that kind in the nation's leading newspapers raised yet again the question of whether polls, valid or not, were implicitly shaping the public image of American religion or, short of that, how polling information was being used. There were several ways to find out. One was to consider the pushback evident in responses to polls and in declining response rates as well as from commentators in the media and academia. Another was to talk with religious leaders.

An opportunity to ask religious leaders what they thought of polls emerged in conjunction with another project in which leaders talked about the challenges facing their congregations and other programs. These were qualitative interviews rather than polls. The religious leaders in the study were chosen purposively rather than at random to provide insights into the variety of roles religious leaders currently play. A hundred fifty leaders participated in the study. They held positions in congregations and in denominational offices and included lay leaders as well as ordained clergy. They were affiliated with more than a dozen denominations and ministered in contexts ranging from large cities to small towns.[9]

The comments from these religious leaders provide a rare view of how people who are not themselves involved in the polling industry but are on the front lines of religious activities think about the information they read and hear about from polls. The leaders were well educated. They held college degrees, seminary degrees, and in a few cases other advanced academic degrees. Seminary training provided them ample opportunities to have discussed research about American religion, and it was clear from their comments that they were familiar with polls. Following the other topics the interviews covered, which included questions about the programs in which each leader was involved and current issues (such as immigration and economic policies), the final section of the interviews posed questions about whether and how the leaders used polls and surveys in their work, how they interpreted the trends about religion that polls have identified, and whether they trusted polling information.

Using Polls and Surveys

To find out if religious leaders were using polls and surveys, and if so, how, each of the leaders was asked, "Do you ever draw on or refer to polls and surveys about religion in your work?" Approximately two-thirds said they did. And if that had been the only piece of information—if that were the kind of yes-or-no question asked in a poll—it would have been a statistic that polling firms like Pew, Barna, and Gallup could have cited as evidence that polls and surveys were an excellent investment of time and energy.

But when the leaders who said they made use of polls and surveys were asked how they used them, a more nuanced picture emerged. A few described specific polling organizations from which they drew information and talked about mentioning polls and survey results in sermons and at meetings. The majority, though, said they rarely made any use of polls and surveys or indicated that the studies they had in mind did not come from brand-name polling firms. For the most part, they described polling as an ambient feature of an information-rich world more than as a tool with specific uses.

One of the pastors typified the few who enthusiastically drew information from polls. He seemed particularly pleased to have been asked if he used polls and surveys in his work. He was the pastor of a small but thriving congregation of first- and second-generation Latino immigrants, many of whom had grown up in Pentecostal or Roman Catholic churches and were now moving into middle-class occupations, sending their children to college, and feeling more at home in a thoroughly Americanized mainstream Protestant denomination. "Yes, yes," he replied when asked if he used polls and surveys. "Particularly from the Pew Research Center and the Alban Institute," the latter referring to the (recently defunct) Virginia-based center of learning, leadership development, and consulting that sometimes conducted studies of congregations but mostly provided expertise about congregational issues through its publications and seminars. Asked how exactly he used the information, he replied, "I talk about it in sermons. I talk about it during Bible studies. And I talk about it when I make proposals for particular ministries." In short, he was a happy user of research, although his reference to particular ministry proposals suggested that the Alban Institute information was probably foremost in his mind.

A Lutheran pastor in his early thirties at what he described as a "theologically conservative" church in the suburbs of a large city in the Midwest was another enthusiastic user of polls and surveys. "I read a lot of surveys and polls from organizations like Gallup, Barna, and Pew," he said, explaining, "They do research on religion in America." He added,

"And then, of course, there are always articles and books being put out that are looking at trends in the church—sometimes drawing on this research, but also sometimes original research. So I'm reading about stuff like that all the time." Like the other pastor, he said he mentions poll results in sermons or in classes at the church. "The trends and statistics are so alarming a lot of times that I'll talk about them with key lay leaders, like the council or the elders, to create a sense of urgency." He tells them that things have to change and that how the congregation delivers its message has to change. "People are naturally resistant to change," he said, but giving them "hard numbers" wakes them up.

Neither pastor sought out poll results by searching websites or looking specifically for them. The information came from authors and publications they trusted. That was true of two other pastors who said they used Barna polls. A pastor of a three-hundred-member congregation in a small town in the Deep South read about a study of Southern Baptists that he found interesting because George Barna ("a Christian pollster") did it. The study said only 17 percent of those polled read the Bible every day, so the pastor mentioned it in his sermon the following Sunday. "It was just a sub-point," he explained, because the main thrust of the sermon, based on the Gospel of John, chapter 17, was that Jesus prayed that God would sanctify Jesus' disciples through the truth. The other pastor was a man in his sixties at a Lutheran church on the West Coast who knew about Barna and trusted him because he had heard him speak and because the congregation received Barna's newsletter. "I'm just not a poll-type person," the pastor said, although he has found it useful from time to time to mention something from a Barna poll to some of the lay leaders at his church.

Most of the pastors who said they occasionally used polls and surveys, though, mentioned other kinds of studies. A woman in her thirties who pastors a small start-up church in the South said the polls and surveys she finds most useful are studies of other church planting efforts. A Lutheran pastor at a large downtown church in the Northeast said he relies "very heavily" on studies conducted by his denomination's research office (noting that he learns more from face-to-face conversations than from looking at graphs). Several Presbyterian clergy noted that their denomination conducts its own surveys of members, clergy, and elders, and is thus able to provide information about issues of interest. One such pastor, who considered statistics "a powerful tool," described how figures from the denomination helped when two of the congregations he was involved in decided to merge. A rabbi in her thirties at a synagogue in New York explained that the studies she keeps her eye on are ones done in "the Jewish religious world," not the general American population polls that usually include too few Jews to be meaningful. "We've done internal surveys of our membership," she said, "to make sure that our perceptions of how people rely on us matches what people are actually looking for." One such study of the membership a year ago, she recalled, used a consultant to develop the questions and to analyze the data. She said the city's federation of Jewish organizations conducted another survey recently with foundation support to examine what was being done about social justice.

A mainline Protestant pastor at an urban church in the Midwest said her congregation had also been part of a citywide survey. The study resembled the ones conducted a century ago during the heyday of the social survey movement. It gathered information about occupations, income levels, population densities, and other aspects of the living conditions of people in the city and then tabulated the data for the geographic areas closest to each of the churches. It was an effort, she said, "to think in a new way about how we are present in our communities and how we need to be present." A priest on the East Coast who sees "all those sort of statistical facts" from the "Pew institute," as part of the general reading he does considered it useful to keep generally informed about the wider society, but the studies that matter most specifically to his work are the diocesan surveys that provide information about demographics, neighborhoods, numbers of children, and church membership. A woman who pastors a predominantly African American congregation not far from the nation's capital also used local statistics, although in her case to challenge the views of denominational leaders and argue for the value of congregational autonomy.

Comments of pastors who did not use polls and surveys provided additional perspective. Nobody said they were opposed to such information on principle and a few went out of their way to say that they were not opposed. However, several offered reasons for not using polls. The closest anyone came to suggesting they might be opposed to polls was a Catholic leader who said he preferred "to go to traditional spirituality rather than the latest poll." A Protestant leader expressed a similar view, asserting that his work was guided by church policy, not by what people thought about church policy. An executive in charge of social justice ministries for another Protestant denomination mentioned Pew's "stuff on religious freedom" but doubted its usefulness. "It doesn't feel like it's interesting," she explained. A United Church of Christ pastor who had recently finished his seminary training noted that it was impossible to avoid polls about religion because they were always in the headlines and on Facebook; however, he did not bring them into his ministry because "there's enough to be scared of than polls," and he thought the church's job was to be a "nonanxious presence" in people's lives.

For other clergy polls and surveys were not on their radar screens. The topic simply did not come up or there were too many other ways of thinking about what needed to be done at their congregations. Several of the pastors, though, explained that they knew about the well-publicized national polls but did not find them useful because the polls either missed the kind of people they worked with or did not represent the attitudes or trends they considered important. This was the reasoning of a United Church of Christ pastor in his fifties at a congregation in New England who said, "Polls and surveys just deal with trends." He was more interested in what was going on in his own congregation, where some of the members thought it might be useful to conduct a survey, but ultimately the congregation decided it made more sense to have people discuss their views than respond anonymously to a survey. The pastor of a predominantly Asian-American congregation in New England expressed a similar view but noted that his congregation had conducted a survey a few years before he arrived.

The pastor of a Mennonite church expressed the view that polls and surveys failed to provide useful information, not only for the needs of his particular congregation but also for other congregations like his. There are all kinds of polls and surveys, he said, about the decline of mainline churches and the rise of evangelicals and the Religious Right. But he likes to think that the Mennonite Church exists apart from that: "We're not a mainline church, and we're not the Religious Right. We're a third way." The Mennonite Church does not conduct its own polls, as far as he knows, and the other polls, in his view, do not speak to the Mennonite Church. A New Jersey Buddhist meditation center leader's experience was similar.

On the whole, pastors' responses to how they did or did not use polls and surveys in their work indicated that they consider *data* helpful, especially when the information pertains directly to their congregations and communities and to congregations like theirs. The data collected within their congregations and communities or by church agencies were more useful than the random headlines they saw about national polls. Polling firms could perhaps take heart that poll results are at least being mentioned from time to time in sermons and classes or in casual discussions. But the operative word is *mentioned*. The pastors who said they sometimes drew information from polls about religion indicated that the information was usually of the most general kind, such as interest in organized religion seeming to decline, or was speculative, such as giving them some hope that progressive religion might be gaining ground against the Religious Right. A pastor at a large Protestant church in New York City, for example, mentioned having read about the rising number of people who are non-religious and he recalled having a conversation about that with someone across the street. Another New York City pastor said his church office receives several daily newsletters about religion, and he knows they some-times mention polls, but he rarely has time to look at them. When specific numbers were mentioned in sermons, pastors noted that the numbers were not the main point. An Episcopal priest in the South who pastors a flourishing suburban church, for example, said he sometimes draws on polls to remind his congregation that Episcopalians nationally are not doing as well. If the average Episcopalian is a sixty-two-year-old Cauca-sian woman, he observed, the denomination needs to start doing things differently.

Making Sense of Trends

A second way to see how religious leaders use polls and surveys is to ask about the trends shown in those studies. Because pollsters put ample stock in their ability to document trends, it is particularly interesting to know if religious leaders find that information credible and, if so, how they interpret it. The interviewers explained to the clergy and lay leaders being interviewed that the final section of the interview included "a few questions about some of the things pollsters and journalists say about American religion," adding, "we're interested in hearing what you think about some of these ideas. For example, you may have read that pollsters think religion is declining in America. Does that seem right to you? Is religion in America declining? What do you think?"

A few of the clergy disagreed and, interestingly enough, those who did were the ones who paid closest attention to polls. The pastor who works with Latino immigrants, for example, said he did not think religion in America was declining but was "taking a different route." Because of the multiethnic community in which his church is located, he considered American religion to be much more "diversified and amplified" than it may have been fifty years ago. He also thought spirituality is changing and yet is still important to most individuals. As evidence, he said, "The Pew Research Center just stated that 89 percent of the American public is spiritual." Despite having a precise percentage in mind, he nevertheless was unsure what to make of it. "What does that mean?" he asked. He figured it might refer to something Christian or something else, but he had no idea.

Nearly all the clergy and lay leaders, though, accepted the view that religion was declining. They did so, taking the statement that pollsters think religion is declining at face value and offering their own interpretations of why that was probably a valid observation. Their responses registered a kind of implicit trust that what the pollsters said was correct. They provided anecdotes and evidence from their own experience, came up with explanations for why this trend was indeed happening, and were able to insert doubts and counter-examples without having to question the main premise.

The woman who pastors a start-up church in the South, for example, recalled that when she was growing up it was expected that people would go to church and that was no longer the case, which meant that "you have greater hurdles to get people to walk through the church doors." Churches in the 1950s, she figured, even though that was well before her time, were the central organizing forces in peoples' lives, whereas that was no longer the case and the decline left people living fractured lives. She thought, too, that a decline had happened in "the hold that religion has over our national and political conversation." Maybe the decline was good, she ventured. Maybe reckoning with it would help the churches refocus their efforts. Perhaps people were still "loosely religious"—maybe because "religion is just a hard word"—but if so, it probably does not affect what they do very much.

The Lutheran pastor whose church has benefited from a citywide survey agreed. The churches were shrinking because they had "become more concerned with preserving what we have and not making people angry" than with "taking the bold stand that we need to." She knew there were still some churches "where the good news is preached and the word proclaimed," but in her community she thought a lot of the churches were "giving people easy answers and false hope" instead of truly preaching the word of God.

Similarly, a recent college graduate who worked part-time for an evangelical church in the Northeast was pretty sure that religion was declining. Being religious is "just not a part of people's routine," he said. "People aren't encouraged within their home or their community" to be religious. "So as a result, I think, people don't feel convicted about it—they don't see it as an obligation, they don't go to services." Religion used to be the norm, he thought, but now it was "kind of like abnormal to be religious."

This was nearly the same view a woman who directs an evangelical inner-city ministry expressed. She thought congregations were declining because people go once in a while to hear someone preach, "if they feel like it," but don't feel obligated to attend every week. She attributed the problem to "bad mentoring" and "bad examples [from] people who call themselves Christians." It had become all too easy to justify not going to church, she thought. "We really have to take a deep look at ourselves," she said, and ask if we really believe God's word and want to be in a fellowship of believers.

Ready acceptance of pollsters' claim that religion is declining is interesting in view of the fact that pollsters themselves disagree on this point. As the Gallup Poll website asserted, "The average percentage who said 'yes' [when asked if they had attended religious services in the past seven days] in 1939 was 41 percent, virtually the same as recorded most recently" and as Gallup president Frank Newport's book about religion affirmed.[10] To see how people would respond to this alternative view, the interviews followed the question about religious decline with this: "Contrary to the view that religion is declining, some statistics suggest that 35 to 40 percent of the public attend religious services every week and that proportion is the same as it was thirty or forty years ago. Does that seem right or is that a statistic you would question?"

Having just agreed that religion was declining, it was harder for interviewees to agree with this statistic as well. The woman in the South, for example, said she had heard of this statistic, but it wasn't true in her community. Maybe churches were growing somewhere else. Maybe the people who were leaving the churches she knew about were joining other churches. Still, she doubted it: "If new people aren't coming to faith, there's just no way that things are going to remain steady."

A priest who knew for sure that organized religion was declining said he would "certainly question" statistics suggesting the contrary. He didn't need polls to show that religion was on the skids. Statistics from his tradition were proof enough. "We are becoming a much more secularized society," he said. It was just easier now for people to stay at home on Sundays reading the *New York Times* or go to Starbucks than to church, and they were not taking their children to church either, which meant a downward spiral that would continue. He knew of churches closing all over the place, so polls showing no decline could not be accurate.

For the most part, though, the people who thought religion was declining found ways to also agree that it was not declining. The Lutheran pastor in the Midwest did some struggling but eventually reconciled the contradictory views. His first thought was that, well, churches were growing in the Southern Hemisphere, but he realized that had nothing to do with claims about churches in the United States. "Those aren't the same places," he acknowledged. "But I think there are communities in which churches are maintaining at least their attendance." Maybe people in those communities felt connected to the tradition of attending church on Sunday mornings. The more he thought about it, the more he figured maybe he had been generalizing too much from his own community. "I think I could believe both in the decline and in the 'maintaining' depending on what communities we're talking about," he concluded.

The young man who was working part-time with an evangelical church pondered the two opposing views for only a moment before deciding that both could be true. He concluded that religion declining was probably just the perception people had because of how it was treated on television and in the movies and at school, whereas maybe religion was actually faring better than that: "That might give people the idea that everybody is leaving church when it's not really true. So at the same time, people are still making [religion] a part of their weekly routine."

The woman at an evangelical inner-city ministry switched gears immediately from what she had been saying about decline to agree that the statistics showing no decline in church attendance were correct. "I would think at least 35 percent attend every week," she said. "I actually believe that." Why? "Those are the same people who went every week thirty or forty years ago, [and] it's that generation of people who are still going." And if that were the case, perhaps the polls were not as representative as they should be—the view of another person who thought the 35 percent surely must be people insulated from the competing demands most families experienced on Sundays.

Swift mental maneuvering was particularly needed to reconcile the popular view that religion, but not spirituality, was declining with the notion that church attendance was actually holding steady. One person contrasted "internal" and "external" religion to suggest that people were still internally religious, but less external about it, but then decided that maybe the growing number of older people (who were still external) accounted for the lack of decline in attendance. Another person thought religion was declining because attendance was no longer expected as a kind of cultural norm, but then attributed steady attendance figures to people still being influenced by those norms.

Although the typical responses included ways to reconcile the different trends, having them juxtaposed did push a few of the people to question the polls' accuracy. The young man at the evangelical church, for example, added, when asked again if he thought the polls showing no decline in church attendance could be accurate, that maybe people who were not going to church said they were. The Mennonite pastor who said national polls were mostly irrelevant to his denomination said the 35 to 40 percent church attendance result "sounds like a Gallup poll," and he just wanted to ask where those Gallup polls were taken. Maybe if they were done in Kansas, they might show that result, but he doubted their accuracy: "That's a Gallup poll and Gallup would have to justify that. I wouldn't be able to defend it."

The conclusion suggested by the ease with which polls showing contradictory trends were reconciled is that poll results may in small ways reinforce what people think anyway, and if an opposite result appears, it is not hard to find some reason why it might be true as well. The implication is not that polls are wrong, but that polls can show almost anything and can be interpreted in different ways. If that is the case, it is consistent with the view of pastors who say they sometimes mention polls in their work but do not put much stock in them unless they are studies that pertain specifically to their church or community. It was evident, too, that pastors and lay leaders found it easier to agree with imprecise than precise polling results. When confronted with the general view from polling that religion was declining, their thoughts went to large "meta-narratives," as one put it, about secularization, people leading busy lives, and even businesses staying open on Sundays. In contrast, the specific claim that church attendance ranged from 35 to 40 percent and was constant invited doubts about how the polls were conducted, where they were done, and the kinds of biases that might be involved.

The leaders did agree with pollsters on one point. Pollsters' response to criticisms about the accuracy of attendance figures has been to argue that, inaccuracies notwithstanding, attendance is still a good proxy for how seriously people take their faith. The leaders, being, as they were, in charge of religious organizations, considered it important for people of faith to be involved in religious organizations. They knew there were exceptions. They understood that people could be spiritual on their own and in their own ways. They mentioned, too, that attendance at worship services needed to be accompanied by efforts to put faith into practice at other times. They nevertheless emphasized the value of taking an active part in a worshipping community. As an evangelical pastor explained, "We believe that a relationship with Christ is the important aspect—a sense of discipleship—and that takes place more frequently and is enhanced in consistent attendance." And as the pastor of a mainline church emphasized, "Attendance is very important for your ongoing faith life; it's just important to be part of an ongoing community of faith and a regular participant in that."

Although they agreed with pollsters that attendance was a meaningful measure of religious commitment, they disagreed, implicitly at least, with polling estimates of attendance. In Gallup polls, approximately 60 percent of American adults hold membership in churches or synagogues, and, of this number, two-thirds attend religious services once a week or almost every week. But when the pastors were asked to estimate how many of their members attended every week (taking account of missing some weeks), the average estimate was 35 to 40 percent, with several as low as 15 or 20 percent and only a few as high as 50 percent.

Plummeting Response Rates

As a final question in the interviews, leaders were asked directly about the low response rates in polls. "Many of the polls we hear about have only a 25 percent response rate, and some are as low as 10 or 15 percent. That means 75 to 90 percent of the people who should have been included in order to have a representative sample did not respond. Does knowing that affect your view of polls, or do you figure you can trust them anyway?"

This information was news to nearly all the leaders interviewed. A few had heard that it was becoming more difficult to do polls, but they had no idea the problem was this serious. They had noted polling information about religion in passing or paid attention to the pollsters they trusted, but had not been sufficiently interested to wade through the pages of website reports to discover that response rates were so low. The most interested leaders assumed the plus or minus 2 or 3 percent margin of error reported in polls was all they needed to know. As far as trusting polls, now that they had considered this information, the leaders divided almost evenly into three groups.

The first group said they would still trust the results because pollsters surely must know what they are doing and, for that matter, the information about religion was really only of passing interest anyway. These leaders—the "trust anyway" group—offered remarks indicating that polling, after all, was something of a mystery and for that reason was a bit like any other brief news item that might grab one's attention for a moment or two but rarely had an impact on one's thoughts or actions.

An example of this first group was the rector of an upscale Episcopal church who said, "I think I can trust them anyway." He thought the "folks that do it do it well enough." He recalled having learned in college that it was possible to draw a sample that was representative of a larger population "if it's done properly." He knew there could be sampling biases and problems with how the questions were asked and the data recorded. But, he concluded, "I generally trust them," adding, "I don't put a ton of weight in them."

A recent seminary graduate at a United Church of Christ congregation similarly acknowledged that he trusts them "a little anyway." He finds them interesting: "They're like curiosities, like, oh, here's something to ponder." But he said his thinking would not be affected one way or the other.

The Mennonite pastor who said he never uses polls anyway was willing to give pollsters the benefit of the doubt. "I'm sure [the late] George Gallup knows a lot more about polling than I do. So when he comes out with a poll, and he makes these conclusions based on whatever he makes them on, and he has a 10 to 25 percent response rate and seems to be satisfied with it, it's like I'll trust the integrity of the research." But having said that, he explained that the reason he pays little attention to polls is because of the assumptions they make about the respondents. He thought most respondents were poorly informed and that polls, especially ones about religion and politics, painted a false picture of religion.

"I would hope the people doing the surveys know what they're doing," another leader reflected. He was unsure if he understood sampling and margins of error enough to know. Another pastor admitted he didn't know quite what to think. He hoped polling organizations were trustworthy. But he acknowledged that he mostly thinks polls are right when they give him the answer he wants to hear and makes him feel good. Yet another considered the best polls the ones that included larger numbers of people, no matter what the response rate was. He assumed that a poll of two thousand people meant that everyone called had responded. It had not occurred to him that as many as twenty thousand calls had been made.

The second group took nearly the opposite view of the first group. Asked if low response rates would affect their view of polls, they said "no" because they had no faith in polls anyway. This "never trust" group believed there were so many problems with polls that low response rates could hardly make things worse. They thought the wording of polls was usually biased or, at best, failed to capture the nuances of what people really believed. In their view, polling was information a prudent person should avoid as much as possible.

A woman in her early thirties who pastors a Presbyterian church illustrated this second group. "I have a general skepticism" toward polls, she said, noting that her husband, a scientist, reinforced her skepticism. Knowing about low response rates did not surprise her or change her view of polls, but she did think it important for people to know that response rates were low.

That was the view of another woman who also pastored a Presbyterian church. She conceded that polls might be useful tools sometimes, but she said she puts about as much stock in them as she does in movie reviews: "For me, it's like, hmm, that's interesting, but I don't depend on them for anything. I don't necessarily think they present accurate information. I think oftentimes it's biased."

The Lutheran pastor who mentioned having benefited from a citywide survey expressed the same general skepticism of polls. "That's the first time I've heard that statistic," she said upon learning about the low response rates. "But I've always kind of known that polls reveal a very limited [kind] of information. I've always had a healthy suspicion of polls, understanding that we shouldn't dismiss them totally, but that they're not a holistic picture of truth."

One of the best-informed leaders expressed nearly the same view. Besides holding a divinity degree and a law degree, he had studied statistics and held a citywide administrative office in his denomination. "I've never trusted polls," he stated categorically. Besides margins of error from sampling, polls were unreliable sources of information, in his view, because of contradictory results and other biases.

Another well-informed leader was a lay member with a graduate degree who had worked in polling in college. He enjoys participating in polls and takes the opportunity to do so whenever he is asked. But he has little faith in them. "I think all polling always needs to be taken with a grain of salt," he said. He knows that some people respond because they believe in scientific data or feel an obligation, but he learned in doing polls that "people who have a strong opinion one way or another" respond while "a lot of moderates get left out."

The third group took the news about low response rates as a specific reason not to trust polls. The "conditional distrust" of this group reflected an interest in polls and a desire to have good polling information, but understood that missing 75 to 90 percent of the people who should have been included posed serious problems. Knowing that response rates were this low made these leaders feel foolish for having taken poll results at face value.

"Now you're hurting me!" one pastor chuckled when confronted with the information about low response rates. He wanted to believe that pollsters were being paid good money to make sure their studies were representative. A lay leader at another church was not surprised. He knew he was one of the 75 percent who did not respond to polls, and he knew that was a source of bias.

A more thoughtful response was that of the man in his early twenties who was working part-time at an evangelical church. Having majored in political science, he immediately recognized that low response rates were problematic. "It does affect the way I view the poll," he said. The few people who responded, he thought, were probably passionate about the topic for some reason. He could imagine his "strong Bible-believing Christian friends" as the kind of people who would respond: "But I don't think they represent the huge bulk of like the middle, the 75 percent. I don't think they represent them at all."

Perhaps the most trusting response was from a priest in his sixties who said any halfwit knows that polls are limited, but you pay attention to them anyway and hope for the best. "I think if it's 25 percent that's not so bad," he said. "I trust places like the Pew institute because even if it's a 25 percent sampling, it's random enough to not have been focused on one particular group." Still, it worried him to know that current response rates even at Pew were significantly lower. "I think 10 to 15 percent is a vastly different thing," he acknowledged.

The pastor of an evangelical church offered one of the most typical responses. "I don't usually think about the low response rate when I see a poll," he said. "I assume that it's accurate—which is dumb! Why do I do that, especially after what you just told me? Wow!"

Polls in Passing

Religious leaders, these responses suggest, are not averse to research, statistical or otherwise, even though they often do not understand the methods involved, as long as it provides meaningful information about their communities and congregations or trends within their denominations. They know about broader trends that matter to their congregations. They are certainly aware that pollsters routinely include questions about religion in their studies. It would be impossible to be unaware of poll results about religion. But if polling firms were under the impression that religious organizations' work was being assisted by polls, they would probably want to reconsider that assumption. The religious leaders who make use of polls say they do so in offhand ways that can usually be taken with a grain of salt.

The way these leaders say they use poll results in sermons is illustrated in the sermon transcripts that pastors sometimes post on websites. One example is a Reformation Day sermon by a Lutheran pastor who referenced a poll done by "Christian researcher" George Barna. "Barna had asked a wide cross-section of Americans a very simple question: What are the most important words you've ever heard? Answer # 1: (no surprise) I love you. Answer # 2: (no surprise either) I forgive you. Answer # 2: (unexpected) Dinner's ready! Come eat!" The pastor then discussed each of the three, arguing that they summarized the gospel message. But several aspects of his polling reference are notable. Barna's credentials are that he is a Christian and has conducted a poll, not that the pastor knows if the results were valid. The quote does not include specific results, and it appears to have evoked laughter, almost as if that is the purpose of polls. Indicating that he had not read the poll results firsthand, he mentioned having heard another pastor quote it in a sermon. It constituted less than 3 percent of the Reformation Day sermon, which included lengthier illustrations about Muhammad Ali, Martin Luther, and Saint Augustine. Still, anyone previously unfamiliar with Barna would now have heard about him.[11]

A more typical use of polls is illustrated in a sermon about heaven in which the pastor mentioned a *Washington Post* article reporting, "88 percent of Americans believe that heaven is a real place," and an ABC News poll that "some 43 percent of Americans believe that their deceased pets will go to heaven." These references occurred near the start of the sermon along with an anecdote about heaven from a recent movie. The point was that "the average person in America today" has a faulty view of heaven, which the pastor proceeded to correct with a forty-minute exposition of biblical descriptions of heaven.[12]

Citing polls to show that Americans are interested in religion but have weak or misguided understandings in need of pastoral instruction is one of the more common uses of polls. Another example was the statement, "George Gallup did a poll a few years ago that said that even 84 percent of the people who never go to church believe that Jesus rose from the dead," in a sermon about the resurrection by prominent megachurch pastor Rick Warren. Stating that people may believe in the resurrection, but not understand it, Warren explained the proper way to understand it.[13]

The other use of polls is to show that even church people are worldly, sinful, or hypocritical. "The findings in numerous national polls conducted by highly respected pollsters like the Gallup Organization and the Barna Group are simply shocking," the pastor of a nondenominational evangelical church told his audience. "Gallup and Barna hand us survey after survey demonstrating that evangelical Christians are as likely to embrace lifestyles every bit as hedonistic, materialistic, self-centered, and sexually immoral as the world in general." Including no numbers, the references nevertheless criticized Americans like those at the pastor's church without directing his criticisms at them in particular.[14]

The ease with which polls found their way into sermons like these was facilitated by websites providing brief excerpts from polls as sermon illustrations. Besides its print magazine, *Christianity Today*, for example, maintained a website with hundreds of sermon illustrations offering insights from polls, such as "stats for atheists," "is God in control of natural disasters," and "Harris results on religion." A subscription website called SermonIndex.net provided a similar service. Serious searchers could also find ample evidence on Barna, Gallup, and Pew websites.[15]

Like the religious leaders interviewed, though, sermons frequently pushed back against polls. For example, in a lengthy sermon titled "Of Polls and Preachers," Southwestern Baptist Theological Seminary professor David Allen cautioned, "One of the leading sources of 'proofiness' in society today is polls," adding that "journalists today are infatuated with polls" because journalists are desperate for news, and polls provide them with "pseudo events." Observing pollsters' and journalists' manipulation of facts and "reckless disregard for the truth," Allen contrasted that information with the "sure word" of truth Christians could find in the Bible.[16]

If religious leaders use polls in these limited and sometimes critical ways, who else uses them, perhaps more extensively? One possibility, suggested by the frequency with which academic journals cite polls about religion, is that researchers may be using polling information extensively. This possibility squares with the fact that poll results have become more readily available and, whether directly or indirectly, establish the topics that are apparently worth studying. Examining articles in peer-reviewed journals that routinely publish social scientific research about religion offers the best assessment of that possibility. During the decade starting in 2001, the five journals in which such research most often appears published more than two thousand articles about some aspect of religion. But the only polls that received more than a few mentions were Pew polls, and those were mentioned in only thirty-five of the articles.[17]

The articles mentioning Pew polls provided a clear sense of how the Pew information was being used. They mentioned Pew studies to indicate that Pew response rates were low and that academic survey response rates were significantly higher. They discussed bias in Pew studies, problems with acquiescence in standard agree/disagree questions, and the Pew foundation's decision to support polling instead of academic research. Several articles mentioned a Pew study in a footnote or included a reference to a Pew report in a lengthy review of the literature or mentioned Pew polls as examples of media coverage of religion. One actually used a 2001 Pew data set, collected at a time when response rates were higher, and another analyzed a more recent Pew study of attitudes toward immigrants, noting weaknesses in the study's wording of questions. On the whole, the articles suggested that social scientists held Pew results in low regard.

References in news sources were far more common. During the years when few of the top social science journals mentioned these polls, the major news media archived in Proquest mentioned them more than five hundred times a year. Prominent newspapers such as the *New York Times*, *USA Today*, *Wall Street Journal*, and *Washington Post* referenced Pew results in stories about conservative religion declining, conversion patterns, curbs on religious freedom, demographics of religion, gays and religion, happiness and religion, intolerance toward religion, Muslims, nonreligion, religion and politics, religious freedom, secularism, trends in religion, and numerous other topics. It would have been difficult for anyone interested in religion not to have been informed in these stories about the latest poll results. And yet, much like pastors' uses of polls, the stories rarely offered more than a brief reference to a poll result, citing it as part of a larger discussion of newsworthy events and their implications. Only fifteen to twenty of the five hundred or so stories per year featured poll results. And the five hundred that mentioned poll results at all were among approximately a hundred thousand per year that mentioned something about religion.

To conclude that polling about religion is inconsequential, though, would be wrong, just as it would be to suggest that round-the-clock news reporting and television advertising has no bearing on American culture. Polling studies demonstrate that polling rarely has discernible effects on election outcomes, but it offers background information that draws attention to how candidates are doing and reinforces implicit perceptions that some issues are more important than others. Polling about religion functions similarly, although with less frequency and less publicity, serving as part of the background information defining the general contours of American religion. It adds marginally to public discussions of how religion is faring and in so doing draws implicit attention to certain aspects of the religious landscape, such as denominational preferences and attendance at religious services. It appears occasionally in sermons and in corridor conversations among religious leaders and academics. If nothing else, it provides journalists with pseudo-events that seem like news.

The prevalence of polls in American popular culture presents a layer of facticity sufficiently thin that a majority of the public suspects it is biased. And yet, polling firms routinely report information about religion ostensibly accurate within a small margin of error, acknowledging only in notes few readers are likely to consult that response rates are embarrassingly low and that many other errors may be present. With few qualms, it seems, writers who are generally careful enough to fact-check minor details about names and dates in other stories report polling results that are not the most reliable data available, but happen to be the most readily available.

8

Taking Stock

AFTER THE 2012 presidential election, an online poll-tracking service produced a list of currently active polling firms. The list included more than 1,200 companies. Collectively, the firms had conducted more than 37,000 polls. Nearly all had been conducted since the late 1990s. The top fifty firms alone were responsible for more than 25,000 polls.[1]

So many poll results were being released that CNN developed a "poll of polls" to average the daily results. A young statistician named Nate Silver gained national attention and a contract with the *New York Times* by producing a poll-based computer simulation predicting the odds of victory for particular candidates.

Hardly any of the polling companies publicized the exact methodology they used or the complete list of questions they asked. Pew, Gallup, and several of the national newspaper polls were among the few that did. It was impossible to know how many of the polls included questions about religion. Chances were high that questions about religious preference, attendance at worship services, and whether a person was born again appeared in many of the polls. Those had become standard practice in making predictions of how the public would vote.

It was not surprising that people were growing weary of being polled. To conduct those 37,000 polls, the polling companies' machines had probably dialed Americans' phones more than three billion times. The average family would have been phoned thirty times. A majority of the calls would have been made at dinnertime, when pollsters hoped at least a few of those called would answer.

Yet there was no denying that polling was a flourishing business. Election campaigns costing hundreds of millions of dollars considered it necessary to conduct regular polls to determine how their candidates were doing. No sooner was an election over than polling for the next election began.

With polls happening every day, no aspect of religion—no aspect at least that might be worthy of a headline or sound bite—escaped attention. Was the pope popular? Did people think the president was a Muslim? Could a Mormon get elected? How much did atheists know about religion? Was religion good for kids? Were religious groups losing ground? Should Democrats talk more about religion? Should Republicans talk less about it? Is Easter important? Did Jesus rise from the dead? Do pets go to heaven? Pollsters had the answers.

Pushback came from many quarters. It happened in letters to the editor, on websites, and in blogs. When it focused on religion, it rarely dealt specifically with polls. It criticized what religion had become, taking pollsters' depiction of it as gospel truth, decrying how it was being "wrenched from the personal and prophetic to the partisan and political," as one critic observed.[2]

But polling was clearly involved. How the public knew religion was partisan and political was apparent not only because public figures talked about religion but also because polls gauged the public's reactions to what they said. Even in arguing that religion was too political, a critic might consider it useful to cite a poll about religion and politics to make the case.

The broader concerns that had been expressed in the late 1990s about declining response rates had done little to deter the major polling agencies from producing polls. Only by paying closer attention to information buried on pollsters' websites would an average consumer of polling information have known how low the response rates had sunk. Pollsters with the greatest credibility satisfied themselves that the information they produced was just as good if it came from 9 percent of the persons they hoped to sample as from 60 or 70 percent. They said little in public releases about the potential problems and did nothing to suggest that trends might be affected. The proof was in the pudding, which meant predicting election outcomes within the same 3 to 5 percent margin of error as every other polling agency.

All seemed well during the 2012 presidential election, with two exceptions. One was the Obama campaign's public postmortem, which acknowledged that it had not relied at all on the usual sorts of national polls publicized in newspapers and on television. Instead, the campaign had focused on swing states and in those locations relied on multiple indicators drawn as much from social media and marketing information as from polls.[3] The Romney campaign, which because of the polls it conducted believed Romney was going to win, acknowledged that the Obama campaign had better information. The other exception was an embarrassing lack of accuracy in the predictions from the nation's most venerable polling firm. Gallup's estimates deviated markedly from those of nearly every other organization.[4]

Gallup's investigation of where it had gone wrong suggested that no single culprit could be identified. Some likely voters had been misidentified. A few time zones and ethnic groups had been underrepresented. An experiment in using listed rather than random landline telephone numbers proved faulty as well. None of the problems indicated anything serious or beyond repair in future studies, the investigation concluded, but clearly the errors did not help the firm's reputation.[5]

None of that would have related to religion had it not been for the concurrent publication of Gallup President Frank Newport's book *God Is Alive and Well*. Citing Gallup's extensive polling involving daily samples totaling some 350,000 individuals annually, Newport argued that Americans were as likely as at any time in the past three decades to consider religion important and predicted that a religious renaissance might be in the making. True, he conceded, a fifth of the public claimed to have no religion, but they should not be considered devoid of religiousness. Only a few were atheists and, for that matter, religion was still exercising an important role in the nation's life. The book received widespread attention. Religious leaders who had worried that God's popularity was declining, one could imagine, breathed a sigh of relief.[6]

With few exceptions, then, the polling community's capacity to produce more information at less cost even in the face of declining response rates and rising public distrust—including information about religion—seemed undiminished. But the problem of declining response rates was gaining some attention within the polling community. Critics recited the usual view that low response rates were not necessarily a problem and that pollsters did not agree on what constituted reasonable rates, but they then pressed the polling community to provide better answers than that. If bias was not necessarily present, better efforts could at least be made, critics said, to name poll results for what they were. In reporting results about Internet use, for example, would it not make sense, one critic suggested, to quit reporting that "one in five U.S. adults doesn't use the Internet" and more truthfully report "of the 9 percent of U.S. adults who respond to telephone opinion surveys, one in five doesn't use the Internet"?[7]

That suggestion, clearly meant to cast doubt on the accuracy of poll results, mostly went unheeded. Commentators on CNN, MSNBC, and Fox News continued to report poll results as "X percent of Americans believe this" or "Y percent of Americans believe that." Only in print journalism did there appear to be an implicit backing away from the view that polls actually represented "Americans." Careful reporting gradually shifted to statements such as "a majority of those responding to a recent Gallup poll" said such and such.

As it had a decade earlier, Pew took up the challenge of examining how biased its information might be. Comparing results from its 9 percent response rate polls with government surveys in which upward of 75 percent responded, it again reported reassuring results. Apparently it did not matter much if hardly anyone responded to its polls. Whatever small discrepancies might be present in the race, age, gender, or geographic location of those who did respond could be weighted away.[8]

But there were some striking differences. Fifty-five percent of Pew's respondents had volunteered for an organization in the past year, compared with only 27 percent in government surveys. There were huge differences in the percentages that said they talked with their neighbors (58 versus 41 percent) and in the percentages having contacted a public official in the past year (31 versus 10 percent). The government surveys did not include questions about religion, but volunteering, talking with neighbors, and contacting public officials were topics shown in other studies to be correlated with greater involvement in religion. The Pew study, in fact, showed that 43 percent of volunteers attended religious services weekly, compared with only 25 percent of nonvolunteers, and adding a weighting factor to compensate for the underrepresentation of volunteers, the estimate of weekly church attendance fell from 35 percent to 29 percent—an error of approximately thirteen million people. "Just what other attributes might differentiate survey respondents from the average American? On most issues that Pew studies, we may never know," one columnist wrote, "because there aren't government benchmarks."[9]

Further analysis of the data did suggest potential biases in several other measures of religion because of the overrepresentation of people who volunteered. Fifty percent of volunteers said most people can be trusted, compared with only 32 percent of nonvolunteers. Only 12 percent of the volunteers were nonreligious, but 18 percent of the nonvolunteers were. Among the former, 40 percent were Protestants, compared with 35 percent of the latter. Forty-three percent of the volunteers were born-again evangelicals, but only 36 percent of the nonvolunteers were. The volunteers were also significantly more likely than nonvolunteers to be Republicans and to agree with the Tea Party.[10]

Declining response rates were also becoming a matter of serious concern among academic researchers. Having prided themselves on studies with significantly higher response rates than those attained by polling firms, it worried them that their own studies were falling short of previous standards. They perhaps did not have quite the incentive that pollsters did to argue that nothing was amiss and that information about trends was as credible as ever. But the grants and contracts on which academic funding depended and the journals in which results were published included response rates among the criteria used in selecting whose work received support and whose did not.

An investigation in 2003 of how the leading social science journals treated response rates found considerable variation in what was expected and what was done. None of the eighteen journals included in the study required that response rates be reported or specified a minimum acceptable level. About a quarter of the papers published provided specific response rate information, though, and most of the others included some information about response rates. Only 5 percent provided no information. In view of declining confidence in polls and surveys, the investigation concluded that more needed to be done to ensure conformity with high standards in academic journals. It recommended that journal editors emphasize "full disclosure standards for reporting survey nonresponse" and that authors be required to meet these standards.[11]

Other evidence documented that response rates were declining even in the most carefully done and most highly respected surveys. In government-funded National Health Interview Surveys, for example, response rates above 80 percent in 1997 fell to 66 percent in 2011. Over the same period, the response rate in National Household Education Surveys declined from 81 percent to 22 percent. In the National Immunization Survey, it dropped from 87 percent in 1995 to 64 percent in 2010. And the Survey of Consumer Attitudes on which national consumer confidence estimates were based registered a response rate below 40 percent by 2004, compared to rates above 70 percent in the late 1970s.[12]

Responding to the concerns, the National Research Council, whose members are drawn from the councils of the National Academy of Sciences, the National Academy of Engineering, and the Institute of Medicine, conducted a major investigation of declining response rates, focusing especially on implications for information obtained by federal statistical agencies. Panelists included distinguished government statisticians and academic survey researchers. The report examined bias associated with nonresponse, approaches to mitigating the problem, and topics on which additional information was needed. It called for research about the public's changing attitudes toward surveys, why people do or do not take part in surveys, and how changes in technology and communication patterns might be contributing to the problem.[13]

Meanwhile, the American Academy of Political and Social Science assembled a team of leading survey researchers to study the problem of declining response rates as well. Led by distinguished scholars with extensive experience in conducting surveys and analyzing survey results, the team documented the numerous ways in which surveys were used to provide valuable national data, described the precipitous decline in response rates, examined its sources and implications, and presented the results of various experiments aimed at curbing the problem.[14]

The reports from these inquiries explicitly agreed that low response rates in polls and surveys are problematic and implicitly concluded that efforts to remedy the problem were likely to have limited success. Focusing on the problem did underscore the importance of attaching greater significance to the results from high-response surveys than from low-response polls. Even though polling information may be easily publicized, that ease should not be the reason for journalists to report polling results as if they were completely credible while ignoring different results from higher-quality studies. The reports also urged researchers to make public the details about response rates and to conduct transparent investigations of potential biases. While addressed chiefly to academic researchers, the reports demonstrated that response rates considerably higher than those in polls could be attained if greater efforts were made. That possibility may have be out of the question for polls that need to be conducted quickly and cheaply, but the reports suggested that money for polls about religion would be better spent on fewer high-quality polls than on more frequent low-quality polls.

The challenge of successfully conducting accurate polls even by expending large sums of money, though, became evident when the Pew Research Center attempted to conduct a landmark study of American Jews. In order to assess trends that took place since previous studies in the 1990s and around the turn of the century, Pew went to great lengths to achieve better results than ordinary political polls. Fielded by commercial polling firm Abt SRBI, the study took four months to complete, involved more than forty thousand hours of interviewer time, and included dialing more than a million telephone numbers. The questions went through two rounds of pretesting, more than two hundred of the interviews were conducted in Russian, and to enhance response rates an incentive of $50 was offered to every eligible respondent. Both landline phone numbers and cell phone numbers were included in the sample. Yet with all that effort, the response rate for the study was only 24 percent for the landline sample and 14 percent for the cell phone sample—an overall response rate of only 16 percent. In short, five-sixths of the people who should have been contacted to make the study truly representative were missing.[15]

The Jewish Americans study lent itself to several competing interpretations of polling's place in American religion. A sympathetic conclusion held, in effect, that flawed information is still better than no information. In this view, the extra time and effort required to elevate response rates from 9 percent to 16 percent were worth it. True, the results might be skewed, but pollsters could be trusted to tweak the data with statistical weights until the results were credible. A less sympathetic assessment wondered if that was truly the best a commercial polling agency could do. Indeed, why was the response rate so low when academic and government surveys were still capable of achieving 60 to 70 percent response rates? Had the public perhaps become so distrustful of commercial polling firms that the die was cast no matter how hard they tried?

As it happened, the most critical responses to the Jewish Americans study underscored another difficulty. Pew's interpretation of the study's key results was that huge numbers of Jews were abandoning religion. The basis for this conclusion was that the percentage of Jews claiming to have no religion had risen from only 7 percent in 2000 to 22 percent in 2013. The problem was that the figure from 2000 was not comparable to the one from 2013 because the earlier study had set aside interviewees with weak Jewish connections. And when comparisons were made with better data collected in 1990, those data showed that about the same proportion of Jews—20 percent—said they had no religion as did in 2013.[16]

Within the polling community itself, the larger question was whether to stick with telephone interviewing at all or to switch to the various online methods that might be cheaper. The argument drawn from the major efforts to test online polling that had been taking place for nearly a decade was not only that it was less expensive; the argument was also that (a) whatever weighting procedures might be needed were no worse than the weighting schemes that were already used in telephone polls to compensate for low response rates, and (b) comparisons of the results to specific questions using the two methods showed few differences.[17]

The debate over the two methods, though, suggested the extent to which the polling industry's decisions depended on in-house traditions. When the *New York Times* and CBS News decided to use online survey panels for their election coverage in 2014, the decision was roundly criticized by several leading pollsters who believed firmly in telephone sampling. Surely the switch to online polling was a bad idea, critics argued, because probability sampling was the only way to generate reliable statistics and, for that matter, many Americans would be excluded because they did not have access to the Internet.[18]

To some in the polling community, the criticisms rang hollow because the low response rates and hefty weighting procedures used in telephone results already rendered the kind of statistical inferences based on accurate probability sampling meaningless. It also seemed disingenuous to emphasize the lack of Internet access when studies showed that as high a proportion of households—more than 80 percent—had Internet access as had landline phones or cell phones.

Few of the discussions in the polling community or among academic survey researchers suggested that polls and surveys would become obsolete or argued that they should. Nor did any of them focus specifically on polls about religion. However, they did underscore the need for further discussions and research about the challenges and opportunities facing investigations based on the collection and analysis of quantitative information. The proliferation of efficient inexpensive polling methods producing data of varying quality, together with the public's apparent fatigue with being polled and its declining confidence in the value of such information, pointed especially to the need for such discussions. The stocktaking of polls and surveys in general suggested the need to consider what the changing impact of polls may have been on specific topics as well. Four such topics bear particular relevance to polling's understanding of religion: generalizations, categories, concepts, and contexts.

Generalizations

Polls imply generalizations. The point of conducting polls in representative samples is to derive results that can be generalized to a population.

The selling point that attracted interest in the first Gallup polls was their ability to produce information generalizable to the American population from a sample of fewer than two thousand people.

Polls that produced generalizations about the national population—about America, Americans, and the American public—were of particular interest. They spoke to the nation's historical awareness of itself as a distinct people. They demonstrated the extent of its distinctness and unity during World War II and the Cold War when national identity and broad social cohesion were greatly valued. Evidence of Americans' pervasive belief in God and comparatively high levels of churchgoing, Bible reading, and prayer contributed to that sense of underlying cultural agreement. If there had always been an idea of something generalizable about religion in America, polls provided grist for those generalizations.

That interest in generalizations about American religion has remained strong. Hundreds if not thousands of polls have reinforced it by describing what Americans in general think, believe, and do in terms of questions about God, attendance at religious services, and the value that individuals attach to religion. Interest in those generalizations is continually reinforced by the fact that national elections occur as often as they do and by evidence that religion matters to how the public, or at least to that part of the public considered likely voters, thinks about candidates and important issues of the day.

These generalizations about American religion are of wide interest and are generally accepted without debate as meaningful information despite the fact that religion in the United States is highly diverse, as is the nation itself, and, indeed, has become considerably more diverse in the decades since polling was invented. That diversity finds acknowledgment most often below the headlines in details of how Americans of different genders, age cohorts, races, or levels of educational attainment responded to the questions asked.

But polls that generalize about American religion privilege the religious beliefs and practices of the majority, suggesting that some abstract notion of "religion" truly characterizes "America" when it may not describe the religious beliefs and practices of the many diverse minority groups that make up the nation very well at all. The majority's responses are privileged for no other reason than the fact that they contribute more than the responses of minorities to overall summary statistics such as percentages and means. One of the consequences is inadvertent white norming.

White norming is the phenomenon of drawing generalizations about the American public, meaning all of the American population, based on evidence that mostly reflects the sampled responses of the white majority. It occurs implicitly in statements about how many Americans believe in God or regularly attend religious services. It may also occur explicitly when generalizations are specifically based on white responses. Both are driven not only by the accepted convention of generalizing about America but also by practical considerations associated with sampling, as in the case, for example, of a poll of a thousand respondents in which perhaps the number of African-American respondents is too small for the polling firm to feel that separate generalizations can be drawn. The problem is exacerbated when racial minorities are underrepresented, as was true in early Gallup surveys. It is present as well in recent low-response polls that attempt to weight underrepresentation away but in so doing skew results in ways that do not reflect differences between respondents and nonrespondents.

White norming provides a useful illustration of how population surveys may produce generalizations that pertain to whoever the majority may be while misrepresenting the minority. The kinds of misrepresentation that may occur can be shown in several examples from actual studies. One example is a comparison of white and black levels of religiosity showing that they may be affected by low response rates. Most national studies confirm the popular impression that levels of religiosity are somewhat higher among African Americans than among white Americans. That difference is consistent and significant in surveys with high response rates.[19] However, in some surveys with low response rates it disappears. The reason it disappears is that early respondents who are white tend in some surveys to attend religious services at higher rates than hard-to-reach respondents who are white, whereas the opposite is true among African Americans. Thus, in surveys including only the easiest-to-reach respondents, white attendance is overestimated and black attendance is underestimated.[20]

A second example of potential bias associated with white norming is evident in a study of trends in religious service attendance among high school students between the 1970s and late 1990s. The author of the study noticed a downward trend in attendance in national samples of students, but when she looked at blacks and whites separately, she discovered that the trend among white students was pronounced while the rates of attendance among black students had not declined. That observation led her to examine the reasons for the difference, which she concluded pertained to differences in students' relationships to working mothers—attendance was affected more by white mothers' increasing involvement in the labor force than by black mothers' longer-term involvement.[21]

A third example suggests the possibility of white norming producing misleading conclusions about religiosity among African Americans. In large national studies in which standard questions about attendance at religious service, being born again, having a religious preference, and considering religion important are taken as adequate measures of religiosity, African Americans register only slightly higher levels of religiosity than white Americans. But in a national study in which African Americans were oversampled and regarded as the focus of the survey, different questions showed much larger differences in levels of religiosity. African Americans were only somewhat more likely than white Americans to attend religious services weekly, but on average they spent about 50 percent more time attending those services. They were also significantly more likely to express religious commitment on other measures, such as praying for and helping fellow members of their congregation.[22]

White norming is only an example of the various ways in which studies that generalize about American religion miss or produce misleading generalizations unless care is taken to consider what exactly the generalizations represent. Religious minorities are another instance in which the problem is frequently evident.

An example from discussions of response rates concerns the presence or absence of Jews in a hypothetical sample survey. In support of the argument that high response rates do not necessarily reduce bias, the hypothetical case has been used of a survey in which the 3 percent of the population who were Jewish did not respond because of being offended by something in how the purpose of the survey was described. If everyone else responded, the argument suggests, the survey would have a 97 percent response rate but would still be biased because of the absence of Jews.

But the example is actually more instructive if it is considered in the real world and apart from questions about nonresponse. In nearly every national poll of a thousand respondents, the response rate among Jews is likely to be as high as among non-Jews but only twenty-five to thirty Jews are included. In this instance, generalizations about American religion involve Christian norming. Any conclusions that may be drawn about Americans' level of religious attendance may be fairly accurate for

Christians but totally inaccurate for Jews. They may be inaccurate not only because Jews composed only 3 percent of the sample, but also because regular attendance at worship services is a better measure of religious commitment among Christians than among Jews or because standard questions about being born again or believing in Jesus do not apply at all.

The literature criticizing conventional polls about religion is replete with examples of biases associated with Christian majority norming. Studies of Jews and Muslims point to the need for greater attention to home practices and to the role of dress and bodily rituals. As the author of one such study remarked, "If pollsters got out from behind their computers and started following religious adherents around for a day or two, they'd find that far more than 20 percent know a whole lot about their religions. Their fingers and ears, noses and feet, *know* how to act, behave, move, and when to remain still." Pollsters' assumptions, the author contended, "betray a larger misconception concerning who religious people are and what they do. Questionnaires are still mired in the mostly-Protestant notion that religious people read holy books and have 'beliefs' in their heads. It makes for good fodder on the religion news circuits but necessarily leaves out the lived realities of religious existence."[23]

Studies of Buddhists and Hindus, as well as some Christian groups, underscore the importance of other topics seldom captured in polls, such as hybridity and multiple religious affiliations. Research on Buddhism in the United States demonstrates especially that the cultural impact of its practices cannot be measured by counting adherents. Many of these criticisms are reminiscent of the concerns about Protestant norming that led to studies that asked Catholics different questions. Critics argue that Protestant norming is evident even in current polling, either directly in the questions asked or in the inferences drawn. The "notion of religion understood as private assent to a set of propositional beliefs," one observer suggests, "depends on Protestant assumptions about what counts as 'religion,' even if we now mask these sectarian foundations with labels like 'Judeo-Christian.'"[24]

To its credit, the polling industry's attentiveness to religious diversity had been evident in such specialized polls as the Jewish Americans study and in comparable efforts to survey Muslims or to conduct sufficiently large studies that results can be reported separately for Pentecostals, Southern Baptists, Mormons, or Catholics. The statistical validity of these studies, of course, varies with sample sizes, response rates, and the screening questions used in the first place.

Among academic scholars of religion, the more serious reservation about polls and surveys' emphasis on generalization is that understandings of the value of generalizations themselves have changed. Social scientists' interests in generalizations during the heyday of polls and surveys rested on the positivistic assumption that these generalizations were *scientific*—meaning that they not only applied to a statistically representative sample but that they also described invariant patterns of human behavior that could be observed under any comparable conditions. But as research has accumulated and few such law-like generalizations have been found, social scientists' attention has shifted toward piecing together the complex factors, processes, and circumstances that shape particular beliefs and actions in particular contexts.

By combining qualitative and quantitative methods, scholars of religion have redirected their attention from generalizations about "Americans," "Protestants," "Jews," or "Southern Baptists" to questions about *how* religious practices are put together in various specific contexts and *what* may be involved in terms of space, communities, bodies, narratives, and social interaction. If anything, the proliferation of polling information about religion has become of less interest to scholars of religion for these reasons than was true a few decades ago.

Categories

Categorization is one of the principal differences between qualitative and quantitative research. An ethnographic study of a congregation may observe that worshippers talk in complex ways about their faith, sometimes citing personal experiences and linking those to the gatherings in which they participate, and sometimes listening to familiar stories from sacred texts. A survey would likely classify worshippers by whether they were men or women, attended every week or less often, and were or were not born again.

Surveys rarely make up categories that have no meaning or relevance at all in everyday life. Or if they do, it would be unusual to find that the categories made much difference to anything else. But surveys are one of the ways that participants and the public who hears about them are invited to think about themselves. When polls are as frequent as they have become, they provide reinforcement for particular categories.

Polls sort people into different religious traditions, denominations, clusters of denominations, levels of religious participation, and varieties of belief. A person may be classified variously as religious, a churchgoer, a born-again Christian, an evangelical, a conservative Protestant, a fundamentalist, a Baptist, or an Independent Baptist. Some of those categories existed independently of polls, but polls have shaped the meaning of others. The Gallup polls that gave evangelicalism new meaning in the 1970s are an example. Despite pushback from evangelical leaders and from social scientists, pollsters intent on documenting trends used the same questions again and again.

In some respects, the polling industry has done a better job over the years of refining the categories in which the public is asked to express itself religiously. Instead of being divided crudely into Protestants, Catholics, and Jews, pollees are sometimes categorized into various Protestant denominational families, such as Baptist and Methodist, and in the most-detailed polls are sorted into particular varieties of Baptists and Methodists. And yet, the simplest categories continue to be used routinely by pollsters intent on little more than showing how some overarching binary, such as born again or not born again, matters in politics. The further problem is that other meaningful distinctions are ignored.

New questions identifying new categories often depend on the occurrence of a significant event, such as the 9/11 attacks. That, or the categories arise from pollsters' whims, like asking if pets go to heaven. When an issue sticks, the categories harden. Soon, the public can be only for abortion or against it—in favor of evolution or intelligent design or both. With good reason, people complain about question wording and look to sources other than polls for better information.

Wiki surveys have emerged as a creative alternative to standard polling. These are open online forums in which interested respondents provide information about topics of potential interest. Unlike the top-down decisions made by pollsters, wiki surveys elicit information quickly and inexpensively from the wider public. By 2012, about 1,500 wiki surveys had been done, collecting information about some 60,000 ideas and involving more than 2.5 million votes. The simple procedure involves posing paired alternatives, asking respondents to make a choice, and using iterations to determine overall preferences.[25] Catholic Relief Services is an example of a religious organization that has used wiki surveys. The method lends itself well to exploring the most and least appealing aspects of worship services, descriptions of religious identities, and priorities for social service activities.

Whether categories are generated inductively or deductively, though, the focus on polls and surveys is to simplify a complex world so that it can be studied through comparisons among a relatively small number of categories. While cognitive science has given support to the claim that human thinking involves such simplifications, the main direction of social science theorizing in recent years has been to argue that these categories are socially constructed and thus more fluid, complex, and arbitrary than might otherwise be supposed. If categories such as race and gender appear as straightforward distinctions in polls, social scientists' interest has shifted increasingly to questions about why the meanings of these distinctions vary from place to place.

The standard polling question asking pollees to respond yes or no with regard to having been "born again" is a case in point. The reason the question persists in polls is because it provides a crude indication of the likelihood that someone will vote Republican or support some political issue, such as legislation against abortion or same-sex marriage. Despite the frequency with which polls have asked the question, polling has done a poor job of illuminating much of what being "born again" means. In contrast, most of the qualitative research on the topic demonstrates that conversion is a process that is narratively constructed and if anything involves more than a binary distinction.

Concepts

The polling community rarely identifies the concepts underlying the questions it asks. Polling nevertheless informs the concepts that interpreters of American religion use. Secularization is one example. Secularization was once understood to have taken place over several centuries and to have consisted of changes in the institutional authority of religious organizations.[26] Polls redefined it. It now meant a measurable decline from year to year in religious attendance and belief in God. Secularization was happening if polls said it was.[27]

Religious "nones" is a related example. The meaning of this concept stems entirely from polls. That meaning is quite different from historical understandings. To be British was to be Anglican and to be Swedish was to be Lutheran, whether one attended services and believed in God or not. Why "none" should have recently become of such interest has seemed curious. Since polling began, the proportion of pollees who attended religious services only once a year or less has never been below

30 percent, and if census statistics about membership in religious bodies are believed, Americans were less religiously involved in the nineteenth century than they were in the twentieth.[28]

Another example is religion itself. The standard "what is your religion" question assumes that pollees share enough of the pollster's understanding of religion to give a meaningful answer. But their ability to answer may be uniquely a function of the frequency with which polls are conducted. Unlike age, sex, and race, religion has no biological referent. Unlike marital status, it has no legal basis. The religion question assumes that people can respond meaningfully even though half rarely attend religious services and are not members of a congregation. Those who do attend may go where the word religion is not used and where people come from different backgrounds. And yet, people willingly answer the question, whether the question reflects how they think about themselves in ordinary life or not.

One of the most significant developments in academic studies of religion in recent years has been an emphasis on religious *practice*—a concept that in polls and surveys easily comes to mean attendance at worship services or frequency of prayer. That understanding of practice has been useful insofar as the study of religious *individuals* is concerned. But it is less useful when interest turns to religious communities and the informal everyday social situations in which religious practice occurs. Unsurprisingly, the religious practices observed in polls and surveys appear to be individualistic and driven by personal interests and dispositions. Those conclusions, however, have increasingly been challenged by studies showing the extent to which seemingly individualistic religious practices are located in social networks and shaped by the institutions with which individuals interact. Understandings of religious practices direct attention especially toward the particular situations in which religious behavior and discourse occur and take on meaning.

Contexts

A further distortion associated with polling is thus to extract responses from individuals with regard only to broad demographic categories such as race, gender, region, and denominational tradition without regard to how religious beliefs and activities become activated in specific situations. The same response to a survey question about yoga may indicate something about religion in one context and not in another. Confucianism may or may not be an appropriate response to "what is your religion?" Church participation may increase the chances of voting Republican in one congregation but have the opposite effect in another congregation. Polls pay little attention to these contextual variations. The information is from individuals and about individuals. It aggregates their responses to create a fictional entity called "the public." In reality, the public is the 9 percent of cooperative people with sampled phone numbers who happen to respond. They believe as individuals, hold religious preferences as individuals, and attend religious services as individuals.[29] About the only thing known about their contexts in where they live. Nothing is known about their friends, who they see in their neighborhoods, and what they talk about with people at work. They are not *at* their places of worship, engaged in prayer, or reveling from a moment of awe. The group style that influences how they talk about their faith is bracketed out.[30]

Polling also assumes firm identities. It taps beliefs and activities stable enough to warrant generalizations. It identifies a decontextualized public describable in percentages about this or that. That information accumulates and registers in the background as apparent facts about people out there with which a person may or may not identify. It invites those comparisons even though the lived experience of religion, as of life itself, occurs in the immediate spaces of daily reality.

Whatever else it may do, polling considers the individual person as the appropriate unit for investigation. The fact that religion is practiced in congregations and among friends and families in everyday life is missed. Those social aspects of religion could be examined in polls. But the polling industry prefers to imagine its results generalizing about individual citizens—usually the ones who expect to vote. Where does one learn about the relationships among like-minded believers and how their practices are connected with clergy, experiences in worship, and the taken-for-granted norms of congregations and communities? Not from polls.

Challenges

The challenges persons interested in religion face in view of the prevalence of polling are of two kinds: ones pertaining specifically to religion, and ones pertaining to polls regardless of the topic. The former are amply discussed. Quantification is of limited value. It gives an aura of precision to say that Pew and Gallup show 90 percent of Americans believe in God, but the numbers say nothing about *what* people believe about God or how they experience God in their lives. Lacking historical background and evidence from archives and qualitative interviews, it is impossible to know if a poll about Americans' attitudes toward Muslims or atheists or evangelical Christians is reason for hope or despair or is yet another meaningless datum.

The challenges pertaining to polling itself are of a different order. Taking the limitations of quantitative information into account, it matters if that information is reasonably trustworthy or not. The response from a growing number of pollees suggests that they think it is not. Academic social scientists' view of polling's trustworthiness is mixed. As long as polling is understood to provide some information about the opinions of some share of the public—as long as any ballpark estimate is better than none—polling is what it is. But if it matters that polling produces dubious results, then caution is warranted.

The question is whether the challenges are so great that polls will—or should—become a relic of the past. A polling industry worth hundreds of millions of dollars and claiming to be the only reliable source of information about major social and political trends is unlikely to let that happen. But there are good reasons to predict its partial demise.

The main threat to polling is big data. During the second half of the twentieth century, polls were the source of big data on anything not covered by the US census. They showcased numbers to outsmart anyone who did not have numbers. But the big data of polls is now outdone by bigger data collected from the likes of Google, Microsoft, and Facebook.

For religion, the polls that have offered little beyond estimates of how many people attend services or belong to different denominations can easily be replaced. Want to know which states are most or least religious? An expensive phone poll of thousands of people is superfluous. A sample-matched Internet poll is cheaper. But even that is unnecessary because Google can report how many searches in each state include words about religion. If poll estimates about churchgoing are off by tens of millions anyway, it may be as instructive to compare weekly variation in Facebook or Twitter mentions about religious participation. And if a political campaign wants to target a message about religion to a particular constituency, it can monitor website hits or send e-mails through friendship networks purchased from social media companies.[31]

What descriptive information of that kind may lack, Web-based experiments can supplement. An expensive national survey is hardly the most economical way to learn if fundamentalist Christians are more likely than nonfundamentalists to favor abortion or despise Muslims. An inexpensive Web-based experiment can pose a variety of implicit and explicit scenarios to see what exactly prompts differences in response. Meanwhile, peer reviewers are raising hard-to-answer concerns about nonresponse and bias in survey data.

The polling elite has called for greater transparency. Transparency means disclosing more of the basic information that polling organizations have come to agree is crucial for assessing the quality of polling results. That includes the method of sampling and interviewing, how many people were interviewed, a statistical estimate of sampling error, the response rate, and the exact wording of the questions asked. When pressed about transparency, the most common response from polling firms is that this information can be found on a website. In addition, the most reputable polling firms make complete data sets available following an initial embargo so that interested persons can conduct further analysis.

That interpretation of transparency has proven to be a half-measure that addresses fewer concerns than it answers. An interesting case in point emerged in conjunction with reports about corrective measures to be taken in view of declining response rates. The proposal was for surveys and polls to move toward a Multi-level Integrated Database Approach (MIDA). MIDA would secure all possible information about the households from which survey samples would be selected and use that information to measure and correct for biases from nonresponse and missing information of other kinds. The data of potential use ranged from household information that telephone companies and the Internet provides or marketing firms might be willing to divulge, to census tract information, to data obtained from screening polls themselves in which questions were asked about household composition and numbers and kinds of telephones. It was a reasonable and attractive idea that took into account how conventional surveys could benefit from big data of other kinds.[32]

But it posed difficulties about how such information could also pass the test of transparency. Simply having that much information at the level of individual households breached standards of privacy that human subjects protection under federal mandate by Institutional Review Boards would in most cases consider unacceptable. If survey organizations had such information, they would not be allowed to make it available for public consumption. In fact, they already sanitize data sets of telephone numbers, addresses, geospatial coordinates, and related information that might make it possible for individual respondents to be identified.[33]

Information of other kinds, though, could reasonably be made available without compromising the privacy of individual respondents. Current practice includes disclosing no information about nonrespondents or about potential respondents who have been screened out for various purposes. Yet some of that information is often available with the data sets from which random telephone numbers are dialed. Such information could help, as the MIDA proposal suggests, in fine-tuning information about differences between respondents and nonrespondents.

A better sense of potential nonresponse bias could be determined if poll results systematically included information about the number of attempts required to reach each respondent. The data sets in which such information has been made publicly available are revealing, but too few of those data sets are available over a long enough period to determine how trends may have been affected by different numbers of attempts and declining response rates. Additional information about which respondents were interviewed first and the days of the week on which the interviews were conducted is sometimes helpful as well.

Other information that needs to be included is implied by concerns about framing and interviewer effects. Although disclosing the exact wording of questions is an important step in the right direction, that information alone is less than satisfactory. The opening statements interviewers use in contacting respondents and telling them what the study is about should always be disclosed. It can make a considerable difference if those opening statements do or do not include the name of the polling company and mention religion, current events, politics, or an upcoming election. Besides that, interviewer instructions should be specified in such a way that further analysis can determine what the effects of those instructions may have been. If a question asks how often people attend religious services, but leaves it to the interviewer's discretion to read a list of categories or not, the results are difficult to compare with other studies in which categories are always read.

Question sequencing, the number of questions asked, respondent fatigue, and interviewer fatigue are additional sources of potential bias. Although these are noted in textbook treatments of survey research, studies documenting bias have suggested growing cause for concern. Omnibus surveys that cover multiple topics can inadvertently introduce bias by adding questions or altering the sequence in which questions are asked. Those biases can affect conclusions about trends. For example, a question about frequency of newspaper reading to which an increasing proportion of respondents respond negatively might elevate the tendency to give negative answers to subsequent questions about other topics. A standard technique for reducing some of the potential bias from question sequencing has been to randomly rotate the order in which questions are asked. However, that information is seldom as fully available as it should be. In addition, response categories that start with a particular option (such as "yes" or "agree") are rarely rotated to start with different options. When respondents are bombarded with rapid-fire questions by an interviewer hoping to complete as many interviews in as short a time as possible, response-set bias can be serious.

Studies of respondent fatigue and interviewer fatigue have underscored additional concerns. One study found that a significant increase in the proportion of respondents who said they had no friends was shown in a subsequent analysis to have attained that result as an artifact of respondent fatigue. Respondent fatigue was evident because the more recent data were obtained through a sequence of questions that communicated to respondents that they would spare themselves from having to answer tedious questions about their friends if they simply denied having any. Further analysis also suggested that interviewer fatigue was involved. Like the respondents, interviewers were eager to avoid asking tedious questions, so they implicitly communicated that denying having any friends was fine.[34]

The bearing of that on transparency is that information needs to be recorded and made available for subsequent analysis about potential biases due to respondent and interviewer fatigue. The recording part is straightforward because interviewing software typically records the time an interview begins, when it ends, and a code indicating who the interviewer was. Making that information available would be the obvious next step.

Transparency, though, is of little value unless opportunities for independent scrutiny and discussion are part of the process. The pushback from polling's critics stems from the fact that pollsters have done their own analyses of potential bias but have been less open to independent analysis or suggestions from critics. An internal analysis that suggests low response rates are seldom a serious problem at all seems on the surface to be about as convenient as police review boards exonerating all the cases they investigate. The concern increases when polling firms confidently report trends over a period of decades but offer no indication of how those trends have been affected by changes in polling methods and response rates.

Pollsters' assertions about transparency fall on deaf ears particularly when the results demonstrate that response rates are so low as to defy any reasonable standard of representativeness. If the response rates are that low, well-funded polling firms with enough money to conduct poor-quality polls every week or month might want to consider spending their money less often and more generously on a few high-quality polls.

Journalists bear responsibility for providing independent scrutiny of polls results instead of taking for granted that the polling industry's reports are credible. When print journalism was more economically viable than it has become in recent years, highly qualified journalists who specialized in reporting specifically about religion were able to include broader reflections and interpretations about poll results from scholars and religious leaders. The current practice is to report only the highlights, leaving it to curious consumers to consult the fine print on websites produced by the polling companies themselves.[35]

The role of academic institutions as settings for independent scrutiny of polls has waxed and waned. The different purposes and styles of research in academic settings and in commercial polling served as a source of constructive tension and criticism during much of the past half-century. The current possibility is that commercial polling has lost so much credibility that academically based researchers will distance themselves from it entirely.

The best way to guard against that happening is in structured settings in which conversation across disciplines, sectors, and styles of research occurs. It makes no sense for polling organizations to host such gatherings without significant input from scholars critical of polling. Nor is it helpful for academic programs to discuss religion as if polling did not exist.

Impressions gleaned from blogs and anonymous online discussions of polling suggest that a certain segment of the public is fed up, frustrated, and angry that polls are in the news as much as they are and yet increasingly of dubious value or validity. It is no longer possible, as polling experts did for many years, to argue that polling and survey research are in their infancy. They are at least in middle age, possibly approaching senility.

"Perhaps the greatest threat to the future of survey data," the editors of the special American Academy project concluded, "is ultimately the lack of public recognition for the importance of statistical and scientific surveys." Whether that threat reflected a deeper anti-scientific,

anti-intellectual sentiment or whether it stemmed specifically from suspicion about the value of polls was unclear. Nor was that the point. It was
a matter of serious concern that required something other than business
as usual. At minimum, the time was ripe for an "industry-wide effort to
improve the image of survey research."[36]

What that means for polls about elections, as well as for studies of
topics such as health and family finances, has been the focus of lively
debate. What it means for religion is more difficult to determine. During
the formative years of national polling, religion was a sideshow, tagged
onto studies of political opinion because it happened to be of public interest. But when entire polls and entire polling firms focused on religion, it
became impossible for religious leaders and scholars of religion to ignore
the public presence of that information. The tendencies then were either
to dismiss it as if it did not matter or to accept it at face value. Neither tendency was constructive.

The criticisms that have become more pronounced in recent years as
a result of the difficulties pollsters face are, in this respect, welcome. The
difficulties should encourage closer and more critical scrutiny of polls
about religion. The scrutiny could be beneficial if it extended from wor-
ries about response rates to a larger discussion about what is being tapped
in polls and whether the investment is worth it. In the absence of such
considerations, little progress in understanding religion is likely. Religion
can be regarded as something so special that nothing about it should ever
be quantified at all, or it can be viewed as a topic that lends itself mar-
velously well to the simple conclusions that polls provide. In either case,
much more about religion remains to be understood.

Acknowledgments

I AM PARTICULARLY grateful to Sera Chung for assistance with archival research and interviewing and to Samantha Jaroszewski, Karen Myers, Grace Tien, and Maggi Van Dorn for assistance in conducting in-depth qualitative interviews. The research was supported with funding provided by the Office of the Provost at Princeton University. Donna Defrancisco and Cindy Gibson provided faithful office assistance, and Jay Barnes kept the technology running smoothly. Courtney Bender, Jon Butler, Elaine Ecklund, and Judith Weisenfeld provided valuable input.

Ideas for the research took shape over many years, starting with my initial exposure to and fascination with surveys of religion in the late 1960s and the opportunity to work as a research assistant at the Survey Research Center at the University of California at Berkeley as a graduate student in sociology in the early 1970s. Charles Glock served patiently and generously as a mentor during those years. In the 1980s, after joining the sociology department at Princeton University, I was privileged to become acquainted with Andrew Kohut at the Gallup Organization and to participate in small ways in several of the religion surveys conducted by George Gallup Jr. Several of my own research projects, starting in the late 1980s, received funding from the Lilly Endowment, Pew Charitable Trusts, and other foundations, which made it possible to include surveys as well as information from qualitative interviews and archival materials. Through those projects, I also served on the board of the General Social Survey and received the Warren Mitofsky Award from the Roper Center for Public Opinion Research.

Directing Princeton University's Center for the Study of Religion provided the opportunity to interact regularly with dozens of graduate students and postdoctoral fellows interested in religion from such disciplines as anthropology, history, political science, religious studies, and sociology. Many of these students have gone on to publish books and pursue careers using various methods and working in polling firms, academic departments, and religious organizations. Interacting with these students, reading their work, and following their careers, as well as consuming information about religion from the media, have prompted the questions I have tried to address here about the relationship of polls to understandings of religion.

Having been as closely associated with the study of religion as I have been, I am keenly aware that my interpretation of the role that polls have played is uniquely my own. I hope that this interpretation garners some agreement, but my larger hope is that it will generate some pointed discussion and further scrutiny of what it has meant for polls about religion to be as common—and indeed as taken for granted—as they seem to be.

Notes

CHAPTER 1

1. F. Scott Fitzgerald, *This Side of Paradise* (New York: Scribner, 1920), 45.
2. Emil G. Hirsch, "Religion in the Home," *Chicago Daily Tribune* (November 27, 1899).

CHAPTER 2

1. Princeton Theological Seminary, letter dated October 31, 1881, Alumni Files, Princeton, New Jersey.
2. John McColl, *Records and Memories of Boston Church in the "Scotch Block,"* *Esquesing Township, County of Halton, Ontario, Canada, 1820–1920* (Georgetown, ON: Boston Church, 1920), 108.
3. Walter Laidlaw, "New York's Latest Movement toward Church Unity," *Outlook* (October 3, 1896), 604.
4. Walter Laidlaw, "Historic Sketch: The Federation of Churches and Christian Organizations in New York City," *Federation* 4 (1905), 1–32, 6.
5. "Federation for Christian Work," *New York Evangelist* (March 19, 1896), 9; "Religious Intelligence: Results of a Religious Canvass in New York," *The Independent* [New York] (October 15, 1896), 13.
6. "Sunday School Scholars Searched Out," *Boston Recorder* (April 28, 1830).
7. Isaac Willey, "Work of the American Bible Society," *New Hampshire Sentinel* [Keene, NH] (January 6, 1870).
8. "State Temperance Society," *New York Tribune* (January 15, 1870).
9. John C. Collins, "Religious Statistics," *Proceedings of the First Convention of Christian Workers in the United States and Canada* (Chicago, 1886), 8–10.
10. "City Church Canvass," *Jackson Citizen* [Jackson, MI] (November 19, 1895).
11. "News and Notes," *Boston Journal* (April 21, 1888).

12. Walter Laidlaw, "A Plea and Plan for a Cooperative Church Parish System in Cities," *American Journal of Sociology* 3 (1898), 795–808; Laidlaw, *Third Sociological Canvass: The Twenty-First Assembly District* (New York: Federation of Churches and Christian Workers in New York City, 1898), 4–5. A researcher who worked on the 1897 survey provided an account of the process: "Provided with the blanks used by the Federation of Churches the investigator knocked at the door of a tenement. Generally a voice from within would call out, 'Come in.' Quite often the voice would ask, 'What do you want?' And the visitor would answer, 'I want to know how many persons are in this family,' or in more difficult cases the answer was, 'I am taking a sociological census,' with emphasis on the last word." Thomas Jesse Jones, *The Sociology of a New York City Block* (New York: Columbia University Press, 1904), 10.

13. "The Census of the United States," *Scientific American* 63 (1890), 132; and for images of the first Hollerith machines, "Illustration 1," *Scientific American* 86 (1902), 269; subsequent developments and uses are discussed in Friedrich W. Kistermann, "The Invention and Development of the Hollerith Punched Card: In Commemoration of the 130th Anniversary of the Birth of Herman Hollerith and for the 100th Anniversary of Large Scale Data Processing," *Annals of the History of Computing* 13 (1991), 245–59; and Friedrich W. Kistermann, "Hollerith Punched Card System Development (1905–1913)," *Annals of the History of Computing* 27 (2005), 56–65.

14. Laidlaw, *Third Sociological Canvass*, 9; Laidlaw, "Historic Sketch," 14, with photos of the pantagraph and Hollerith electric tabulating machine on the following page.

15. "The Federation of Christian Churches," *New York Evangelist* (October 1, 1896), 7.

16. Initially termed "sanitary areas," they were called "census tracts" by the 1930s; Walter Laidlaw, "Federation Districts and a Suggestion for a Convenient and Scientific City Map System," *Federation* 4 (1906), 1–6; H. W. Green, "The Use of Census Tracts in Analyzing the Population of a Metropolitan Community," *Journal of the American Statistical Association* 28 (1933), 147–53; Nancy Krieger, "A Century of Census Tracts: Health and the Body Politic (1906–2006)," *Journal of Urban Health* 83 (2006), 355–61; Jon Butler, "Protestant Success in the New American City, 1870–1920: The Anxious Secrets of Rev. Walter Laidlaw, PhD," in *New Directions in American Religious History*, ed. Harry S. Stout and D. G. Hart (New York: Oxford University Press, 1997), 296–330.

17. The quote from Low in Harrison's letter is from Samuel McCune Lindsay's introduction to W. E. B. Du Bois, *The Philadelphia Negro: A Social Study* (Philadelphia: University of Pennsylvania Press, 1899), ix–x; "Historic Sketch," 1–32, especially pages 6 and 28 on Low's involvement.

18. Letter to Whom It May Concern from University of Pennsylvania Provost Charles C. Harrison, August 15, 1896, W. E. B. Du Bois Papers, Special Collections and University Archives, University of Massachusetts Amherst Libraries.

19. Family Schedule, Condition of the Negroes of Philadelphia, Ward 7, University of Pennsylvania, December 1, 1896, Du Bois Papers; W. E. B. Du Bois, *The Autobiography of W. E. B. Du Bois: A Soliloquy on Viewing My Life from the Last Decade of Its First Century* (New York: International, 1968), 198.

20. Du Bois, *The Philadelphia Negro*, 63; Du Bois mentions Laidlaw's 1896 and 1897 surveys in New York but does not indicate if Du Bois and Laidlaw were in contact during that time; Samuel McCune Lindsay, who as an assistant professor at the University of Pennsylvania advised Du Bois's project, was likely to have known Laidlaw after moving to Columbia University in 1907.

21. Walter Goodnow Everett, "Review of *The Philadelphia Negro: A Social Study*," *American Historical Review* 6 (1900), 162–64, quote on page 163.

22. Du Bois, *Autobiography*, 199–200.

23. W. E. B. Du Bois, "The Study of the Negro Problems," *Annals of the American Academy of Political and Social Science* 11 (1898), 1–13; quote on page 16.

24. Du Bois, *Autobiography*, 198.

25. Aldon Morris, *The Origins of American Sociology: The Untold Story of W. E. B. Du Bois* (Berkeley and Los Angeles: University of California Press, 2014); Phil Zuckerman, "The Sociology of Religion of W. E. B. Du Bois," *Sociology of Religion* 63 (2002), 239–53.

26. "Slum Expert on St. Louis Work," *St. Louis Dispatch* (March 29, 1900); George H. Nash, "Charles Stelzle: Apostle to Labor," *Labor History* 11 (1970), 151–74.

27. Stelzle, quoted in "Slum Expert on St. Louis Work."

28. Charles Stelzle, "The Workingman and the Church: A Composite Letter," *Outlook* 67 (July 27, 1901), 717.

29. Ben Primer, *Protestants and American Business Methods* (Ann Arbor, MI: UMI Research Press, 1978).

30. Richard P. Poethig, "Charles Stelzle and the Roots of Presbyterian Industrial Mission," *Journal of Presbyterian History* 77 (1999), 29–36.

31. James R. Barrett, "Women's Work, Family Economy, and Labor Militancy: The Case of Chicago's Immigrant Packinghouse Workers, 1900–1922," in *Labor Divided: Race and Ethnicity in United States Labor Struggles, 1835–1960*, ed. Robert Asher and Charles Stephenson (Albany: State University of New York Press, 1990), 249–66.

32. "Ministers' Union," Associated Press (April 8, 1904); "Labor Scorns a Pastor," *Chicago Daily Tribune* (April 11, 1904).

33. "Labor Scorns a Pastor"; "Tolstoy Blames Lawmakers," *Chicago Daily Tribune* (February 10, 1904).

34. Charles Stelzle, *A Son of the Bowery* (New York: George H. Doran, 1926), 87.

35. Laidlaw, "Historic Sketch," 13.

36. Martin Bulmer, "The Social Survey Movement and Early Twentieth-Century Sociological Methodology," in *Pittsburgh Surveyed: Social Science and Social*

Reform in the Early Twentieth Century, ed. Maurine W. Greenwald and Margo Anderson (Pittsburgh: University of Pittsburgh Press, 1996), 15–34.

37. Men and Religion Forward Movement, *Outlines for Social Service Institutes*, undated pamphlet, Charles Stelzle Papers, Box 13, Columbia University Library; "First Meeting of Eight Days' Men and Religion Campaign," *Boston Herald* (January 14, 1912); Charles Stelzle, "Survey Work—Charts and Diagrams," *Macon Telegraph* (January 14, 1912).

38. Bureau of Social Services, "Social Survey Series," Stelzle Papers, Box 10.

39. Charles Stelzle, *American Social and Religious Conditions* (New York: Fleming H. Revell, 1912), quotes on pages 202, 204, and 205.

40. Men and Religion Forward Movement, *Sociological and Religious Survey of Seventy American Cities*, April 1912, Stelzle Papers, Box 14.

41. Stelzle, *A Son of the Bowery*, 110.

42. An example of the apparent need to fend off this confusion was a front-page story in the *Fairport Herald* (Fairport, New York) announcing: "Charles Stelzle and his staff of expert sociologists (not Socialists) have been engaged by the four Protestant churches, Congregational, Free Baptist, First Baptist and First Methodist, to make a religious and social survey of Fairport and the contiguous territory." "Religious and Social Survey of Fairport" (December 3, 1913).

43. George E. Bevans, "How Workingmen Spend Their Spare Time" (PhD diss., Columbia University, New York, 1913), which includes information about Stelzle's role and the Bureau of Social Service; Stelzle, "How One Thousand Workingmen Spend Their Spare Time," typed notes, Stelzle Papers, Box 1.

44. Shelby M. Harrison, "A Social Survey of a Typical American City," *Proceedings of the Academy of Political Science in the City of New York* 2 (1912), 18–31; Shelby M. Harrison, "Trends in the Study of Local Areas: Social Surveys," *Social Forces* 11 (1933), 513–16. Robert E. Park, "*The Social Survey* by Carol Aronovici and *Community Action Through Surveys* by Shelby M. Harrison," *Journal of Political Economy* 25 (1917), 752–53.

45. Stelzle to Henry Sloane Coffin, September 18 and 29, 1914; Stelzle Papers, Box 4; Stelzle, "Consultant and Promoter," typescript, Stelzle Papers, Box 5; Stelzle, Circular Letter, October 13, Stelzle Papers, Box 15; "Social Engineer's Suggestions for Our Social Evils," *Wilkes-Barre Times Leader* (March 19, 1914).

46. "Public to be Polled on Religious Views," *New York Times* (November 22, 1926).

47. Stelzle Papers, Boxes 6 and 11, with Stelzle's typed summary and clippings from newspapers published in December 1926, including the questionnaire under the headline, "Your Religion: What Do You Believe?"

48. "In the Driftway," *The Nation* (January 12, 1927), 38.

49. "Youth Gives the Lie to Gossip," *Literary Digest* (April 30, 1927); besides belief in God, the questions asked about belief in immortality, prayer, the divinity of Jesus, biblical inspiration, church membership, attendance at religious services, religious upbringing, and religion as a necessary element of life for the

individual and community; each asking for a "yes" or "no" response, Stelzle Papers, Box 11.

50. Stelzle Papers, Box 10.

51. Stelzle, "Digging Up Social Facts," undated typescript, Stelzle Papers, Box 5.

52. Charles Stelzle, *A Report of the United Religious Survey Committee as Prepared by Its Staff for the Comity Commission*, March 4, 1931, typescript, Stelzle Papers, Box 16.

53. Charles Stelzle, "Rockefeller, Jr., Scores Employers for Ignorance of Great Labor Problems," *Rockford Morning Star* [Rockford, IL] (March 25, 1917).

54. Interchurch World Movement of North America, *World Survey*, 2 vols. (New York: Interchurch Press, 1920).

55. Fosdick's brother, Harry Emerson Fosdick, pastored New York City's First Presbyterian Church from 1918 to 1925, where he became a prominent critic of fundamentalism.

56. "Effectiveness of Protestant Church Work of Springfield," *Springfield Republican* (April 17, 1922); Worth M. Tippy, "The Value of the Social Survey for Religion," *Journal of Religion* 2 (1922), 402–17, discusses church surveys.

57. Jeffrey K. Hadden, "H. Paul Douglass: His Perspective and His Work," *Review of Religious Research* 22 (1980), 66–88.

58. Robert S. Lynd and Helen Lynd, *Middletown: A Study in American Culture* (New York: Harcourt, Brace, and World, 1929).

59. Sarah E. Igo, *The Averaged American: Surveys, Citizens, and the Making of a Mass Public* (Cambridge, MA: Harvard University Press, 2007).

60. W. Lloyd Warner, *Yankee City* (New Haven, CT: Yale University Press, 1963); Arthur J. Vidich and Joseph Bensman, *Small Town in Mass Society: Class, Power, and Religion in a Rural Community* (Urbana: University of Illinois Press, 1958).

CHAPTER 3

1. "Triangle Presents Premiere Tonight," *Daily Princetonian* (November 21, 1941); "Triangle Revue Slated to Appear Again Friday," *Daily Princetonian* (November 26, 1941); "New Triangle Production," *Daily Princetonian* (November 28, 1941).

2. "Public Opinion Institute Surveys Many Social, Economic, and Political Problems," *Daily Princetonian* (June 23, 1938); Williston Rich, "The Human Yardstick," *Saturday Evening Post* (January 31, 1939), 8–9, 66–71.

3. William Allen White, "New in Democracy," *Emporia Gazette* (November 19, 1938); and "Take a Look," *Emporia Gazette* (August 24, 1940).

4. George Gallup, "Fact-Finding Organization Without Political Views," *Dallas Morning News* (May 21, 1938). (Hereafter George Gallup is cited as GG.)

5. Jay Franklin, "Cockeyed Poll," *Cleveland Plain Dealer* (July 28, 1938).

6. Sarah E. Igo, *The Averaged American: Surveys, Citizens, and the Making of a Mass Public* (Cambridge, MA: Harvard University Press, 2007), discusses the letters.

7. GG, "Testing Public Opinion," *Public Opinion Quarterly* 2 (1938), 8–14; quotation on page 14.

8. Gallup Polls conducted in February and March, 1937; iPOLL Databank, Roper Center for Public Opinion Research, University of Connecticut; GG, "The Favorite Books of Americans," *New York Times* (January 15, 1939); the 1935 poll results are summarized in "Twenty-Two Problems Named Most Frequently in Today's Poll Survey," *Cleveland Plain Dealer* (December 15, 1935).

9. GG, "Church Lotteries Disapproved by Protestants in Poll," *Dallas Morning News* (June 3, 1938).

10. Percentages here are from the Roper Center iPOLL Databank and differ slightly from those initially reported in 1939 press releases.

11. GG, "The Gallup Poll: Churches," *Baltimore Sun* (March 19, 1939).

12. GG, "Religious Faiths of American People Analyzed in Survey," *Dallas Morning News* (December 10, 1944).

13. GG, "96 Per Cent Believe in God," *Atlanta Constitution* (December 10, 1944).

14. "Two Churchmen Report," *Oregonian* [Portland, OR] (January 9, 1944); Daniel A. Poling, "Americans All," *Oregonian* (December 29, 1945); "Polls on Religion Mean Little," *Christian Century* (April 3, 1940), 437–38; "Public Opinion Polls Are an Inexact Science," *Christian Century* (January 10, 1945), 36.

15. O. M. Walton, "Clergymen on Peace," *Cleveland Plain Dealer* (July 5, 1936); Walton W. Rankin, "Religion in Review," *Cleveland Plain Dealer* (April 25, 1937); "Hampden Pastors Hear Program for Church Plebiscite," *Springfield Daily Republican* [Springfield, MA] (October 21, 1937); Dorothy Thompson, "Youth and Opportunity," *Augusta Chronicle* (November 28, 1939); Gerard Donnelly and Albert Whelan, "National Catholic College Poll," *America* (November 18, 1939), 145–47.

16. The Roper poll was conducted in October 1944 with 1,249 nationally representative personal interviews; iPOLL Databank, Roper Center.

17. F. Stuart Chapin, "Progress in Methods of Inquiry and Research in the Social and Economic Sciences," *Scientific Monthly* 19 (1924), 390–99.

18. James Lowell Hypes, *Social Participation in a Rural New England Town* (New York: Bureau of Publications, Teachers College, Columbia University, 1927).

19. George A. Lundberg, "The Newspaper and Public Opinion," *Social Forces* 4 (1926), 709–15.

20. Carle C. Zimmerman, "Types of Farmers' Attitudes," *Social Forces* 5 (1927), 591–96.

21. "Dr. Gallup Outlines Opinion Surveys," *Princeton News* (January 19, 1939).

22. "The Public's 'Remarkable' Intelligence," *Augusta Chronicle* (February 27, 1939).

23. U.S. House of Representatives, *Hearings Before the Committee to Investigate Campaign Expenditures* (Washington, DC: GPO, 1945).

24. Adam J. Berinsky, "American Public Opinion in the 1930s and 1940s: The Analysis of Quota-Controlled Sample Survey Data," *Public Opinion Quarterly* 70 (2006), 499–529.

25. "How Gallup Poll Taps Public Opinion," *Christian Science Monitor* (October 5, 1940); "Light on Gallup Poll," *Chicago Daily Tribune* (October 16, 1940).

26. Hugh T. Kerr Jr., "Books and the Book," *Theology Today* (1946), 247–48; Arnold Rose, "Opinion Polling: Science or Business?" *Commentary* 4 (1947), 483–87.

27. "True Patriot Must Practice Religion, Says Archbishop Cushing," *Boston Globe* (February 12, 1945); "Materialism Our Greatest Enemy," *Anniston Star* [Anniston, AL] (January 18, 1848); "Americans and God," *Time* (November 1948).

28. "99 to 1," *Time* (October 20, 1952).

29. John E. Gibson, "God in the United States," *Los Angeles Times* (March 30, 1952).

30. President Harry S. Truman, "Address at a Luncheon of the National Conference of Christians and Jews," November 11, 1949, American Presidency Project, University of California at Santa Barbara.

31. President Harry S. Truman, "Address Recorded for Broadcast on the Occasion of the Lighting of the National Community Christmas Tree on the White House Grounds," December 24, 1950, American Presidency Project, University of California at Santa Barbara.

32. National Opinion Research Center poll of 1,272 persons, November 1950; iPOLL Databank, Roper Center.

33. "A Gallup Poll to Be Pondered," *Christian Century* (February 27, 1952), 237.

34. National adult survey of 1,291 people conducted by the National Opinion Research Center, University of Chicago, November 1952; iPOLL Databank, Roper Center.

35. Roper and NBC polls conducted in 1952; iPOLL Databank, Roper Center.

36. Poll of 1,602 people conducted by the Gallup Organization, March 28 to April 2, 1953; iPOLL Databank, Roper Center.

37. President Dwight D. Eisenhower, "Remarks Recorded for Program Marking the 75th Anniversary of the Incandescent Lamp," October 24, 1954, online by Gerhard Peters and John T. Woolley, American Presidency Project, University of California at Santa Barbara.

38. "Midwest Favored in Poll on Location," *Christian Century* (April 16, 1952); Walter W. Van Kirk, "Survey Cites Need to Put Best Beliefs into Action," *Christian Science Monitor* (February 23, 1952); "Teach Us to Pray," *Christian Science Monitor* (November 24, 1952).

39. Hubert Kay, "What about the Polls This Year?" *Saturday Evening Post* (September 8, 1956), 44–45, 70–72.

40. "Ike's Faith," *Time* (April 13, 1953).

41. "President Urges Self-Discipline," *New York Times* (November 10, 1954).

42. Will Herberg, *Protestant, Catholic, Jew: An Essay in American Religious Sociology* (New York: Doubleday, 1955).

43. "The American Religion," *Time* (September 26, 1955); "Counting the Lord's House," *Time* (April 29, 1957); Will Herberg, "There Is a Religious Revival!" *Review of Religious Research* 1 (1959), 45–50.

44. Robert N. Bellah, "Civil Religion in America," *Daedalus* 96 (1967), 1–21. Notably, in contrast to the impression of uniform belief in God in Gallup polls, Bellah observed that God was "a word which almost all Americans can accept but which means so many different things to so many different people that it is almost an empty sign" (p. 3).

45. James Ward Smith and Leland Jamison, eds., *The Shaping of American Religion* (Princeton, NJ: Princeton University Press, 1961), is an interesting four-volume example of separate essays treating the history and culture of various denominations and traditions.

CHAPTER 4

1. "The Aftermath of Mars: An Interview with Professor Hadley Cantril," *Princeton News* (February 9, 1939).

2. Paul F. Lazarsfeld, "An Episode in the History of Social Research: A Memoir." In *The Intellectual Migration: Europe and America, 1930–1960*, ed. Donald Fleming and Bernard Bailyn (Cambridge, MA: Harvard University Press, 1969), 270–337.

3. Jean M. Converse, *Survey Research in the United States: Roots and Emergence, 1890 to 1960* (Berkeley and Los Angeles: University of California Press, 1987).

4. David Riesman, "How Can We Study the Formation of Public Opinion?" *Public Opinion Quarterly* 13 (1949–1950), 741–51; David Riesman and Mark Benney, "The Sociology of the Interview," *Midwest Sociologist* 18 (1956), 3–15; David Riesman, Nathan Glazer, and Reuel Denney, *The Lonely Crowd: A Study of the Changing American Character* (New Haven, CT: Yale University Press, 1950).

5. T. W. Adorno, Else Frenkell-Brunswik, Daniel Levinson, and R. Nevitt Sanford, *The Authoritarian Personality* (New York: Harper and Brothers, 1950).

6. L. L. Thurstone and E. J. Chave, *The Measurement of Attitude: A Psychophysical Method and Some Experiments with a Scale for Measuring Attitudes toward the Church* (Chicago: University of Chicago Press, 1929); L. L. Thurstone, "Attitudes Can Be Measured," *American Journal of Sociology* 33 (1928), 529–54.

7. Gordon Allport, *The Individual and His Religion: A Psychological Interpretation* (New York: Macmillan, 1950); William James, *The Varieties of Religious Experience* (London: Longmans, 1902).

8. Details about the founding of these organizations can be found in Jeffrey K. Hadden, "A Brief History of the Religious Research Association," *Review of Religious Research* 15 (1974), 128–36; and William M. Newman, "The Society for

the Scientific Study of Religion: The Development of an Academic Society," *Review of Religious Research* 15 (1974), 137–51.

9. Hadley Cantril, "Educational and Economic Composition of Religious Groups: An Analysis of Poll Data," *American Journal of Sociology* 48 (1943), 574–79.

10. Joachim Wach, "Review of *Southern Parish, Vol. I: Dynamics of a City Church* by Joseph H. Fichter," *Journal of Religion* 32 (1952), 139–41; Helen Rose Ebaugh, "Joseph Fichter: Lightning Rod and Loyal Critic," *Sociology of Religion* 57 (1996), 339–44.

11. R. Bentley Anderson, "Pride and Prejudice in New Orleans: Joseph Fichter's 'Southern Parish,'" *U.S. Catholic Historian* 24 (2006), 23–46; quotation on page 25.

12. Converse, *Survey Research in the United States*, 284.

13. Charles Y. Glock, *A Life Fully Lived: An Autobiography* (Coeur d'Alene, ID: Manuscript, 2001), 112–16; Charles Y. Glock and Benjamin B. Ringer, "Church Policy and the Attitudes of Ministers and Parishioners on Social Issues," *American Sociological Review* 21 (1956), 148–56; Benjamin B. Ringer and Charles Y. Glock, "The Political Role of the Church as Defined by Its Parishioners," *Public Opinion Quarterly* 18 (1954–55), 337–47; Charles Y. Glock, Benjamin B. Ringer, and Earl R. Babbie, *To Comfort and to Challenge: A Dilemma of the Contemporary Church* (Berkeley and Los Angeles: University of California Press, 1966).

14. Gerhard E. Lenski, "Social Correlates of Religious Interest," *American Sociological Review* 18 (1953), 533–44; Bernice McNair Barnett, "The Life, Career, and Social Thought of Gerhard Lenski: Scholar, Teacher, Mentor, Leader," *Sociological Theory* 22 (2004), 163–93.

15. Gerhard E. Lenski, *The Religious Factor: A Sociological Study of Religion's Impact on Politics, Economics, and Family Life* (Garden City, NY: Doubleday, 1961).

16. Charles Y. Glock, "Review of *The Religious Factor* by Gerhard Lenski," *Political Science Quarterly* 77 (1962), 152–54. Peter Berger, "Review of *The Religious Factor* by Gerhard Lenski," *Social Research* 28 (1961), 370–72.

17. Samuel Z. Klausner, "Methods of Data Collection in Studies of Religion," *Journal for the Scientific Study of Religion* 3 (1964), 193–203.

18. Charles Y. Glock and Rodney Stark, *Religion and Society in Tension* (Chicago: McGraw Hill, 1965).

19. Gary T. Marx, "Religion: Opiate or Inspiration of Civil Rights Militancy among Negroes?" *American Sociological Review* 32 (1967), 64–72; Seymour Martin Lipset and Earl Rabb, *The Politics of Unreason: Right Wing Extremism in America, 1790–1970* (New York: Harper and Row: 1970).

20. Examples include Ted R. Vaughan, Douglas H. Smith, and Gideon Sjoberg, "The Religious Orientations of American Natural Scientists," *Social Forces* 44 (1966), 519–26; Edward C. Lehman Jr. and Donald W. Shriver Jr., "Academic Discipline as Predictive of Faculty Religiosity," *Social Forces* 47 (1968), 171–82; and S. Lee Spray and John H. Marx, "The Origins and Correlates of Religious

Adherence and Apostasy among Mental Health Professionals," *Sociological Analysis* 30 (1969), 132–50.

21. As two examples, Susan M. Stolka and Larry D. Barnett, "Education and Religion in Women's Attitudes Motivating Childbearing," *Journal of Marriage and Family* 31 (1969), 740–50; and Edward A. Suchman, "The 'Hang-Loose' Ethic and the Spirit of Drug Use," *Journal of Health and Social Behavior* 9 (1968), 146–55.

22. David J. Ludwig and Thomas Blank, "Measurement of Religion as Perceptual Set," *Journal for the Scientific Study of Religion* 8 (1969), 319–21; Richard A. Hunt, "The Interpretation of the Religious Scale of the Allport-Vernon-Lindzey Study of Values," *Journal for the Scientific Study of Religion* 7 (1968), 65–77; and Milton Rokeach, "Part I. Value Systems in Religion," *Review of Religious Research* 11 (1969), 3–23, illustrate these contributions.

23. Jon P. Alston, "Social Variables Associated with Church Attendance, 1965 and 1969: Evidence from National Polls," *Journal for the Scientific Study of Religion* 10 (1971), 233–36.

24. Daniel Bell, "Religion in the Sixties," *Social Research* 38 (1971), 447–97.

25. Jackson W. Carroll and David A. Roozen, "National Sample Questions on Religion: An Inventory of Material Available from the Roper Public Opinion Research Center," *Journal for the Scientific Study of Religion* 12 (1973), 325–38.

26. Myer S. Reed Jr., "The Sociology of the Sociology of Religion: A Report on Research in Progress," *Review of Religious Research* 15 (1974), 157–67.

27. Yoshio Fukuyama, "The Uses of Sociology: By Religious Bodies," *Journal for the Scientific Study of Religion* 2 (1963), 195–203; quote on page 203.

28. Glock, *A Life Fully Lived*, 186.

29. Russell Middleton, "Do Christian Beliefs Cause Anti-Semitism?" *American Sociological Review* 38 (1973), 33–52; Rodney Stark, Bruce D. Foster, Charles Y. Glock, and Harold Quinley, *Wayward Shepherds: Prejudice and the Protestant Clergy* (New York: Harper and Row, 1971); Merton P. Strommen, "Religious Education and the Problem of Prejudice," *Religious Education* 1 (1967), 52–59; Glock, *A Life Fully Lived*, 187–88.

30. Andrew Greeley, "The Protestant Ethic: Time for a Moratorium," *Sociological Analysis* 25 (1964), 20–33.

31. Andrew Greeley, *Religion and Career: A Study of College Graduates* (New York: Sheed and Ward, 1963).

32. Andrew Greeley and Peter H. Rossi, *The Education of Catholic Americans* (Chicago: Aldine, 1966).

33. John Schmalzbauer, *People of Faith: Religious Conviction in American Journalism and Higher Education* (Ithaca, NY: Cornell University Press, 2002), 93.

34. Peter Berger, *The Noise of Solemn Assemblies* (New York: Doubleday, 1961); *The Sacred Canopy: Elements of a Sociological Theory of Religion* (New York: Doubleday, 1967); *A Rumor of Angels: Modern Society and the Rediscovery of the Supernatural* (New York: Doubleday, 1969).

35. Robert N. Bellah, "Religious Evolution," *American Sociological Review* 29 (1964), 358–74, quote on page 372; see also Bellah, *Beyond Belief: Essays on Religion in a Post-Traditionalist World* (New York: Harper and Row, 1970); Bellah, *The Broken Covenant: American Civil Religion in Time of Trial* (New York: Seabury, 1975); Robert N. Bellah, Richard Madsen, William M. Sullivan, Ann Swidler, and Steven M. Tipton, *Habits of the Heart: Individualism and Commitment in American Life* (Berkeley and Los Angeles: University of California Press, 1985), especially p. 395 on polls.

CHAPTER 5

1. George Dugan, "Evangelical Leaders Map National Campaign," *New York Times* (October 7, 1967).
2. Russell Chandler, "50 Million 'Born Again' in U.S.," *Los Angeles Times* (September 23, 1976).
3. Kenneth L. Woodward, "Born Again!" *Newsweek* (October 25, 1976).
4. "Counting Souls," *Time* (October 4, 1976).
5. Kenneth S. Kantzer and Carl F. H. Henry, *Evangelical Affirmations* (Grand Rapids, MI: Zondervan, 1990).
6. James Franklin, "What Does Religion Mean to You?" *Boston Globe* (November 14, 1976); Kenneth Briggs, "Gallup Poll Finds New Evidence of the Religious Character of U.S.," *New York Times* (September 12, 1976); Lewis Lapham, "The Easy Chair," *Harper's* (September 1, 1976); Seymour Martin Lipset, "The Election Is Now a Real Contest," *Washington Post* (September 5, 1976).
7. "Religion in America," a poll of 2,783 adults conducted by the Gallup Organization for *Catholic Digest*, November 1965, questions and responses available at the iPOLL Databank, Roper Center for Public Opinion Research, University of Connecticut.
8. US Senate, Committee on Government Operations, "Citizens View Government Survey," conducted by Louis Harris and Associates, September 1973, questions available at iPOLL Databank, Roper Center.
9. US House of Representatives, *Public Opinion Polls: Hearings before the Subcommittee on Library and Memorials of the Committee on House Administration* (Washington, DC: GPO, 1972).
10. Melvin Maddocks, "Does Gallup Speak Only to Roper?" *Christian Science Monitor* (April 15, 1974).
11. George Gallup, "Pollsters, Not Prophets," *Society* (September/October 1976), 19–25.
12. George Will, "Can We Really Measure 'Public Opinion'?" *Newsday* (November 10, 1977).
13. "George H. Gallup Jr.," *Town Topics* [Princeton, NJ] (November 30, 2011).

14. The handbook for clergy, *What My People Think*, is mentioned in the caption of a photo of Davies and Gallup in *Town Topics* (June 3, 1971).

15. "Presbytery Rejects Ordination of Gays," *Chicago Tribune* (December 17, 1977).

16. Stories included in the *Baltimore Sun, Boston Globe, Chicago Tribune, Christian Science Monitor, Los Angeles Times, New York Times, Philadelphia Tribune, Pittsburgh Courier, Wall Street Journal,* and *Washington Post,* archived in the ProQuest Central database.

17. Kenneth A. Briggs, "A New Voice for Religion: Vox Populi, Vox Gallup," *New York Times* (June 25, 1978).

18. "Evangelical Christianity in the U.S.," a poll of 1,553 randomly selected respondents conducted from November 10–13, 1978 by the Gallup Organization for *Christianity Today*; codebook from iPOLL Databank, Roper Center.

19. The smaller number was also the one suggested by further analysis of the *Christianity Today* data in James Davison Hunter, "Operationalizing Evangelicalism: A Review, Critique, and Proposal," *Sociological Analysis* 42 (1981), 363–72; and James Davison Hunter, *American Evangelicalism: Conservative Religion and the Quandary of Modernity* (New Brunswick, NJ: Rutgers University Press, 1983).

20. Hunter, *American Evangelicalism.*

21. Marjorie Hyer, "Poll Shows Evangelicals Support Nuclear Freeze," *Washington Post* (July 8, 1983); Kenneth L. Woodward, "How the Bible Made America," *Newsweek* (December 27, 1982); Charles Austin, "Theologians Note Growing Consensus on the Divinity and Humanity of Jesus," *New York Times* (December 25, 1982).

22. John Dart, "U.S. Religion Leaders Depend on Poll Data," *Los Angeles Times* (February 5, 1984).

23. George Gallup Jr., *Religion in America* (Princeton, NJ: Princeton Religion Research Center, 1984).

24. Ronald Reagan, "Remarks at the National Religious Broadcasters Association Annual Convention," *Public Papers of the Presidents* (January 30, 1984); the speech, which was Reagan's first following his announcement for reelection, was so enthusiastically received that fundraiser Richard A. Viguerie figured the assembled conservatives would not only vote for Reagan but cancel their vacations for him; quoted in Lou Cannon, "Reagan Starts by Stirring Passions," *Washington Post* (February 5, 1984).

25. Paula Schwed, "Prayer in School Advocates Push for Constitutional Amendment," *United Press International* (March 1, 1984); "School Prayer," *MacNeil/Lehrer Report* (May 6, 1982).

26. W. A. Criswell, "If the World Has Any Hope," *Criswell Sermon Library* (August 14, 1988).

27. Sandy Johnson, "New Group Aims to Support Religious Right in Politics," *Associated Press* (July 18, 1986).

28. "Virginia Church Gets Gallup to Poll on Restoring Latin Mass," Associated Press (November 14, 1984).

29. Clara Germani, "Moral Majority Stumps for 'Traditional Values,'" *Christian Science Monitor* (July 13, 1984); Robert Furlow, "Many Share Robertson's View of Divine Guidance, Gallup Says," Associated Press (December 8, 1986).

30. "Moral Majority Gains in Poll on Recognition," *New York Times* (January 24, 1982); Charles R. Babcock, "Blending Charity and Politics," *Washington Post* (November 2, 1987).

31. Kenneth A. Briggs, "Politics and Morality: Dissent in the Catholic Church," *New York Times* (August 11, 1984); Robert Wuthnow, *The Restructuring of American Religion: Society and Faith Since World War II* (Princeton, NJ: Princeton University Press, 1988).

32. Rushworth M. Kidder, "Gallup's Poll of Pacesetters Suggests the Shape of the Year 2000," *Christian Science Monitor* (July 23, 1984).

33. Patsy Perrault quoted in Lisa Paikowski, "Christian Market Inspires Ad Duo," *Adweek* (October 1, 1990).

34. "World News Tonight with Peter Jennings," *ABC News* (April 1, 1991).

35. David Holahan, "Opinion Polls Everywhere, But No One Calls on Us," *Christian Science Monitor* (July 17, 1986).

36. Ellis Cose, "Do We Ask Too Much of Polls?" *Time* (February 19, 1990).

37. Kenneth A. Briggs, "Political Activism Reflects Churches' Search for a Role in a Secular Society," *New York Times* (September 9, 1984).

38. Dan Rather, "Anti-Abortion Expand Efforts; Are Using Public Relations Firms," *CBS Evening News* (April 6, 1990).

39. "Americans Do Mix Religion and Politics: Polling Methodology Means Mixed Results," *CNN* (October 20, 2004).

40. Douglas S. Massey and Roger Tourangeau, "Where Do We Go from Here? Nonresponse and Social Measurement," *Annals of the American Academy of Political and Social Science* 645 (2013), 222–36.

41. "What Is an Evangelical" and "Statement of Faith," National Association of Evangelicals (2012), online.

42. Conrad Hackett and D. Michael Lindsay, "Measuring Evangelicalism: Consequences of Different Operationalization Strategies," *Journal for the Scientific Study of Religion* 47 (2008), 499–514.

43. Frank Newport and Joseph Carroll, "Another Look at Evangelicals in America Today," Gallup Poll (December 2, 2005), online.

44. Mark Chaves, *Congregations in America* (Cambridge, MA: Harvard University Press, 2004); Nancy Tatom Ammerman, *Bible Believers: Fundamentalists in the Modern World* (New Brunswick, NJ: Rutgers University Press, 1987); *Religious Landscape Survey* (Washington, DC: Pew Research Center, 2008), electronic data file.

45. Larry L. Bumpass, "The Measurement of Public Opinion on Abortion: The Effects of Survey Design," *Family Planning Perspectives* 29 (1997), 177–80.
46. *Evangelical Manifesto* (2007), online.
47. Sarah Kropp, "Press Release: Most Unmarried Evangelical Millennials Have Never Had Sex," *National Association of Evangelicals* (November 29, 2012); "Sex and Unexpected Pregnancies: What Evangelical Millennials Think and Practice," Gray Matter Research (May 2012), online.

CHAPTER 6

1. Burns W. Roper, "Evaluating Polls with Poll Data," *Public Opinion Quarterly* 50 (1986), 10–16.
2. Stephen Schleifer, "Trends in Attitudes Toward and Participation in Survey Research," *Public Opinion Quarterly* 50 (1986), 17–26.
3. Jibum Kim, Carl Gershenson, Patrick Glaser, and Tom W. Smith, "Trends in Surveys on Surveys," *Public Opinion Quarterly* 75 (2011), 165–91.
4. These reasons and other views of polling were examined in a 2001 poll conducted for the Kaiser Family Foundation by Princeton Survey Research Associates; iPOLL Databank, Roper Center for Public Opinion Research, University of Connecticut; my analysis of the electronic data file.
5. Kim et al., "Trends in Surveys on Surveys."
6. C. Kirk Hadaway, Penny Long Marler, and Mark Chaves, "What the Polls Don't Show: A Closer Look at U.S. Church Attendance," *American Sociological Review* 58 (1993), 741–52.
7. Unchurched Americans Survey, April 1978; Evangelical Christianity in the U.S., November 1978, iPOLL Databank, Roper Center.
8. World Values Survey, May 1990, iPOLL Databank, Roper Center.
9. Polls asking about attendance at religious services, iPOLL Databank, Roper Center.
10. General Social Surveys, iPOLL Databank, Roper Center.
11. Hadaway, Marler, and Chaves, "What the Polls Don't Show," 748.
12. Michael Hout and Andrew Greeley, "What Church Officials' Reports Don't Show: Another Look at Church Attendance Data," *American Sociological Review* 63 (1998), 113–19; C. Kirk Hadaway, Penny Long Marler, and Mark Chaves, "Overreporting Church Attendance in America: Evidence that Demands the Same Verdict," *American Sociological Review* 63 (1998), 122–30; Stanley Presser and Linda Stinson, "Data Collection Mode and Social Desirability Bias in Self-Reported Religious Attendance," *American Sociological Review* 63 (1998), 137–45.
13. C. Kirk Hadaway and Penny Long Marler, "How Many Americans Attend Worship Each Week? An Alternative Approach to Measurement," *Journal for the Scientific Study of Religion* 44 (2005), 307–22.

14. Tom W. Smith, "A Review of Church Attendance Measures," *American Sociological Review* 63 (1998), 131–36.

15. C. Kirk Hadaway and Penny Long Marler, "Did You Really Go to Church this Week? Behind the Poll Data," *Christian Century* (May 6, 1998), 472–75.

16. Hunter Baker, "Is Church Attendance Declining?" *Christianity Today* (November 8, 2007), summarizing Stanley Presser and Mark Chaves, "Is Religious Service Attendance Declining?" *Journal for the Scientific Study of Religion* 46 (2007), 417–23.

17. Rebecca Barnes and Lindy Lowry, "7 Startling Facts: An Up Close Look at Church Attendance in America," Church Leaders (2006), online.

18. Andrew Walsh, "Church, Lies, and Polling Data," *Religion in the News* 1 (1998), 1–7.

19. Frank Newport, "Questions and Answers about Americans' Religion," Gallup (December 24, 2007), online.

20. Daniel Burke, "God Is Alive and Well in America, Says Gallup Chief," *Religion News Service* (January 7, 2013).

21. Mark Chaves, *American Religion: Contemporary Trends* (Princeton, NJ: Princeton University Press, 2011), 42–54.

22. Frank Newport, "Americans' Church Attendance Inches Up in 2010," Gallup (June 25, 2010), online.

23. Mark A. Chaves, *National Congregations Study, 1998 and 2006: Codebook* (Ann Arbor, MI: Inter-university Consortium for Political and Social Research, 2006).

24. Pew 2006 Religion and Politics Poll, total N of 2,003; Pew Religious Landscape Survey conducted from February through August, 2007, total N of 35,556; and Pew Early February Poll, conducted in January and February 2008, total N of 1,502; electronic data files; weekly attendance at religious services among pollees with no college education, respectively for women and men, 41 percent and 39 percent in the Early February Poll; 50 percent and 32 percent in the 2006 poll; and 45 percent and 33 percent in the Religious Landscape Survey. The Early February Poll preceded the attendance question with questions about employment, economic conditions, and employee financial benefits; the other polls preceded the question about attendance with questions about religious teachings, religious beliefs, abortion, homosexuality, creation and evolution, and churches engaging in politics.

25. Andrew M. Greeley, "Habits of the Head," *Society* (May/June 1992), 74–81.

26. Wade Clark Roof, *A Generation of Seekers: The Spiritual Journeys of the Baby Boom Generation* (San Francisco: Harper San Francisco, 1993).

27. Robert D. Putnam, *Bowling Alone: The Collapse and Revival of American Community* (New York: Simon and Schuster, 2000).

28. Robert D. Putnam and David E. Campbell, *American Grace: How Religion Divides and Unites Us* (New York: Simon and Schuster, 2010).

29. James S. Coleman, "Social Capital in the Creation of Human Capital," *American Journal of Sociology* 94 (1988), S95–S120.

30. Alejandro Portes, "Social Capital: Its Origins and Applications in Modern Sociology," *Annual Review of Sociology* 24 (1998), 1–24.

31. Robert D. Putnam, *Better Together: Restoring the American Community* (New York: Simon and Schuster, 2003).

32. D. Michael Lindsay, *Faith in the Halls of Power: How Evangelicals Joined the American Elite* (New York: Oxford University Press, 2008), 82–83.

33. Kathleen Teltsch, "2d Largest Philanthropy Widens Role," *New York Times* (August 27, 1990).

34. In the *Christian Science Monitor, New York Times, Philadelphia Tribune,* and *Washington Post,* 238 articles mentioning the Pew Charitable Trusts appeared from 1990 to 1999, compared with 51 from 1980 to 1989.

35. An example of efforts that expanded beyond evangelicalism was support for Princeton University's Center for the Study of American Religion. Deborah Kovach, "Princeton Scholars Form Religion Center," *Trenton Times* (February 26, 1991).

36. Peter Steinfels, "The News Media and Religion: A Changing Mood that Bodes Well for the Nation's Believers," *New York Times* (April 30, 1994).

37. Joel Carpenter quoted in John Dillin, "TV Networks Blind to Role Religion Plays in the US, Major Study Says," *Christian Science Monitor* (March 8, 1994).

38. Laurie Goodstein, "White Evangelicals 'A Powerful' Bloc," *Washington Post* (June 25, 1996).

39. Stephanie Strom, "Pew Charitable Trusts Will Become Public Charity," *New York Times* (November 7, 2003). Idem, "New Pew Trusts Merging Works into One Body," *New York Times* (April 27, 2004).

40. At the end of 2003, the "centers of excellence" included NYU's Center for Religion and Media, Yale's Center for Religion and American Life, USC's Center for Religion and Civic Culture, the University of Missouri's Center for Religion and the Professions, the University of Pennsylvania's Center for Research on Religion and Urban Society, Emory's Center for the Interdisciplinary Study of Religion, Princeton's Center for the Study of Religion, the University of Virginia's Center on Religion and Democracy, Notre Dame's Erasmus Institute, and Boston University's Institute on Religion and World Affairs.

41. Surveys using Pew and alternative wordings about religious service attendance are included in the iPOLL Databank, Roper Center.

42. The number of media mentions is from the ProQuest Central digital database and for each period refers to the number of times in which all media in the database include the words "religion," "poll" or "survey," and "Pew."

43. Fouad Ajami, "The Falseness of Anti-Americanism," *Foreign Policy* 138 (2003), 52–61; quotations on page 54. Darren Sherkat, "Where to Stick that Poll?" Sherkat's blog (January 25, 2008), wherkat.wordpress.com.

44. Norval D. Glenn, "The Trend in 'No Religion' Respondents to U.S. National Surveys, Late 1950s to Early 1980s," *Public Opinion Quarterly* 51 (1987), 293–314.

45. Michael Hout, Claude S. Fischer, and Mark A. Chaves, "More Americans Have No Religious Preference: Key Finding from the 2012 General Social Survey," *Institute for the Study of Societal Issues Press Summary* (March 2013).

46. Pew Forum on Religion and Public Life, "'Nones' on the Rise: One in Five Adults Have No Religious Affiliation," Pew Research Center Press Release (October 9, 2012); "In U.S., Rise in Religious 'Nones' Slows in 2012," *Gallup Poll News Service* (January 10, 2013).

47. Michael Hout and Claude S. Fischer, "Why More Americans Have No Religious Preference: Politics and Generations," *American Sociological Review* 67 (2002), 165–90.

48. Otis Dudley Duncan, "The Rise of the Nones: A Paleostatistical Inquiry," *Free Inquiry* 24 (2004), 29–31.

49. Pew Forum, "'Nones' on the Rise."

50. Stephen Vaisey, "Motivation and Justification: A Dual-Process Model of Culture in Action," *American Journal of Sociology* 114 (2009), 1675–715.

51. Chaeyoon Lim, Carol Ann MacGregor, and Robert D. Putnam, "Secular and Liminal: Discovering Heterogeneity among Religious Nones," *Journal for the Scientific Study of Religion* 49 (2010), 596–618.

52. General Social Survey, 2008 Panel Wave 2, electronic data file. Wade Clark Roof, *Spiritual Marketplace: Baby Boomers and the Remaking of American Religion* (Princeton, NJ: Princeton University Press, 1999), 131, also observed significant changes in responses to questions about religion in panel data collected in the late 1980s and mid-1990s.

53. Lim, MacGregor, and Putnam, "Secular and Liminal," 615; see also Conrad Hackett, "Seven Things to Consider When Measuring Religious Identity," *Religion* 44 (2014), 396–413.

54. Committee on House Administration, *Public Opinion Polls: Hearings before the Subcommittee on Library and Memorials* (Washington, DC: House of Representatives, 1972).

55. Daniel Schorr, "Opinion Pollsters Get Few Responses," National Public Radio (April 19, 1992).

56. Helen Crossley, Burns Roper, and George H. Gallup Jr., "Present at the Creation," *Public Perspective* (April/May 1996), 13–15; quotations from page 15.

57. Andrew Kohut, "Possible Consequences of Non-Response for Pre-Election Surveys," Pew Research Center for the People and the Press (May 16, 1998).

58. Pew Research Center for the People and the Press, "Response Rate Project: Codebook," August 11, 1997, iPOLL Databank, Roper Center.

59. My analysis of the electronic data file; the data file is available from the Roper Center. In data weighted to compensate for demographic differences, 35 percent in the standard version said they were born again compared with 32 percent in

the rigorous version (a difference of approximately seven million people), and 8 percent in the former were nonreligious compared with 10 percent in the latter.

60. These results are drawn from my analysis of the 1973 General Social Survey, electronic data file, courtesy of the Inter-University Consortium for Social and Political Research; see also Appendix A of the General Social Survey Codebook for details about sampling design and weighting.

61. Scott Keeter, Courtney Kennedy, Michael Dimock, Jonathan Best, and Peyton Craighill, "Gauging the Impact of Growing Nonresponse on Estimates from a National RDD Telephone Survey," *Public Opinion Quarterly* 70 (2006), 759–79.

62. Robert M. Groves, "Nonresponse Rates and Nonresponse Bias in Household Surveys," *Public Opinion Quarterly* 70 (2006), 646–75.

63. "Religion and Public Life Survey," Pew Research Center, conducted July 2005; electronic data file.

64. R. Emmett Tyrrell Jr., "God and Man and FDR," *American Spectator* (June 21, 2012), spectator.org.

65. "Methodology," Rasmussen Reports (June 10, 2013), describing the automated survey process conducted for all Rasmussen Reports surveys conducted by Pulse Opinion Research LLC, online.

66. "64% Believe in God of the Bible," Rasmussen Reports (December 30, 2012), online.

67. "OK City: Bothered by Religious 'Bling'?" SurveyUSA Breaking News (November 12, 2007); "New Hampshire Voters: Religion Not a Factor," SurveyUSA News (December 3, 2007), online.

CHAPTER 7

1. Pew Research Center and Associated Press/Yahoo Polls conducted from January to September 2008; courtesy of the Roper Center for Public Opinion Research, University of Connecticut.

2. Polls conducted among national samples by Gallup in September 2011 and Harris in February 2010; courtesy of the Roper Center for Public Opinion Research.

3. Steven Shepard, "Americans Don't Trust Polls," *National Journal* (September 4, 2013).

4. Topline results from Kantar's Path to Public Opinion Poll, September 4, 2013; us.kantar.com.

5. Steven Shepard, "Sorry, Wrong Number," *National Journal* (May 29, 2013). Mark Blumenthal, quoted in an interview with Dana Stanley, "Evaluating Survey Quality" (July 2, 2012), online at http://researchaccess.com.

6. Rodney Stark, "The Myth of Unreligious America," *Wall Street Journal* (July 5, 2013).

7. Carl Bialik, "Tracking Religious Trends Takes a Leap of Faith," *Wall Street Journal* (October 13, 2012).

8. "LifeWay Study Adds Doubts to Pew Poll's Results," *Religion Today* (July 1, 2008). John S. Dickerson, "The Decline of Evangelical America," *New York Times* (December 15, 2012), online.

9. The interviews were conducted under my supervision as part of a project on religious leaders' responses to contemporary cultural challenges by a team of researchers from May 2013 to April 2014, including telephone and in-person interviews using semi-structured questions and lasting from one hour to more than four hours and averaging approximately an hour and a half. Approximately two-thirds of the interviews were with clergy engaged in congregational work, and one-third with lay leaders in congregations or clergy doing noncongregational work. The project included interviews with leaders from each of the major Protestant denominations as well as from nondenominational congregations, Roman Catholic parishes, and synagogues.

10. Frank Newport, "Estimating Americans' Worship Behavior: Survey-based Estimates Have Value," Gallup Poll (January 3, 2006), online; Frank Newport, *God Is Alive and Well: The Future of Religion in America* (Princeton, NJ: Gallup Press, 2012).

11. Delmer L. Chilton, "Reformation Sunday" (October 30, 2011), lectionarylab. blogspot.com.

12. Calvin Wittman, "Heaven Can Wait," *LifeWay Christian Resources*, undated, www.lifeway.com.

13. Rick Warren, "What Difference Does Easter Make?" undated, www.preaching. com.

14. Scott Carson, "Get Real: Taking Sin Seriously," Grace Church, undated, www. gracechurchwi.org.

15. "Sermon Illustrations," *Christianity Today*, undated, www.preachingtoday.com.

16. David Allen, "Of Polls and Preachers," *Theological Matters* (September 24, 2012), online.

17. The journals were the *American Journal of Sociology, American Sociological Review, Journal for the Scientific Study of Religion, Review of Religious Research*, and *Social Forces*, archived in JSTOR, with 2,115 articles identified with keyword "religion" from January 1, 2001, through December 31, 2010.

CHAPTER 8

1. Our Campaigns, online at www.ourcampaigns.com. The firms having conducted the largest number of polls were SurveyUSA, Rasmussen, Public Policy Polling, and Quinnipiac. Gallup came in fifth. Pew ranked thirty-first.

2. Barry Lynn, "Is America Too Damn Religious?" ABC News (February 1, 2007), online.

3. "Obama Campaign Polls: How the Internal Data Got It Right," Huffington Post (November 21, 2012), online.

4. "Gallup Presidential Poll: How Did Brand-Name Firm Blow Election?" Huffington Post (March 8, 2013), online.

5. "Gallup Poll Reveals Four Reasons It Got the 2012 Election Wrong," Huffington Post (June 4, 2013), online; "Gallup 2012 Presidential Election Polling Review," Gallup, Inc. (June 4, 2013), online.

6. Frank Newport, *God Is Alive and Well* (New York: Gallup Press, 2012); Daniel Burke, "God Is Alive and Well in America, Says Gallup Chief," *Religion News Service* (January 7, 2013).

7. Will Oremus, "Minority Opinions," Slate (May 17, 2012), online.

8. Pew Research Center for the People and the Press, *Assessing the Representativeness of Public Opinion Surveys* (May 15, 2012), www.pewresearch.org.

9. Oremus, "Minority Opinions."

10. Pew Methodology Survey, January 4 to 8, 2012, electronic data file, weighted data. The trust question, to which 37 percent of Pew respondents said most people can be trusted, was worded identically to one in the General Social Survey, in which only 32 percent gave that answer.

11. Timothy Johnson and Linda Owens, "Survey Response Rate Reporting in the Professional Literature" (paper presented at the annual meeting of the American Association for Public Opinion Research, Nashville, TN, 2003).

12. Richard Curtin, Stanley Presser, and Eleanor Singer, "Changes in Telephone Survey Nonresponse Over the Past Quarter Century," *Public Opinion Quarterly* 69 (2005), 87–98; J. Michael Brick and Douglas Williams, "Explaining Rising Nonresponse Rates in Cross-Sectional Surveys," *Annals of the American Academy of Political and Social Science* 645 (2013), 36–59.

13. Roger Tourangeau and Thomas J. Plewes, eds., *Nonresponse in Social Science Surveys: A Research Agenda* (Washington, DC: National Academies Press, 2013).

14. Douglas S. Massey and Roger Tourangeau, "Introduction: New Challenges to Social Measurement," *Annals of the American Academy of Political and Social Science* 645 (2013), 6–22.

15. Pew Research Center, *A Portrait of Jewish Americans: Findings from a Pew Research Center Survey of U.S. Jews* (Washington, DC: Pew Research Center, 2013).

16. J. J. Goldberg, "Pew Survey about Jewish America Got It All Wrong," Forward (October 18, 2013), online.

17. Stephen Ansolabehere and Brian F. Schaffner, "Does Survey Mode Still Matter? Findings from a 2010 Multi-Mode Comparison," *Political Analysis* 22 (2014), 285–303; Daniel Cox, Robert P. Jones, and Juhem Navarro-Rivera, "I Know What You Did Last Sunday: Measuring Social Desirability Bias in Self-Reported Religious Behavior, Belief, and Identity," *Public Religion Research Institute* (May 17, 2014), www.publicreligion.org.

18. Nate Cohn, "Explaining Online Panels and the 2014 Midterms," *New York Times* (July 27, 2014); Drew DeSilver, "What *The New York Times*' Polling Decision Means," Pew Research Center (July 28, 2014), www.pewresearch.org.

19. Weekly religious service attendance among African Americans ranged from 7 to 12 percentage points higher than white attendance in General Social Surveys conducted from 2002 to 2010.

20. Sufficient information was included in a 2005 Pew poll to compare weekly religious service attendance among blacks and whites for easier- and harder-to-reach respondents. Had only three call attempts been made, the poll would have achieved a 21 percent response rate and among both blacks and whites 43 percent attended weekly. However, among respondents reached with four or more callbacks, yielding a 32 percent response rate overall, 38 percent of whites and 46 percent of blacks attended weekly. A potentially related problem is that weights to compensate for underrepresentation of certain demographic categories generally do not take into consideration specific combinations of those categories; for example, in the Pew poll 28 percent of white respondents were age sixty-five and older while only 16 percent of black respondents were.

21. Sabrina Pendergrass, "An Analysis of Differences in the Weekly Religious Service Attendance of Black and White Youth from 1976–1996" (senior thesis, Department of Sociology, Princeton University, 2002).

22. National Survey of American Life, 2003, electronic data file, courtesy of the Inter-University Consortium for Political and Social Research; in which 3,570 African Americans and 891 white Americans were included, showing the following among blacks and whites, respectively: weekly religious service attendance, 40 percent and 35 percent; spending three hours or more on a typical weekend at church, 66 percent and 39 percent; spending two or more hours a week at church for other church activities, 65 percent and 49 percent; helping church people very often, 34 percent and 20 percent; feeling very close to church people, 49 percent and 39 percent; watching religious television at least one hour a week, 65 percent and 30 percent; listening to religious radio at least one hour a week, 67 percent and 34 percent; and asking someone to pray for them at least once a week, 56 percent and 39 percent.

23. S. Brent Plate, "Why Pollsters Still Don't Get Religion," *Religion Dispatches* (September 29, 2010); S. Brent Plate, "The Problem with Ranking 'Bible-Minded' Cities," *Religion Dispatches* (January 27, 2014); Lynn Davidman amply demonstrates the importance of the embodied knowledge that polling typically ignores in *Becoming Unorthodox: Stories of Ex-Hasidic Jews* (New York: Oxford University Press, 2014); Iddo Tavory and Daniel Winchester offer a similar argument that includes observations among Muslims and Jews in "Experiential Careers: The Routinization and De-Routinization of Religious Life," *Theory and Society* 41 (2012), 351–73.

24. Molly Worthen, "American Christianity and Secularism at a Crossroads," *New York Times* (December 23, 2012); the first of the two quotes is one that Worthen attributes to Northwestern University political scientist Shakman Hurd.

25. Matthew J. Salganik and Karen E. C. Levy, "Wiki Surveys: Open and Quantifiable Social Data Collection," Working Paper, Princeton University, Center for Information Technology Policy, 2012; Matthew Salganik, *Bit by Bit: Social Research in the Digital Age* (Princeton, NJ: Princeton University Press, 2015).

26. Among the many discussions of secularization, one of the more useful is Philip S. Gorski, "Historicizing the Secularization Debate: Church, State, and Society in Late Medieval and Early Modern Europe, Ca. 1300 to 1700," *American Sociological Review* 65 (2000), 138–67.

27. Nicholas J. Demerath III, "Trends and Anti-Trends in Religious Change," in *Indicators of Social Change*, ed. Eleanor Bernert Sheldon and Wilbert E. Moore (New York: Russell Sage Foundation, 1968), 349–445; Jeffrey K. Hadden, "Toward Desacralizing Secularization Theory," *Social Forces* 65 (1987), 5887–611; Norval D. Glenn, "The Trend in 'No Religion' Respondents to U.S. National Surveys, Late 1950s to Early 1980s," *Public Opinion Quarterly* 51 (1987), 293–314.

28. Roger Finke and Rodney Stark, *The Churching of America, 1776–2005* (New Brunswick, NJ: Rutgers University Press, 2005).

29. Paul Lichterman, "Studying Public Religion: Beyond the Beliefs-Driven Actor," in *Religion on the Edge: De-centering and Re-centering the Sociology of Religion*, ed. Courtney Bender, Wendy Cadge, Peggy Levitt, and David Smilde (New York: Oxford University Press, 2012), 115–36.

30. On group style, see Nina Eliasoph and Paul Lichterman, "Culture in Interaction," *American Journal of Sociology* 108 (2003), 735–94.

31. Besides straightforward counts of social network information, possibilities of combining big data approaches with content analysis are described in Paul DiMaggio, Manish Nag, and David Blei, "Exploiting Affinities between Topic Modeling and the Sociological Perspective on Culture: Application to Newspaper Coverage of U.S. Government Arts Funding," *Poetics* 42 (2013), 570–606; and on alternative polling predictions based on network assumptions in Internet sample-matching panels, see David Rothschild and Justin Wolfers, "Forecasting Elections: Voter Intentions versus Expectations," Working Paper, Microsoft Research and Applied Statistics Center (January 23, 2013) and "A Data-Driven Crystal Ball," Microsoft Research (September 29, 2014), http://research.microsoft.com.

32. Tom W. Smith and Jibum Kim, "An Assessment of the Multi-level Integrated Database Approach," *Annals of the American Academy of Political and Social Science* 645 (2013), 185–221.

33. The concern about confidentiality of data is noted in Douglas S. Massey and Roger Tourganeau, "Where Do We Go from Here? Nonresponse and Social

Measurement," *Annals of the American Academy of Political and Social Science* 645 (2013), 222–36.

34. Claude S. Fischer, "The 2004 GSS Finding of Shrunken Social Networks: An Artifact?" *American Sociological Review* 74 (2009), 657–69; Anthony Paik and Kenneth Sanchagrin, "Social Isolation in America: An Artifact," *American Sociological Review* 78 (2013), 339–60.

35. The American Association of Public Opinion Research (AAPOR) announced a "Transparency Initiative" in 2010, but four years later few results had been achieved. Of 140 polls, only 24 percent described sampling frames in news releases and fewer than half acknowledged weighting or stratifying their data at all; only three of the 140 disclosed response rates: "How Much Can We Trust the Polls? A Look at the Industry's Transparency Problem," Huffington Post (October 3, 2014), online.

36. Massey and Tourganeau, "Where Do We Go from Here," 235.

Index